OUR FOUR BOYS

OUR FOUR BOYS

Foster Parenting Retarded Teenagers

MARTHA UFFORD DICKERSON

 SYRACUSE UNIVERSITY PRESS • 1978

Many thanks to Dave Rosen and Jerry Provencal of Macomb-Oakland Regional Center for their constant support and interest in the four boys who were placed in our home from that agency; their cooperation and guidance has been invaluable to Wade and me as we lived our lives as foster parents; to Ken Kenny for his assistance to me in the early days of sorting my jumbled thoughts into some logical order; to Janet Christian for typing, retyping, and critically reacting; and, especially, to Dr. "C," Director of the Institute for the Study of Mental Retardation and Related Disabilities, who used many strategies to motivate and sustain me through a very challenging process of publicly sharing a very private experience.

Library of Congress Cataloging in Publication Data

Dickerson, Martha Ufford.
    Our four boys.

    1. Foster parents—United States—Biography.
2. Mentally handicapped children—United States—Biography. I. Title.
HQ759.7.D5   301.42'7   78-5642
ISBN 0-8156-0146-8

Manufactured in the United States of America

To Jori and Frosty, who made parents of us.

MARTHA UFFORD DICKERSON is Program Associate in Social Work, Institute for the Study of Mental Retardation and Related Disabilities, University of Michigan, Ann Arbor. She is in clinical practice with families and is also an instructor of graduate students from many disciplines. She has developed and conducts workshops on parenting skills, human fulfillment, and developmental disabilities. Wade Dickerson, a self-employed businessman who took early retirement, developed an interest in foster parenting and devised the practical management of foster parenting their four boys.

Contents

Foreword, WILLIAM M. CRUICKSHANK   ix

The Way We Were   xiii

1 From Parenting to Foster Parenting   1

2 The First Two Foster Sons Arrive   19

3 The Boys' Backgrounds   31

4 The First Few Months   41

5 Others Joined Us   53

6 Introducing Routines   67

7 The Goal—To Raise Men   85

8 Learning to Be a Family Member   99

9 The Wonder of Words   119

10 New Experiences   133

11 Ownership   161

12 Difficult Behavior   177

13 Living with Foster Children   197

Foreword

MARTHA AND WADE will not enjoy this introduction to Martha's book, for they are private people deeply in love with each other and with their two generations of family. Martha is a colleague and a friend of mine; Wade is a friend with a deep voice, quiet and intense, firm and kind, who makes a hole-in-one per year at Hickory Hills. Martha has a soul-saving sense of humor, a capacity to empathize objectively, and an ability to structure her life to the benefit of everyone with whom she comes in contact. Wade, a bit less well known to me, is simultaneously a person of compassion and one with a will of steel when firmness is required to the benefit of The Four about whom you will read in this stirring book.

How many foster parents are there in the United States? What would they be like if they were all lined up by height, by color, by disposition, by genuine concern for children, by age, by religion, by compassion, by honesty, by emotion, or by a myriad of other characteristics which, woven into a firm fabric, together constitute what parents by any name or with any adjective should be—natural, step, foster, my, our, their? In this book the reader will quickly become acquainted with two persons who are the epitome not only of what children seek in their "own" parents, but of what society seeks in the modern-day foster parent.

A swimming pool is built because boys need it. Youth are taught to ride bicycles because this learning provides independence. A visit to a hotel overnight with its pools, saunas, and hot tubs is undertaken because young men need experiences with their (foster) parents as a family group. A youth is disciplined ("Go sit on the bot-

ix

tom stair for a couple of minutes until you can remember how we behave at the dinner table"). A crying head is held until a disappointment passes. A hand is shaken when a genuine success is experienced. A responsibility is assigned which is within the youth's ability to achieve, and a genuine response is given when achievement is realized. These are some of the planks in the charter for growth which Martha and Wade have established for their two families—natural and foster—each but a few years apart in time.

These parents believe in the dignity of man, and they plan for and practice ways in which four defeated youths can learn to hold their heads high as men—as men with dignity. Their lives are shared with their friends as well. A few months before this book's manuscript was in any recognizable form, Martha had a birthday. Birthdays are important any year, but Martha's birthday party was also an occasion for recognizing Phillip, his leaving adolescence and entering adulthood. He was now eighteen. A birthday dinner was carefully planned to include ten persons—the boys, Martha and Wade, and four guests. Phillip, now an adult, poured the wine for those eligible to drink it, and he proudly poured his own first glass. What a celebration! A symbol of adulthood was achieved with dignity and caution. Wade securely presided at one end of a long family dining table; Martha's eyes beamed at the other end of the table. But what of the remaining three boys? They too had their recognition that day and contributed to Martha's celebration. Tom made the green salad; Andrew the peanut bread ("Have some more, Dorothy; have some more"); and Mark, after several practice runs, the magnificent seafood casserole. A game of pool, a visit to see the bicycles, a stop to be shown the huskies and the pool frozen over, the programming of appropriate welcoming behavior and showing off one's sleeping rooms—all these and more were couched in an environment emphasizing personal worth, learning, humor, and above all, dignity. These things do not just develop; they must be planned and nurtured.

As a colleague of Martha's, I have had the pleasure of taking these young men by twos as my guests for luncheon at a private eating club. Reading the early pages of this book, one quickly realizes that growth, following intensive effort on the part of Martha and Wade, has taken place in the young men—growth which permits them to be welcomed as guests, essentially undifferentiated from others, by those who are eating and conversing nearby. As I write these paragraphs I remember that a promise is outstanding to Mark to repeat the experience "to go and eat lunch where we did before." We will do that before this book is in your hands, and it will have been with pleasure. Formerly confined to an institution, boys who had no future fortunately found their way into a home where they were aided to grow with dignity into youth and adulthood. Two foster parents had to cause this to happen. Never could it have happened otherwise. It is what professional people speak of as normalization.

This book contains a message for foster parents anywhere—a story of hope and achievement. Indeed there is a general message here for all parents, both foster and natural, and a particular message for every natural or foster parent of a severely mentally retarded child or youth. There is a challenge in the pages of this book for every institutional employee, including the director or superintendent. Residential life can be brought to a level of near equation with this foster family. Directors of state departments of mental health and social services and legislators of state governments will find a testament in this book's story of what should be legislated and what should be administratively brought to reality for every mentally retarded youth in every state. This book's story can be heartening to all members of parent groups—the local, state, and national associations for retarded citizens.

But this foster-family autobiography, related in complete honesty, is the story of two committed people. Foster parents should never become foster parents unless commitment and recognition of the value and worth of the individual are uppermost. Foster parents who function from any other base perform a hollow service, perhaps often a disservice. Martha and Wade may be seen as unique, but they should not be viewed as such. They should be the models for foster parents everywhere. Martha had to be urged to tell their story and to share the feelings of their son and their daughter. In so doing, a story has flowed of how they have brought a sense of dignity and worth to four youths who had neither of these. They have assisted Tom, Andrew, Phillip, and "my special friend" Mark each to be able to say in his own way, "I know who I am." Until I know who "I am," I am nothing. Out of nothing but potential these two parents have created something which can be of value to the boys, to themselves, and to the communities in which the four boys may eventually live as adults.

Ann Arbor, Michigan
Spring 1978

William M. Cruickshank

.

The Way We Were

FROSTY WAS HOME for Christmas. Not only was Frosty home for Christmas, he *made* Christmas. He prepared gifts for each of the foster boys who live with us, and arranged to take care of the children a couple of nights over the holiday so that Wade and I could go out with friends. The fact that this happened at Christmas 1976 made the previous three years of our life worthwhile.

Just before Christmas in '73 our twenty-four-year-old son, Frosty, had told us that he could not spend Christmas in our home because he could not tolerate the way Tom and Andrew behaved. They were the two children we had taken in to live with us. Tom and Andrew were disruptive, noisy, demanding children who had little control of their behaviors and had little sense of how to take care of their personal needs. Three years later, Frosty was home for Christmas and home included *four* foster sons: Phillip, aged eighteen; Mark, sixteen; Andrew, sixteen; and Tom, fourteen. Each of the foster sons had retardation, as well as other complications. During the three years all of us had grown in understanding, acceptance, and in knowing how to get along with other people.

It was a lovely Christmas. The children helped in all of the preparations. We put the tree up two weeks before Christmas so that we could enjoy it as long as possible. Electric candles were placed in all of the upstair windows. Outdoors Frosty hung a long string of twinkle lights in the lilac bush near the swimming pool.

The children took responsibility for the electric candles placed on the windowsills on the second floor. Mark went outdoors each evening to connect the lights that were on the lilac bush. The lights on the tree indoors were left for Wade. We placed wax candles all over the main part of our home—one time there were eighteen candles burning! With all the candles and the twinkling lights on the trees, the house had a magic about it.

It was the first time that the boys had bought Christmas presents for Wade, Frosty, and me. Mike, a social worker who works part time in our home, helped them with this errand, and the gifts were thoughtfully selected. Socks for Wade, soap-on-a-rope for Frosty, and for me they had found lipstick and fingernail polish that matched. They had a lot of fun wrapping the presents and keeping them hidden until the proper time. Two of the children did well keeping secrets, but two wanted to talk. Wade and I had to keep reminding them, "Don't tell us or we won't be surprised."

Phillip, the oldest boy, had hooked a beautiful rug for his mother. He wrapped the gift as well as a wreath that he had made to take home to her. Two or three days before the holiday Phillip's stepfather picked him up for his Christmas visit. Phillip was very confused as he went out the door. He wanted to go home for the holiday, but he wanted to stay with us too. He had to come back a couple of times to hug me and shake Wade's hand and wish us Merry Christmas. It was nice to know that he felt that much a part of our home. We gave him packages to carry home to put under the tree so that he would have some of the Dickerson warmth, too, under his tree at home.

Two days before Christmas Tom's grandmother came to visit. She had not been able to visit Tom for a couple of years because of illness in the family. He had spoken of her often during the time and with much longing. Wade and I were apprehensive as to how he would handle the visit for some of the earlier visits had been disastrous. Wade spent a lot of time with Tom the morning of the visit, talking with him about the appropriate ways he should act when his grandmother came. Wade explained to Tom that he was going to have to tell his grandmother that Tom could not have sugar because it wasn't good for him and when grandmother took him out Wade would be asking her to avoid candy. Wade had felt that it was important to discuss this with Tom ahead of time so that Tom would not be embarrassed by the conversation that would need to take place when grandmother arrived.

Grandmother came and grandpa too. Grandpa was not able to get out of the car because of his ill health. Nevertheless, grandmother took Tom on a short shopping trip and out for lunch. He came back with several new articles of clothing and a new flashlight. Grandmother had brought him a large bag of homemade cracker jack to share with the others. It had been a good visit. He had behaved well and was able to get through the experience without a tantrum—a big difference from the last time his grandmother had come to call.

On Christmas Eve Andrew entertained his family around the Christmas tree at our house. His father, mother, brother, and two sisters arrived at 7:00 P.M. to spend some time with him. They brought him gifts which were placed under the tree. He, in turn, had gifts for each of his parents. It had been a special time for Andrew and me when we had shopped for those gifts. We had gone to a gift shop that specialized in candles, and he had selected a beautiful blue Christmas candle for his mother. He was careful as he carried that package and wrapped it for he was very anxious that his mother be pleased.

Christmas Eve by the lighted tree Andrew gave his Christmas gifts to his parents. His mother was pleased with the candle and understood how important it was to Andrew to give her a gift that was like some of the things that he enjoyed in his foster home. I prepared a tray of eggnogs for Andrew to serve his family. He was a gracious host and served the eggnog as though he were used to the task. Wade and I left Andrew and his family alone for the visit. All we know about what occurred were the remarks that his mother and father made as they were leaving. The glow on Andrew's face revealed a great deal, too. He was very proud of himself because he had entertained his parents in his home. The next day when we unwrapped the Christmas presents he was anxious to open first the gifts that his parents had brought to him. Two days after Christmas Andrew's mother and sisters came back to pick him up to take him home for a twenty-four-hour visit. He was a happy boy.

Mark was to have no visitors and this was difficult to accept. A few weeks before Christmas, Mark had had an emergency call from his twenty-year-old sister. The sister had asked that Mark be allowed to visit their mother who was in the hospital and seriously ill. This visit was arranged and Mark spent a couple of days with his sister and his mother's fiance. During the visit Mark's relatives had promised him many things, including a Christmas visit, gifts, his own apartment, and a dog. When he returned home Wade and I were dubious that these gifts would be forthcoming. We were under the impression that there had been many years with no family contact. We asked Mark's social worker to check with the sister and mother to determine whether these promises were to be fulfilled and found that it was not going to be possible for any of the promises to be kept.

At the most, Mark could hope to see his sister if she came for a visit during the month of December, possibly on her birthday. Mark had prepared for his sister's birthday and had made her a gift. He was aware of the birthday when it arrived and was very disappointed when the sister called to say that she had no transportation and would not be able to see him. He had the impression that his sister was going to call him later in the month but as the holiday drew closer and closer Mark began to accept the fact that no one was going to be in touch with him for the Christmas holiday.

Three or four days before Christmas, Mark decided that he was going to pack his suitcase and walk down the street to find his sister. When this happened Wade suggested that it was rather foolish to make such a decision when Mark did not know where his sister lived and Wade did not know either. Wade told him that he would try to contact the social worker to see about arranging for a contact between brother and sister. However, the sister had moved, and her whereabouts were unknown. Mark was distraught and wanted to leave to look for her. Wade took the position that "if you have to go, you have to go. If you are saying that you don't want to stay here for the holidays, but you want to go out and look for your sister, nobody is going to tell you that you cannot do that." It was wise that Wade got out his suitcase and said, "Be careful that you take the things you really need, Mark." Giving Mark the message that it would all right to leave also freed Mark to rethink his decision. He began to realize that he was not fighting Wade, and that it was all right for him to want to find his sister. Wade told him it would be nice if he could see her. Mark decided not to leave the house.

I had called home for some other reason and Wade suggested that I talk to Mark on the phone. Mark and I visited for a while. Finally he told me that he guessed that he was going to put his suitcase away. He was going to wait for me to come home, and we could talk some more about what was real about looking for his sister.

When I returned home that evening we sat and talked. After a few minutes of letting him know that I understood and supported him, I clearly delineated three factors that we could not change for Mark. One fact was that he had seizures. The second fact was that we did not know where his sister lived, and third, we could not take him to see his mother. Those were three conditions that we could not change as his foster parents. No one could change the fact that he had seizures. The situation regarding his mother and his sister could only be resolved by the social worker from the agency. I went on to ask him what would be accomplished if he left a place where he was cared for, respected, and loved to go off on a cold winter day to try to solve three problems that he was not prepared to solve. He thought about this a long time and decided that he really wanted to stay where he was because he was being given care and attention and he was learning how to take care of himself when he had seizures. By working with the social worker perhaps he could figure out how to get in touch with his sister.

At the end of the conversation I said, "Mark, it hurts a lot not to have visitors when the other three boys are having them. I understand that. Maybe we could do something special that could make up a little bit for the fact that you didn't have visitors." I asked him if he would like to have me plan an outing just for him that the other boys would never do. He was pleased with the proposition and eagerly asked, "You won't ever do the exact thing with the other kids?" I promised that I would not. I talked with Wade and Frosty about what would be a reasonable experience for Mark to have that the other children would not have. We decided that Frosty and I would take Mark to see the movie "King Kong" and then out to dinner. Mark was thrilled. He got to ride in my car, which rarely happens because the boys usually ride in the station wagon, and he got to go out with Frosty whom he idolizes.

Two or three times during the outing Mark said to Frosty, "Will you be my 'really' big brother?" Frosty said, "Well, what would that mean, if I were your 'really' big brother? What's in it for you, what's in it for me?" After lots of conversation, they decided that Frosty would not be his really big brother, because that was impossible. Frosty explained to Mark that he never had a really big brother either, that he could not be a really big brother for Mark, but that he could be a *very special friend.*

Many other things happened during Christmas of '76. The boys received sports equipment, radios, and clothes. The gifts were highly individualized and nobody was troubled because the presents were not exactly the same for everybody. Each boy was able to accept the fact that the gifts were based on his particular interests and preferences. The children were involved in preparing the special food and serving the holiday meals. Christmas time was a good time. Tom acted out and Mark had a seizure under the Christmas tree, but Frosty was home for Christmas and that was an affirmation for Wade and me. Frosty stayed home because the children had grown so much. Their behaviors had improved to the extent that he found them tolerable to be around and sometimes fun. But most of all and more important than anything else, Frosty along with his father and mother had come to know four boys as individual boys and not as disabled children. This book is intended to describe what happened in the Dickerson family between November '73 and January '77.

One might say that what started as an involvement with two retarded boys became a commitment to four adolescents who needed help growing up. I am reminded of a quote by W. H. Murray:

> Until one is committed, there is hesitancy, the chance to draw
>   back,
> The moment one definitely commits oneself then Providence
>   does too,
> A whole stream of events issues all manner of unforeseen
>   incidents and meetings,
> And material assistance which no man could have dreamt
>   would have come his way.

And so it is with this book. I never dreamed I would write a book, certainly not one that would describe our family and our growing pains. But here it is. I hope the book will help other foster parents as they raise children who have limitations, for I have described parenting techniques that the boys helped us to develop, use, and evaluate. I have described the positive effects that constant, consistent parenting had upon boys who had been deprived for a long time.

Wade, a retired man, made an enormous difference for four youngsters. It is still uncommon for a man to be the primary parent in any household, yet in our home Wade has been the foster father to four boys. I hope this book will serve as encouragement for other men who contemplate becoming the primary parent for their children. As Wade became the key parent in our home, I needed to become the secondary parent and that was not an easy change for me. Wade and I found no one in our circle of acquaintances who could guide or advise us as we attempted to learn new ways of dividing parental responsibilities, so this book is an attempt to provide some guidance to parents who prefer or need to meet such responsibilities in a new way.

I have tried to describe candidly the feelings of frustration, anger, resentment, and futility that we experienced, as well as the moments of joy, exhilaration, pleasure, and fulfillment. It has been hard work, often tedious and boring, but it has also been rewarding, invigorating, and satisfying to accept the challenge of retardation. As a way of sharing our experience I have described how things happened, with what result, and how Wade and I felt about it.

The book includes a description of the Dickersons before we became a foster family. It describes our selection of the children, preparation of the physical and social setting, introduction of the children to our home, daily activities and routines, determination of the growth needs of each boy, constructive behavior management, crisis intervention, and future plans.

This book deals mostly with Tom and Andrew, the first of our foster sons, and to a lesser extent with Phillip and Mark, who joined our family later. Wade and I are the foster parents in the experience, and our biological children, Jori and Frosty, are transiently involved in the experience. As it is appropriate, other persons are introduced who played an important part in the boys' lives—Frank, John, Noni, Jane, Dwight, Cindy, Bill, and Mike.

Fall 1977   Martha Dickerson

OUR FOUR BOYS

1

From Parenting to Foster Parenting

WADE WAS FIFTY-TWO when he assumed the responsibility of primary parent to our second family. He had retired from self-employment a few years earlier. An only child, Wade was born and raised in Michigan, and he went to college in Vermont, where we met. After a period in the service during World War II he became a partner in his family's hardware business. I grew up in Vermont, the middle in a family of three daughters. Our mother had died when I was fourteen, and our father had remarried when I was seventeen.

I used to tease Wade about marrying me for my family. He had been immediately accepted into the open, frank, noisy, and warm atmosphere that existed in my family home. He was impressed with the easy way my stepmother and Dad could accommodate to the comings and goings of three daughters and their friends. He enjoyed the spontaneity of "stay for dinner, there's enough for one more." He respected the involvement of each family member in the activities of the community. I did not realize until much later the great contrast my home life presented for him. He had grown up alone, the center of attention. He had owned many things but had known few of the experiences common in large families. His family had entertained seldom, and he had been encouraged to keep his friends outside of the house.

When we married there was little doubt that Wade wanted to establish a home that was similar to my Vermont family. Early in our relationship we talked about raising many children. We wanted them for us and we wanted them to be companions for each other. It never entered our minds that we might not be good parents. As the years went on we had two children, first our daughter, Jori, and two years later our son, Frosty. Both children were planned and anticipated with much joy.

To our chagrin, we were very uncomfortable as young parents. The babies' apparent fragility and inability to communicate staggered Wade and me. We were apprehensive that out of ignorance we would do something that would hurt the children or that would not be in their best interests. Somehow, more by good luck than by good management, we survived the first two or three years of parenting. When the children began to talk in sentences and began to take responsibility for some of their actions, we relaxed as parents and began to enjoy them. Preschool, early school years, adolescent years, teenage years, and their twenties were challenging and joyful. We felt loving about our children and loved by them. To have been their parents has been the finest thing to have happened to us individually or as a couple. There have been times during thirty-two years of marriage when Wade and I have had difficulties, but never has there been a problem about accepting, respecting, and honoring the other person as a parent to our children.

Jori and Frosty were bright, curious children, given to much exploration and experimentation. They have had exciting lives and have had the freedom to find their own interests and friends. There were times when we were concerned as parents about the process that Jori or Frosty were in for a period of time. As the years unfolded we were never disappointed with the result of that process. Both Jori and Frosty attended Michigan State University.

Jori pursued an interest in social work and ultimately found herself in Anchorage, Alaska, where she was married. She and her husband have worked for agencies that served children in crisis through residential programs. After three years they decided to relocate in Maine on a small farm, where Jori stays home to be primary parent of their young daughter, and her husband continues to work in a social agency. They are very busy reclaiming an old farm and establishing it as an ecologically balanced, self-sustaining organic farm for their own use. They are competent adults who appear to be able to turn their hands to anything. They are well read and conversant about the affairs of the day and are actively involved in the life of the small community where they live.

Our son Frosty was born with sand between his toes and itching to travel. We tell the story in our family that Frosty received a *National Geographic* magazine subscription for his fifth birthday and that he made the resolution that he would visit all the places he saw illustrated. Frosty has spent the years since college traveling around the world. He has been to more places than I can think to name. He spends his summers in a logging camp in Alaska, saves his money, and indulges his love for travel the balance of the year. Frosty is a giant of a man who has many interests that go along with his excellent health. He enjoys golf, skiing, and rock hunting, but he does not enjoy children. Frosty says that he really does not like little kids much. Although this is his frequent assertion, we often notice that his gentle behavior with little people contradicts this statement.

Down through the years Wade and I had the privilege of having many children in our home. Jori and Frosty brought home their friends and some of them became our friends. Wade and I were involved in many different types of activities that supported the children as they developed relationships with friends in the community. During the early years of our marriage I took primary responsibility for the children because Wade was off to business for the major part of the day and week. He was an involved parent, however, when he was home. He enjoyed sports and athletic activities with the children, swimming with them regularly and playing golf. He was always available to do helpful things to complete particular projects for school.

Once the children were both in school I decided that I wanted to go back to college and complete an undergraduate degree. Wade was supportive in this effort, and subsequently I completed a master's program in social work. From the time I resumed my education our parenting responsibilities became more evenly divided. For the last twenty years of our marriage there has been no division of labor that could be called "his work" or "her work." We have approached tasks by deciding who had the time and energy to do what needed to be done most effectively. This attitude toward family management and parenting meant that many jobs were done in an untraditional manner. Several nights of the week meals were prepared by father. Sometimes Wade managed the car pool. It usually fell to me to attend such things as parent conferences because they could be scheduled around my hours of attending school. As a result of this sharing of responsibilities for home management and parenting, an atmosphere was created where Jori and Frosty were comfortable in approaching either one of us with their problems or concerns. As the years went by the children teased us and said that they thought that Frosty could always get his way with mother and that Jori could always get her way with father. It may have been somewhat true, but I think that might have occurred even had we been traditional parents all through the years.

Wade and I learned very early how vulnerable we were as parents to the children's manipulation. We learned that the only way we could protect ourselves from being put into a corner was always to check out with the children, "Did you ask your mother? What did she say?" Or, "Dad and I will talk about this with you."

We tried to set few limits for our children, but the ones that we did establish we mutually supported. Early on Wade and I determined that certain things would become routine within our family. As a family we would eat dinner together and maintain an acceptable level of cleanliness and order in regard to bathing and laundry. We would attempt to provide each family member with a certain area to keep their own things without fear of intrusion from any other family member and without unnecessary monitoring. Down through the years Wade did a better job than I of respecting Jori's and Frosty's right to privacy of space and time. He could close his eyes to the total confusion that surrounded their activities on occasion. I found that extremely distressful and periodically went on rampages and insisted that bedrooms be cleaned and things be put away. Sometimes I gave in to the idea that it was easier to do it for them, and I never understood, then, why this was not appreciated.

Our two children have become adults for whom we have great respect. We have little apprehension about their ability to take care of themselves in a complicated world. The children brought tremendous joy, excitement, and warmth into our home. The traditional things—holidays, birthdays, pets, hobbies, games—were experiences that we all shared in such a way that we thoroughly enjoyed the meaning of "family." Wade frequently commented on how different he was experiencing his family of choice as opposed to his family of origin. No doubt the children enjoyed many things with their father to an unusual extent because Wade was making up for time he had lost as a little boy.

Since we never did become comfortable with babies we decided soon after Frosty's birth that we did not wish to have any more biological children. However, we knew that we wanted to be involved with children and adolescents throughout our lives. We knew that we should not burden Jori and Frosty with our need to be around young people and our need to continue to be parents. We talked a lot about starting a camp where we could spend the summers with children in a free, growth-producing situation. During the early years of our marriage we used to look at sites and dream of the camp that we would develop in some part of New England. As the years went on we began to recognize something about ourselves that certainly would be an impediment to owning a camp. Neither Wade nor I give a hoot about taking care of large areas of land. Neither one of us enjoys yard work or gardening. We began to realize that the maintenance and supervision of a camp was beyond our interest and ability.

We began to modify the dream and talk about developing an after-care home for emotionally disturbed children. We were aware that many children who achieved stability in institutions did not have the resource of a stable family to accept them on discharge. While never considering developing a treatment home for emotionally disturbed children, we did want to provide a warm, secure home atmosphere for a child in lieu of an unstable family home once the therapy process had been completed. We used to think we might be able to manage three or four teenagers in this setting. The dream became so much a topic of our discussion and planning that we took steps to do it. After preliminary discussions with an agency with whom we wished to work, we examined property that would accommodate a larger group of people. Finally, the cooperating agency selected a teenaged boy they wished to place in our home.

Wade met the young man many times, came to feel a strong attachment to him, and believed that he could be of help to him as he struggled to find his way back to an acceptable life style. There were many complications about the placement's becoming a reality. Eventually the teenager decided that he preferred to live in a setting more familiar to him and closer to his family. Wade was very disappointed and hurt, and he felt rejected. As is his habit when he is extremely pained by some incident, he withdrew to lick his wounds. He is not open to discuss his feelings at such times. It was difficult for me to see him cope with this disappointment for it had happened to him soon after he had retired and was looking for new interests in his life.

The boy's decision not to come to live in our home made Wade reconsider all of his thoughts about early retirement and his dream of creative activity for the rest of his life. When Wade had decided to retire we had lengthy conversations as to what that meant to our relationship, especially in terms of my wanting to continue to work professionally. Since I had completed a master's degree in social work just two years before Wade's retirement, I was not ready to give up that important piece of experience. We talked about how we would feel if I was out in the work world every day and Wade was living on a less structured plan. Wade said that he could be comfortable with my working as long as I was excited about my work, but that he would find it difficult to see me doing boring, frustrating work if he was carving his life to suit himself.

I had worked many years before and during graduate school in the field of the aging, and I had always wanted to have more experience working with adolescents and young adults. Through a friend I made a contact with an agency that was serving adults with retardation who were being returned to the community after years of living in an institution. My friend was providing group services on a part-time basis to some of these young adults and invited me to visit a couple of sessions. I was apprehensive as I went to meet these young people for the first time. Prior to this my experience with retardation had been limited to providing recreational programs on three different occasions to a group of children. I recalled all kinds of misinformation as I drove to the meeting place that night. I wondered if the young adults would "look and sound" retarded. Would they have vacant faces and grasping hands? Would I know what to do, what to say? Would I be turned off by their "strangeness"? After two hours with the group and observing my friend with them, I realized that I had met some people with whom I would like to work.

In a matter of weeks I became a civil service employee for the state of Michigan assigned to the Wayne Regional Center for the Mentally Retarded. I was given the assignment of working with adults with retardation as they learned to cope with the challenges of the inner city. One of my earliest experiences was working with a group of seven women who had been placed in a group home. My task was to help the young women become comfortable enough with the city bus so that they could go downtown to the center where other activities and services were available to them. I met for several sessions in the group home with the young women while they learned about such things as the appropriate clothing to wear outdoors in the winter and the attention a person gave to herself before she prepared to go out for an afternoon with other people. After five or six sessions it was time to teach the women how to use the public bus. Conversations with a friend prepared me for the fact that there were twenty-one specific behaviors that had to be learned in order to use the bus independently.

I was terrified at the thought of helping seven women with retardation learn the twenty-one particular behaviors that they needed in order to go across the inner city of Detroit to the downtown area to the center. I recruited my retired husband as a volunteer to help me. We looked for books in the library to give us some clues, directions, or guidelines as to how to train people who were severely retarded to get around a community independently. Some materials had been prepared on how to "mobility train" the person who was blind that gave encouragement but little specific help. Since we found none, we proceeded on the first of many of our trial-and-error experiences. Together, over a period of several days, Wade and I successfully trained seven women to use the city bus. In the process we learned which of their behaviors were dysfunctional for them as they lived in the city. Within the institutional setting they had been permitted to speak to all adults that they met and in many instances spoke to them in endearing terms such as "dearie," "daddy," "mummy," and so forth. The first time we rode the bus with the seven women scattered to take available seats, Wade was embarrassed to have a thirty-year-old woman screech at him, "Daddy, Daddy, Daddy Wade, wait for me, wait for me." He said afterwards he felt like a jerk to have this attention focused on him. He realized also how vulnerable it made the woman appear.

We talked about the enormous challenge to the person with retardation who returned to the community after years in an institution. The person needed to learn new functional behaviors in order to survive. The person also needed to unlearn many behaviors that had worked previously but which now made them targets of ridicule. During the three years I was with that agency Wade devoted many volunteer hours to the program when it was necessary to have an additional responsible adult to accompany me and the young adults to community activities such as the state fair and the ball game. Wade was a willing volunteer and over the years developed some warm relationships with several of the young people. It made my working experience richer because I was able to come home and discuss the challenges of and my concerns with and in behalf of my clients. We discussed the issues of guardianship, sexuality, parents' rights, premature institutionalization, and normalization.

I guess it. should not have come as a surprise to me that in January 1973 a new goal emerged for us as a couple, and a new plan evolved as to how we would use our time in the next few years. "Why do we wait until we find the dream property to have the dream house for emotionally disturbed adolescents?" "Isn't that kind of dumb?" "We're getting older." "Why don't we do something right now about people who are in institutions and should not be." "Why don't we see if we can find three or four children and help them find their way into the community earlier." In January 1973 I began to realize that all of our talk focused on one topic. Our goal was becoming firm.

We began to realize there was a way to be involved, and so we started to investigate the idea of becoming training/foster parents for adolescents who were retarded. We began to explore the different things that would have to happen in order for this to become reality for us. The very first issue that needed to be confronted was a career decision for me. In order for us to move in the direction of licensure, I needed to leave civil service. It was considered a conflict of interest in the state of Michigan to be working for the Department of Mental Health as a civil service worker and, at the same time, have a contract as a foster parent. The first big decision was whether or not I was willing to give up a job in order to be a parent again. It took no time at all for me to decide I was willing to give up my state job and civil service status, but I was not willing to say that I would give up my career. This meant that Wade and I had to discuss anew the issue of my continuing as a professional person. I knew that I wanted to be involved professionally, at least on a part-time basis, for many more years, but I was willing to take one year off to establish a new family at home. We agreed that I would spend up to, but not more than, a year away from professional commitment so that I could help establish a secure and stable home within which to raise retarded children. It was clearly understood between us that at the end of a year I would again be away from home for at least part of a work week.

We came to realize that if I was going to be away from home for a good percentage of time, that would have a bearing on the age and the sex of the children we should have in our home. We recognized the realities of prejudices in our state about the primary parent and the sex of the child living in the home. We realized that we would be subject to criticism if Wade was a primary parent to a houseful of girls or to a coed situation. Since Wade would be the primary parent this was the factor that led us to the decision to raise boys. Since neither of us felt very comfortable with young children, we wanted to work with children at least ten years old. We thought that a boy with retardation would have many behaviors comparable to a much younger child and that that would be challenging enough for us without adding the problems of parenting little persons. We talked of building a family around one boy to whom we would make the commitment to provide a home until he was eighteen. Then we would seek other children to balance the family according to the youngest member's needs. We spent days and days exploring these ideas with many different people. Some people tried to discourage us because of our age, but a few gave us some encouragement. We went on with our plans and dreams. We decided that I would resign my job as of June 1, 1973, and then we would take a lengthy vacation in preparation for our new commitment.

When we were firm in our intention to foster parent boys over the age of ten with retardation, we contacted the Macomb Oakland Regional Center, which made a number of services available to us. We went through the procedure of filling out the application forms to become foster parents. We were interviewed. We were evaluated. Wade and I took eight sessions of training to learn how to be foster parents. We told the agency social worker that we would be available to accept boys in our home in October of '73, explaining that we wanted a period of time to prepare ourselves psychologically for our new responsibilities.

I well remember the social work interview when we were questioned about the type of children that we would have in our home. Wade and I had decided that since he would be the primary parent for many years he should have selection of the children. We discussed with the social worker the type of children with whom we would be willing to work. I was a silent participant in this lengthy interview because I was trying to honor the agreement that Wade would have the decision about the selection of children. I found it interesting that Wade told the social worker that he felt that he could handle almost any kind of children. She kept asking him questions about different types of limitation and to every situation he would respond, "Oh, I think I could handle that," or "I think that that would be OK." Those were the answers that he gave to her when she asked about epilepsy, cerebral palsy, blindness, hearing loss, retardation, and behavioral problems. Always the same answer, "Oh, I think that that would be OK. I think I could manage that."

He told the worker that he would first like to have an opportunity to observe children with problems of hyperactivity and epilepsy because he was unfamiliar with these problems, but he was willing to take a look at this kind of situation to see if he felt that he could manage it. He said he would be willing to visit the institution to meet different children to get some sense of his feeling about being able to build workable relationships with children who had different limitations. I was very nervous during this whole conversation. I thought, "My God, what is he committing us to. He doesn't know what the hell he's talking about. We'll have a houseful of demanding children and we won't know what we're doing."

Finally Wade said to the social worker, "There's just one thing that I don't want. I could not tolerate a child who had a history of abusing animals. I would find that intolerable. In our home animals are respected almost as much as people. I would not want to have to teach a child how to respect animals. Please do not select a child for our consideration who has a history of abusing animals." The worker and I both looked at him in amazement. I think it was the first time that she had ever heard a potential foster parent make such an unusual request. After the social worker left, I asked Wade about his position and he explained to me: "After all, our Siberian huskies are big animals and they're old. They should not be expected to have to learn to accommodate to children's behavior at this late stage. I want any kids who come to live with us to be able to accept immediately the need to respect Kai and Ziggie."

During this process one of our friends spent a great deal of time with Wade and me forcing us to address the whole issue of our motivation for taking on these children, our expectations about this involvement, and our stability in terms of being able to reach a commitment. He persisted in being the devil's advocate in the discussions. This served a good purpose for Wade and me because his questions and challenges forced us to think through and plan preventively in many ways that we otherwise would not have recognized. We acknowledged that we were leaving behind a life stage that permitted a lot of freedom to come and go, freedom to travel, freedom to make spontaneous decisions. He asked us to consider what it would mean to us to be tied down. There were times during this discussion that I questioned whether or not he believed that Wade and I would be suitable parenting people for children other than our own. It was a source of dismay for me. Later, after we had lived through the experience, I realized what a true friend he had been to ask us all the difficult questions and to force us to address many issues in advance. During the three years we have been foster parents, he has been one of our consistent supporters and a resourceful friend.

Our conversations with this friend helped us think about how we could protect our need for privacy. The idea of having live-in help came to us as a way of meeting our needs to be away from the children while knowing they were well cared for. We realized it would be growth producing for the boys to have contact with adult models other than their foster parents, but this was a secondary consideration in our planning stage. Thinking of ways to attend to our own needs, we realized that we would want time out of the home away from the children, and there would be times when we would want time within our home separate from the children. As we began to think of the idea of help we decided that we would attempt to employ male students in the graduate school of social work. This had to do with our experience in the past with several young friends who had gone through the graduate school of social work under great financial stress. We knew how glad they had been to find part-time work to defray some of their expenses. We began to consider the idea of having at least 10 hours a week of input from such a student. We thought of this as time spent with the children in growth producing activities. Also, it would provide Wade and me with the opportunity to be separate from the children.

The more we thought about this idea the more we began to think that it would be a perfect situation if we could find a male graduate social work student to live in our home for the length of time that he was in his graduate program. We believed that we could afford to provide a student with board and room, $200 a month salary, and the use of a vehicle in exchange for 75 hours a month work with the boys. We assumed that many of those hours would be times when the children were asleep. We theorized that to have such a person in our home would develop a kind of model family for our foster boys and provide model male behaviors at various life stages. We began to conceptualize that the student would be something like an older brother. We knew of one couple who had indicated interest in what we were doing. We wanted them to come to our home on a monthly basis to stay with the children for 36–48-hour blocks of time so we could have lengthy periods away.

As we began to think about how we would provide supervision for our children we began to realize that our seven-room house was not quite large enough for our endeavor. We began to consider renovating a larger house that my husband also owned a block down the street. It was the house that had been his boyhood home and had been in his family for several generations. The house was considerably larger and we realized it would provide for more privacy for everyone concerned.

June 1973 found Wade and me ready to take an extended holiday. We had fulfilled all the requirements for licensure and were contracted to work with the Macomb Oakland Regional Center. We had a firm commitment to take two boys into our home in the fall. We had taken the training provided. I had resigned from my position. The decision had been made to renovate the larger house and the tenants had been notified that they would need to move out by September of 1973. Wade and I packed our van for the long trip to Alaska where we intended to spend many days camping with Jori and her husband. Frosty planned to join us there so that we could have a final family vacation before Wade and I started on our second family.

Many, many hours of driving along the Transcanada and Alcan Highway were spent discussing and drawing the renovation plans for the big house. Every detail was discussed and rediscussed in terms of the function it would serve for the children and the parents. We decided that we wanted to create a kind of home that would allow for maximum expression of individual preference by every family member. The big house was ample enough to allow for two large twin bedrooms, two single bedrooms, a bath, and a playroom on the second floor. The first floor allowed for a living room, dining room, kitchen, and then a parents' suite. The suite contained a bedroom, sitting room, dressing room, and bathroom. It was arranged so that it could be closed off from the rest of the house if we so desired. Since the sitting room was adjacent to the dining room it could be incorporated easily into the total floor plan when we planned to entertain a large group of people. One of the wisest decisions Wade made was to create the parents' suite. It proved to be the safety zone where, as parenting people, we could retreat, rest, and recover in order to return to the challenges of parenting.

It was planned that one single bedroom would be for the use of the live-in worker, a second single bedroom would be for the use of our son on his rare visits or as a guest room. The two large twin bedrooms would ultimately be used by three or four boys. We planned to add a large porch on the rear of the house and to make the yard a childsafe play area that would eventually include a swimming pool and a tartop area half the size of a basketball court.

Hours and hours were spent planning, designing, and figuring. We believed that we would be able to renovate, furnish, and equip the larger facility for the amount of money we could recover for selling our seven-room home. It was on this basis that we made our plans. We had many heated discussions as to what furnishings we would keep and/or discard. We were suddenly faced with the realization that by making this move we had far too much furniture and much of that was inappropriate. In order to make the new facility functional for the children, we needed to take a whole new approach to furnishing the playroom, bedrooms, and dining room. What should we do with all the furniture that was in storage in attics, garages, and cellarways? There were several pieces of furniture that had been in Wade's family for years that he wanted to keep. Especially important to him were three Chinese rugs that he wanted to use in our new home. We had some spirited quarrels, discussions, arguments about the practicality of using some of the furnishings in the way he wished to use them. My idea of a childsafe home was, in retrospect, not much different from a traditional institution. Truthfully, I had envisioned a dining room with a bare tile floor. I thought that fragile furniture and objects should be stored for the duration of our second family. Wade was adamant that this would not be the case. He insisted that children could learn to live with beautiful things and learn to take care of them. I knew he was wrong. I knew that he was going to regret his decision, but there is no changing his mind when he is so determined. The issue of whether or not to use the rugs in the living areas became a topic that could not be discussed.

We talked a lot about the advantages of having two children live with us at our present house as we went through the process of renovating and moving into the new house. We anticipated that the children would develop a sense of ownership, pride, and concern because of this involvement. We anticipated that they would experience this as an affirmation of their right to be so involved. We did not begin to anticipate all of the good things that would happen ultimately for two boys because of this plan.

As luck would have it, in late May of 1973, just prior to terminating my work, I talked with the Director of Social Work at the Institute for the Study of Mental Retardation and Related Disabilities at the University of Michigan about the possibilities of my joining the staff there as a Program Associate in Social Work. I was very attracted to the institute and to the program as it was described to me. I was interested in working there on a part-time or full-time basis. So Wade and I had left for Alaska knowing that I had indicated interest in resuming professional involvement. Whether or not this would happen depended on the institute's decision. It had been our original intention that I would stay home up to a year to help Wade in the process of establishing a family and to be helpful in all the extra work involved in renovating and moving into a new home. But suddenly here was a professional opportunity, and I did not wish to lose it. We needed to negotiate again what this would mean to us in terms of starting a family. Wade was supportive, feeling that one had to take opportunities when they came along, and it seemed logical that I continue professional involvement in the field of retardation. We decided that one of the first things that would happen, if I took full-time employment, would be to hire a person to help with the heavy cleaning in our home on a once-or-twice-a-week basis. We agreed to line up people to help us upon our return in the fall.

We began to think about how we were going to manage the children. Who was going to be the decision maker? Who was going to have the final say in the household? We really had to think this through. We recognized, without any planning or deciding, that I had become the primary decision maker during the course of raising our biological children because Wade had been at work many of the times when there were decisions to be made. He had always been involved in the planning, but the day-to-day decisions had been made by the parent-in-residence, who happened to be me. It became increasingly clear to us that we would not have this pattern with our second family because I was going to be away a good share of the time and Wade would be with the children most of the time.

We began to realize that Wade was truly going to be the primary parent. I had some difficulty with that. Down through the years I had become quite comfortable with the power of motherhood, and certainly the community within which we lived supported that situation. There were not too many working mothers and stay-at-home fathers in our suburban area. I wanted the freedom to be away, but I was not ready to give up the privileges and authority that I had experienced in the earlier years. The only way that I could honestly make the commitment to Wade that I could accept him as the final decision maker was on the condition that he promise always to consider my feelings and suggestions. We talked about this a great deal, even discussing the different types of situations

that might come up that he would have to handle. After these discussions I was able to say to him that in a crisis situation I could be
comfortable with his making the decision and that I would accept
his decision as final. We agreed that all planning and goal setting
would always be subject to discussion between the two of us. Wade
assured me that in every instance that it was possible he would sit
down and discuss with me point by point a plan of action, a strategy,
an intervention. Once the decision was made I agreed to accept the
decision. I considered this the second most critical agreement Wade
and I made as we approached parenting for the second time. Our
first big decision had been to recognize and prepare for our need for
privacy.

By the time we reached Anchorage and joined our children we
had solidified our plans. By the time we were with them we were in
concert on all of our plans, strategies, and on the timetable. We
thought we were prepared to take on the discussions with our children, but we were naive. We had expected that we could make an announcement as to how and what we were doing, that there would be
a certain amount of curiosity and then instant statements of support from the kids. I had assumed that they were so involved in
their own lives that they would have only passing interest in what
we did. It came as no new statement to our children that we were so
committed, because they had always known that we wanted to do
something on this order. But they were not prepared for the carefully thought-through plan of work their father and I presented to
them in the summer of '73. I had anticipated they might be somewhat disturbed about the fact that we were selling or were planning
to sell the home that they had lived in for years, but we were pleasantly surprised to find that was not a concern. Jori could remember
living in her father's old house as a very little girl years before.
Frosty told us that he had always loved the old house and was
pleased to think that we were going to move back into it to make it
home again.

Jori was supportive about the idea of our raising more children.
That was not too surprising, since a few years earlier when we had
celebrated our twenty-fifth wedding anniversary she had suggested
to us that we have more children—an appalling thought. Her husband was equally supportive. Their work had helped them realize
how important parenting surrogates can be for children who are for
some reason or other unable to be with their own family. Jori really
believed that children would be better off living with us than in an

institution, but she wanted assurance from us that there would always be a bedroom in our house for her brother who was still unmarried. She said to us, "I'm on my way to establishing my own home and I don't need a place to go. But until Frosty has that kind of relationship and commitment to somebody else, then I want to know that my brother always has that in your home." We reassured Jori that we had planned for Frosty. It was heartwarming to us as parents to hear her express such a bonding, loving concern for her brother.

Frosty was overtly and instantly critical of "the whole damn plan." "You must be insane" was the least extreme statement he made. "You've got us kids raised and off doing our own thing and you're at a place in your lives where you can come and go as you please, travel, do what you wish, and carry minimal responsibility. Why in hell would you want to tie yourselves down to raise more children? And *retarded* kids!" He was traveling a great deal and he could not conceive why anyone would want to be tied down. "Look how hard you're going to have to work again. Why should you want to take on so much work. And especially with children who are not going to make a lot of progress." The whole issue of the retardation was one he had difficulty in handling with us. He would have found it initially easier to accept that we were going to take children into our home who were ill and would get well. To work with children who had retardation and who would never become high achievers was difficult, nearly impossible, for him to comprehend. He felt that there was a large need in the child care field for parents such as ourselves, "but if you're going to be crazy enough to do something like that, why don't you work with children who have a greater potential for achievement?" It was interesting that after several days Frosty said to us, "Well, if you're really going to remodel the old house this winter, I just might come home and help."

And Frosty did. He came home in December of 1973 and spent four months helping in the remodeling job. When he came home and met the children he stayed at our house for two days. Then he said to his father, "I don't want to live in this house with these kids right now. I'm going to live down in the other house while I'm working on it. Even though we're tearing down stairways and taking down walls I can always find a place to put up a cot. I'll find a place somewhere down there to sleep. I'll come home for dinner, but that's all I can take." To me he said, "It's important for me to do it this way, Mother, because I really don't like to be around the kids that much." I respected him for being so straight and it was easy to make arrangements for him to live in the other house. It has been interesting over the three years to watch what has happened with Frosty and the boys. With exposure has come tolerance. With tolerance has come understanding, and some acceptance and liking. But I'm ahead of myself.

2

The First Two Foster Sons Arrive

BY MID-SEPTEMBER OF 1973 we had returned to Michigan and I had signed a contract at the Institute for the Study of Mental Retardation and Related Disabilities. Wade contacted the social worker at Macomb Oakland Regional Center to say that we were home and ready, willing, and able to receive children. In a matter of days the social worker arranged for Wade to visit the state institution from which the boys would be placed. The institution Wade visited that fall was a huge, old facility that accommodated several thousand residents. He observed several children in a classroom and visited the dormitory where they spent their non-school hours. Several children had been considered appropriate for placement, and Wade selected from that group the boys he wished to have in his home. When Wade came home after spending a day at the institution he said to me, "Well, I picked the boy around whom I want to build a family and you are not going to like him." I wondered why. He said, "Oh, he will be a chore. He is just one troubled kid. He's constantly moving and his mouth never closes. He is a wheeler, a pistol. He is going to be very, very difficult." So I said to him, "Why in the world did you select him as your number-one choice?" He answered, "Because he's such a fighter, I think he wants to survive. I think he wants to get out of that system. I think he's fighting so hard that somebody ought to help him. There was a time or two in that classroom when that kid asked a question that was sensible and it should have been answered and nobody paid attention."

Wade said if he was able to have Tom, the second child should be a very obedient, docile, manageable child, for, as he said, "I'll

19

have my hands full with Tom. And I think it ought to be balanced by the second child being a more manageable kid." Wade told me that the choice for the second boy was between a child named Andrew and a child named Phillip. His inclination was to choose Andrew because Andrew was closer to Tom's age. Ultimately Tom, eleven, and Andrew, thirteen, were his choices. Wade indicated to the worker at the institution that he would consider Phillip for placement in the future if he were still in the institution. However, he knew that he wanted many months to work with the two boys to help them feel at home and to accomplish the move into a larger house. He told the placement social worker that if, in a year's time, everyone was surviving well in the family setting he would be willing to come back to the institution to select a third boy. Phillip would be an acceptable choice, and this, too, turned out to be the way it was.

We started work on renovating the old house early in October. Wade employed a carpenter and his assistant to work with him on complete reroofing, rewiring, replumbing, repainting, and landscaping. It was a lengthy process. It was good to have the month of October to get started on the renovation process and to get some sense of what the demands of that would be. Nevertheless, we were anxious and found it difficult to understand why the agency took so long to place the children after Wade had been to the institution.

Finally, Tom and Andrew were brought for a forty-eight-hour period to visit us in our home. Wade and I were nervous as we ate breakfast that Monday morning, wondering what we had let ourselves in for. What were the children going to be like? It was with apprehension and relief that we answered the door at about 10:30. Two social workers from the institution stood there with two boys, Tom and Andrew. Andrew said not a word, but Tom was loudly saying, "I want to get back in the car. I want to go back. I don't want to stay here. I don't want to stay here." The social workers urged him to come in. He entered the house and immediately saw our cat, Boots. Instantly he started chasing her around the house and quickly caught her. He brought her into the living room and sat down and began to stroke her. I tried to explain to him how to hold the old cat, but he was too excited at having this animal in his arms to listen. Bootsie, sixteen years old, was used to being treated gently, but during this encounter she was extremely patient. I think Bootsie knew that the boys were loving her, but they did not know how to love her gently. In any event Tom was able to get past those

first terrifying moments in our strange home because this lovely old
cat allowed herself to be touched, squeezed, and loved. Andrew was
as nervous about being there as Tom but not quite as verbal about
it. He looked around at everything, picked up various things around
the house, studied them, and put them down. After a half hour the
workers decided that they were ready to leave. Tom and Andrew
were comfortable enough to stay. They did not even walk to the
door as the social workers left.

When we were alone, I said to the boys, "Are you hungry?
Would you like to help fix lunch?" They thought that was a good
idea. I let each of them have an apple as they went into the kitchen.
As they munched their apples, they watched me start fixing lunch.
It was a very simple lunch and they both wanted to be involved in
helping to prepare it. Tom put water in the kettle and added the hot
dogs. He had the job of standing at the stove to watch and tell me
when the hot dogs boiled. He also unwrapped rolls, put them in a
pan, and placed them in the oven to warm. Andrew agreed to set the
table. I put all the necessary articles on a tray. He carried it into the
dining room and set the table slowly and well. When he was done he
quietly came out and watched the rest of the process in the kitchen.
Tom learned how to use tongs to take hot dogs out of the boiling
water and place them in the rolls. Andrew served applesauce.

The children were very hungry, but it was interesting to note
the difference in the way they ate. Andrew ate very slowly and
deliberately, but Tom ate as though there were no tomorrow and he
would never see food again. He rammed the food into his mouth and
tried to take another bite while his mouth was full of food. My husband and I said nothing about their eating habits or table manners
because we were waiting to see how they behaved. We tried to have
a conversation at lunch. Tom gave only yes and no answers, but Andrew was curious and asked all kinds of questions. Unfortunately,
the catsup poured too easily and the boys used far too much. I asked
them if they wanted an extra roll so they would not have to have all
that soupy stuff. This was not acceptable. It dawned on me that
they were delighted to have as much as they wanted. They were deliberately using more than was appropriate. As they finished lunch
they wanted to know, "What are we going to do now?" I explained
that we were going to tidy up after lunch. We would wash our hands
and do the dishes. Tom wanted to know if we had a vacuum cleaner,
asked if he could vacuum, and did the dining room. While he was involved in this, Andrew and I did the dishes. Andrew had learned

that dishes were rinsed and stacked before they were put in a basin to be washed. He was a little unsure as to how to rinse dishes, but he thoroughly enjoyed drying and stacking the dishes. He quickly learned to sort the silverware into the various notches in the silver-tray. When the inside chores were done, we went outdoors to do a chore.

We had deliberately selected a chore to see how well they could manage staying in the yard and following directions for a simple task. The job was to load seventy-five bricks into the van, ride down to the other house, and unload them. It was interesting to watch the boys try to do this task with us. Tom's interest lasted all of two trips, carrying two bricks at a time. After two trips he was bored. Andrew was not interested in getting his hands dirty. He was more excited about climbing in the van and looking at all the parts of the vehicle. Once again we put no demands upon them because we were interested in finding out how well they could follow directions. When we were done we climbed into the van and the children imme-diately got into the back seat and fastened their seatbelts. We went down the street and proceeded to unload the bricks. Andrew en-joyed placing the bricks in a neat pile. When the task was done we told the boys that we were going to the cider mill.

We had selected the cider mill because we thought it would not be crowded on this day. We would have an opportunity to observe the children in a free, community-type experience. We were about five miles from home when both Tom and Andrew began saying they had to go to the toilet. I played a hunch and gambled that they were nervous and were using this as a ploy, and I found out that this was true. During their visit with us whenever they became unsure about the situation or did not know how to cope, the first thing they said was that they had to go to the toilet. We went on to the cider mill and they were excited by the sights and sounds. They were ap-prehensive about trying cider because it was unfamiliar to them, but when we explained it was like pop, they tried it and enjoyed it. We bought doughnuts, which were familiar to them.

At the cider mill the boys spotted a little girl, fourteen or fifteen months old, toddling around between the tables. The boys wanted to pick her up. I told them that they could not pick her up because we did not know her and we did not pick up strange children that we did not know. They accepted my explanation but they did not like it. I realized that they had little opportunity to be around little chil-dren and they were wanting to be loving to the little girl. However, their behavior could be easily misconstrued in a place such as the cider mill.

After we returned home the boys wanted to know if they could watch television. Their interest lasted about two minutes and they wanted to flip the channels, explore Wade's desk, and take all the magazines and books off the bookcases and magazine racks. Wade and I sat with the children in the den and tried to engage them in conversation and games but with little success. Finally I left to prepare dinner while Wade monitored the children.

When dinner was ready, Andrew again set the table and Tom helped put the food on the table. They were delighted with the menu: baked chicken, mashed potatoes, vegetables, tossed salad, and milk. We were pleased at how they tried to imitate our behavior at the table. They tried to eat the chicken with their knife and fork, but soon they were picking up the drumsticks. We told them that this behavior was acceptable as it was difficult to eat chicken without using fingers. We noticed that both the boys had a tendency to use far too much salt. We thought this might have something to do with the dearth of salt shakers at the institution dining table. They enjoyed eating salad; they wanted to have more and more. When the main course was completed I told them the kinds of ice cream from which they could choose. The boys were pleased with the "welcome" cake. It was surprising to me how quickly Andrew got into the routine. He wanted to help put away food and dry and stack the dishes. Again Tom wanted to vacuum.

During dinner we explained to the boys that Frank would be working with them too, that he would come after dinner to meet them and have popcorn, but only after the chores had been completed.

Shortly after the chores, Frank arrived. He sat down and visited with the boys for a few minutes before we started the bath procedure. We told the boys that they could decide whether they wanted a tub bath or a shower. Tom chose a tub bath so he was going to bathe downstairs. Andrew chose the shower. Both boys did quite well bathing. They were able to soap their bodies and rinse themselves. Tom needed to be reminded to pick up his dirty clothes and hang up his towel. Andrew folded every article of clothing he took off. When the baths were done we gathered around the dining table and made popcorn.

The popcorn popper is the type that you can see through and watch the popcorn popping. The boys enjoyed this. It was less than an hour and a half since dinnertime and Tom had certainly eaten an adequate dinner, but he ate two large bowls of popcorn. We began to realize that we would have to help Tom from overeating.

Soon it was time for bed. The two boys would be sharing a bedroom. We went upstairs with them and they climbed into their beds. Andrew was willing to settle down but Tom was very, very active, bouncing and yelling. I sat on the bed and put my hand on his arm and talked with him until he began to settle down. I realized he was trying to keep himself awake so I said I would sit in the chair until they were asleep. After a half hour the boys were asleep.

The next day the boys were up as soon as they heard me taking my shower. There were lots of things that came out such as, "Why are you using the boys' bathroom?" It seemed to Tom and Andrew that all the bathrooms in the house were exclusively for the use of men. They could not understand how I could use the same bathroom because at the institution boys and girls had separate bathrooms. I had to go to work that day so the boys helped to prepare breakfast. I explained that I would be gone all day. Andrew walked me to the door and told me that he would have the table set when I returned. Subsequently, I found that the boys had a very good day.

After breakfast they went outdoors with my husband to play ball and other games and watched him as he mowed the lawn. At no time would they go near his dogs. They were very fearful of them. After lunch they went to a nearby lake, and again Wade noticed their nervousness and their requests to go to the bathroom as a way of getting out of a situation. He had anticipated this and had reminded them both to go to the bathroom before they started on their ride. As they pressured him to go to the toilet he told them they would have to act grown-up and wait. Out in the country they got out of the car to walk around on the nature trail. Tom spotted an old, discarded child's pacifier lying on the ground. He immediately grabbed it and placed it in his mouth. It was difficult to get him to give it up. The boys were very frightened and wanted to get back in the car. Wade did not force them. The reason for the trip was to find out just what they could manage, so he let the children get back in the car and they returned home. They had some free time to play and then they helped him fix dinner. When I arrived home everything was going smoothly. They had made a big kettle of chili and there was salad and vegetables. The boys were eating very well but we noticed again they were using far too much seasoning. When I asked the children what kind of ice cream they would like, I was pleased that Andrew felt comfortable enough to say that if there was any applesauce he would rather have that. I found out that one of Andrew's activities during the day had been to make a thorough inventory of the refrigerator to find out what was in it.

Wade went out in the evening. We had decided to follow our usual routines so the boys could get used to our comings and goings. Frank came, visited with the children for a few minutes and took over supervising bathtime. Both boys decided on a shower and Tom wanted to use the hair dryer that he had discovered in the upstairs bathroom. While Frank supervised the bathing of one boy, I was with the other in the study, trying to read a story. The baths were uneventful. While I was trying to read a story to Tom, he snuggled down into my lap and said very clearly, "I want titty." I didn't even give a facial clue that I had heard. However, I think that Tom felt that he had been heard because he started saying other things like, "I want titty. I like pussy." While this was going on Andrew came into the room and giggled and thus supported Tom's behavior. When I did not respond the incident came to an end. We had asked the boys to call us by our first names, and several times during the evening they both asked, "Where's Wade?" Frank and I told them several times that Wade had gone out for the evening and they would see him in the morning. They were interested in where I worked and I told them that I was at the university. They wanted to know if I was a secretary. I tried to explain to them what I did but it made no sense to them. Again we started the bedtime procedure and when they climbed into bed Tom needed a lot of help to calm down. As he began to get drowsy he said to me, "Where is Daddy?" I assumed that he meant Wade. I wondered if it would have helped to calm him if I had let him have a cup of milk. In any event that evening the boys said to me, "Do we have to go back tomorrow?" I answered, "Yes, your visit is over." I explained to them that this had been a trial time and they had to go back the next day.

The next day my alarm went off at 6:30 and I got up to take my shower. As I opened my door both boys were standing there. They evidently had been awake for some time but had been quiet so as not to awaken us and I commended them on their consideration. They wanted to know if Daddy had really come back. "Is he really there?" Again they asked if they really had to go back and I said, "Yes." I had breakfast with the children and for the second time I allowed them to choose exactly what they wanted for breakfast and prepared it for them. One of them had bacon and eggs and the other had cold cereal. I explained to them that I had to leave because I had an appointment in the city. Again they wanted to know if they had to go back. I said they did.

Andrew became very upset and went into the study and threw himself face down on the sofa. I found out later that he spent the major part of the morning in that position. Tom followed Wade around the entire morning. When the workers from the institution arrived he threw his arms and legs around Wade and hung onto him for dear life. The boys did not want to leave Wade and our home, but they had to. Wade assured them that as far as he was concerned he was planning on their return. I had thought that most people who were institutionalized would prefer to be at home or some other place in the community. The boys' wish to stay with us seemed to confirm this impression. The boys did have the right to refuse to live with us and stay in the institution, and their parents or legal guardians also had the privilege of refusing the particular placement.

Two weeks were to pass before the children would come to live with us permanently. During those two weeks the children would be given complete physicals and be completely outfitted with new clothing. During that time Andrew's family had the option of coming to visit us to determine whether or not they approved of the placement arranged for their son. The agency social worker made arrangements for the children with the local school district so that upon coming to live in our home the boys would be enrolled immediately in special classes. Andrew came from a family of six, and they live not too far from our home. When Wade and I learned this we had some misgivings about accepting a boy for placement in our home when the parents lived so close by. It turned out that the parents shared our concern. Wade and I had a lengthy conference with the agency social worker. We came to the agreement that any work that would need to be done with the family was the agency's responsibility. We agreed to provide the agency with all the information that was needed to keep the family aware of Andrew's progress. It would be the agency's responsibility to decide what information would be shared with the family. We agreed that any visits between Andrew and his family would be arranged through the social worker and we would be notified when Andrew would be visiting his parents.

The social worker called about the end of October and said that Andrew's family was interested in meeting us. They wanted to know where and with whom their son would be living. Within a few days the father and mother arrived along with a brother and two sisters. Wade and I were pleased that the family cared so much for Andrew that they had arranged to have all of the children out of school to come to meet us.

It was a brief visit and the social worker was not there. It was apparent that the social worker had discussed our credentials with the parents and told them we would be running a training home in addition to providing a parenting experience for Andrew. During the visit the parents asked many pertinent questions about the opportunities their son would have in our home. They were interested in knowing where he would be attending school. They wanted to know what kinds of recreational experiences he would have. Wade explained to the parents that he would be taking Andrew out into the community to a variety of activities that would introduce Andrew to the kinds of things that most boys enjoyed. Andrew's father and mother shared some anecdotal information about their son as a little boy when he still lived at home. They told us that for the last several years their visits with him had been primarily on Sunday afternoons when they had gone to the institution to see him. Occasionally they had taken him for a ride to get an ice cream cone. His visits back home had been brief and infrequent. They told us that they would look to us to make recommendations as to the types of gifts that they should give their son at Christmas time. They acknowledged that it might make Tom uncomfortable if they provided too many things for Andrew, and they asked us to provide them with the direction that they needed. Andrew's parents expressed some concern that they might run into their son in a store or on a street sometime. Wade assured them that was quite unlikely for some long period of time because Andrew would not be in the community alone in the foreseeable future. On the off chance that Andrew would run into his family members in any public situation Wade expected that Andrew would greet them casually.

The visit was a comfortable experience for Andrew's family and for us. We separated knowing that they had accepted Andrew's placement in our home because we were able to provide a training experience for him. We had spent a great deal of time emphasizing that we had no intention of being father or mother to Andrew. Rather we intended to help him have a better understanding of his relationship to them as members of his family. At our request Andrew's family agreed to pick him up the day after that first Christmas holiday because we wanted to involve the children in Christmas preparations and we wanted Andrew to experience the rest of the holiday in our home. This was no problem for the family as Andrew had not been home for Christmas for years.

We were informed by the social worker that since Tom was a ward of the court there would be no one visiting our home on his behalf.

It was an exciting time waiting for the children to move in. Finally on Tuesday, November 3, 1973, our dream began to become real. Two boys became part of our family.

The boys arrived before lunch so Wade prepared it with them. After lunch he took them to the school they would be attending. When I returned home that evening the boys were already home from school. Wade told me they were delighted to be back with us. They were excited to be back in the house, to see Wade, to see me, to see the cat Bootsie. They seemed to understand that they had come to live with us for a period of time. After dinner, which was the first of many chaotic meals, Frank arrived, bringing a man's hair dryer as a gift for the boys, a welcome home present. He recalled with them that on their earlier visit to our home they had been fascinated by my dryer. Frank thought it would be appropriate for them to have one of their own. That evening I helped with putting the boys to bed. We introduced the routine that we would follow for many many weeks. The boys showered, got into their pajamas, and got into bed, and I stayed upstairs with them until they were asleep.

The next day the boys were to attend school for only half a day because of parent-teacher conferences, so we did not have the task of packing lunches. It was a good thing because the first morning the excitement about selecting clothes to wear to school was almost more than the boys could manage. The institution had provided them with complete new wardrobes: several pairs of trousers, underclothes, shirts, and shoes. To my eyes it was a very dull selection. All of the trousers were olive drab or gray gabardines and all the shirts were pastel short-sleeved T-shirts. But they were new and they were theirs. Each boy had a difficult time deciding what to wear on the first day to school. Finally, they were dressed, with a great deal of help from Wade and me. We went downstairs for breakfast and initiated what we hoped would be a routine for some time. They were permitted to choose what they wanted for breakfast, within reason. It was very difficult for the children to choose. They wanted everything—now! Somehow we managed to get through a hectic breakfast. Wade and I made the first of many changes in plans. Wade decided that on school days Wade would plan breakfast and on weekends we would allow the boys to choose.

Finally the boys went off to school. This was a big event for it was their very first day on the school bus. Since we live on a busy street Wade walked from the front door to the school bus and saw the boys safely onto the bus. Upon their return in the evening he went to greet them. The bus driver reported that the boys had been excited on the bus and had been unruly and noisy. Fortunately, Wade took this report in stride for it was the first of several such reports that we were to receive. After lunch the boys went out into the yard to play and to be with Wade. They did not understand the chores that he was doing and gave little evidence of wanting to rake leaves with him. But they wanted to be with him, as close to him as possible. At times, he said, he felt as though they were glued to him. And so we started.

3

The Boys' Backgrounds

AS FOSTER PARENTS we were not provided with lengthy case material about any of the children. Initially, we knew very little about their families, causes of retardation, rationale for placement in the state institution, or about the training programs that they had experienced while there. We were told the boys had been considered ready for community placement and there were certain things they had learned in the state institution. We received an introductory letter describing each boy.

Here was the introductory letter about Tom.

> Tom—born July 15, 1962—was admitted to Oakdale Center March 4, 1969, with the diagnosis of encephalopathy associated with prematurity and underlying convulsive disorder. His IQ was tested at 35 on the Stanford Binet, October 8, 1973. Prior to admission, Tom's behavior was characterized by extreme hyperactivity. He suffered from parental neglect. Today he is an attractive boy who tends to his own needs in dressing, toileting, and bathing with supervision. He eats well using all utensils. He is quite verbal, with several foul words in his vocabulary generally used when frustrated. There are no physical deformities or handicaps. His present medication is Dilantin, 1 grain TID, and Mellaril 25 mg TID.
>
> Tom gets along well with peers, and attention from adults is especially enjoyed by him. In his leisure he enjoys bike riding, as well as most outdoor activities. He is generally good natured; however, he exhibits occasional temper outbursts when not allowed his own way, but he is not aggressive. It has been noted that Tom has a fear of dogs; however, we are finding that repeated exposures seem to lessen his fear.

Tom has been enrolled in a trainable school program on a full-time basis. This should be continued in the community. He could also benefit from speech therapy. Tom continues to be hyperactive and highly destructive. In view of his hyperactivity it is felt that a home which would provide structure would be necessary for a successful placement."

It is a fair statement to say that the letter was written so as not to discourage placement for Tom, and it is just as well. Wade asked the social worker why Tom was taking Dilantin and Mellaril; he was told that Tom had a history of seizures and that the medicine kept them under control. There is little question in my mind but that Wade and I would have been terribly discouraged if we had known all of the complexities of Tom in the early days of living together. It turned out that Tom, in truth, has strengths on which to build; at the same time he had as many problems as he had strengths.

As the years passed we learned some of the events that contributed to Tom's problems. Tom had a twin brother, considered normal. In the same family was a sister two years older. We learned that the three children were born to very young parents. The father was in the service and the mother had little assistance in coping with her small children. For many reasons and as the result of several incidents, the children were removed from their mother's care. From age two, Tom had been in a variety of different settings. He had lived briefly in other foster homes and subsequently he had landed in the state institution. Later we were to learn that his behavior in the state institution had been so extreme and out of control that there were times he had to be contained and isolated.

We were told that Tom was a court ward when he was placed in our home and that no family members had any interest in him. Hence we were surprised after a few weeks when his paternal grandmother contacted us and wanted to come to see him. This was arranged and we learned that she had tried to keep in touch with Tom through the years and had visited him periodically wherever he had been living. We were glad for Tom that this contact had been established.

When Tom was placed in our home he had extremely short hair; it looked as though he might have had a haircut or rather had his head shaved two weeks prior to coming to our home. His hair was so short that you could see little spots all over his head where hair was noticeably missing. We had to live with Tom for a period of time to realize that those spots were places where he had pulled the hair out by its roots. The first time Wade bathed him he noticed bruise marks on certain parts of his body which we determined later were a result of his pinching himself. His arms, from his thumb knuckle all the way up to his elbow, were covered with bite marks. In some places there was callous-like tissue where he had bitten himself. There were times when we observed him banging his head. Frequently he tried to bite, pinch, or kick anyone around him. Often he directed this behavior toward Andrew. His temper tantrums were numerous and extensive. It was not unusual to have five or six temper tantrums a day, lasting as long as half an hour.

Tom destroyed things but only things that belonged to him. Soon we realized that he destroyed the things that meant the most to him. His grandmother gave him a transistor radio for Christmas 1973. She had not been away from our home five minutes before he demolished the radio. Obviously he wanted it but apparently he could not cope with keeping something that meant so much to him. Tom frequently screamed at the top of his lungs, to the point of hoarseness. He had a vocabulary that was extensive in its profanity and obscenity. His favorite words were a series of ten sexual words that he recited over and over again starting with "Pantyhose, pantyhose, pussy, and prick."

Tom never walked, he ran. He jumped constantly. If he was standing, waiting for Wade to unlock the car so that he could get into it, he would jump up and down waiting to get in the car. If he was sitting in a chair, he was bouncing up and down. He wet the bed and his clothes, soiled his clothes, and spread feces. Tom put anything that appeared edible into his mouth. There were even times we saw him pick over trash and put things in his mouth.

Tom had no controls from within himself and objected vociferously, continuously, and loudly to any controls imposed upon him by anyone else. Hyperactive, yes. Hostile, yes, Destructive, yes. In many ways a very offensive little boy whose behaviors were so severe that they were impediments to his achieving a decent experience in the community. Fortunately for Tom and for us, we did not realize how offensive his behavior was until we had become quite attached to him and quite taken in by his need to be loved and his need to love someone.

Tom was a manipulator. Along the way he had learned some interesting phrases. He would sidle up to you and say, "Oh, you look pretty today, my you look nice today," and immediately follow it up with a "Can I have . . ." statement. Tom came to us with many

fears. He was afraid of dogs and of thunder. He was afraid to go outdoors, of being alone, and of the dark. He had a pattern for managing his fear. First he would scream, and if by screaming he was not
helped from the frightening situation, he would move into a full-
scale tantrum. We quickly recognized that Tom thoroughly enjoyed
all food. If he could put it in his mouth he enjoyed it. If it was sweet
he liked it better; if there was a great amount of it he was delighted!
His love of food was to serve us well during the many months ahead.

    Where to start with Tom? We were dismayed; there were so
many things that needed immediate attention. Which behaviors
should we ignore, which ones work on? As in the case of Andrew,
Wade convinced me that we needed to focus on helping Tom acquire
complete independence in everything to do with toileting. Wade believed that as soon as Tom knew that he was like other teenage kids
in toileting, he would have something to be proud of about himself.
To help Tom master toileting was the first short-term goal set for
him. The second short-term goal was to help him eliminate his foul,
obscene, profane language, which was so offensive it would be impossible to take him out into the community to do any of the things
that would be growth producing for him. The third most important
thing was to help Tom learn other ways of managing his frustration
—ways other than having a tantrum. He needed to begin to understand his own behavior and to be responsible for it. He needed to
learn that he could not go through life screaming out his anger in
every situation. During those first few weeks of getting to know
Tom and the complexities of his needs, Wade and I were very discouraged. We were frightened about what we had taken on and felt
ill prepared and inadequate as we faced this big challenge. We clung
to the knowledge that we were willing to try and that we would do
our level best. But we were afraid.

    The letter of introduction about Andrew read as follows:

> Andrew, born 6/8/60, was admitted to Oakdale Center 7/6/66 with
> diagnosis of "encephalopathy due to anoxemia at birth." Tested
> 10/17/73, he received an estimated score of 35.
>
> Prior to admission Andrew would not accept discipline at home
> and was a disrupting influence in the family. Today Andrew is even
> tempered and reasonably cooperative and obedient. He is active, loves
> outdoors play, and gets along well with peers. He is affectionate and
> especially enjoys attention from adults. Any real sense of direction or
> persistence is lacking in his activities and his attention span is quite

limited. A certain amount of supervision is required, especially when out-of-doors, as he has been known to chase trucks.

Andrew washes and dresses himself, brushes his own teeth, and has acceptable eating habits. He is an attractive boy who is neat and clean in appearance. His speech is fairly good but he is vague and wandering in his attempts at conversation. Medication is Vitasol, one teaspoon daily; thiamine 15 mg TID. Andrew has been a full-time student in a trainable school program. This should be continued in a community with speech therapy incorporated in the program.

Since we had met Andrew's entire family prior to his placement in our home, we knew that he was the third child in a family of four. He has a brother five years older than himself, a sister three years older, and a sister two years younger. The sister, Terri, the youngest in the family, was the one family member whom Andrew talked about. Andrew was an attractive boy with blond hair, hazel eyes, fair complexion, and a well-built body. He moved gracefully and easily, as an athlete does. He was quick to copy any behavior that he saw done by the adult in charge. He sat at the table and watched what the adult did in terms of picking up a spoon, knife, or glass and tried to imitate the action. He was apt to walk one step behind the adult, frequently attempting to hold his or her hand.

We did not live with Andrew long before we realized that his hands got into all kinds of trouble. He was forever taking big and little things apart. He got into all kinds of mischief after making sure no one was watching. When confronted about his behavior he had one of two responses. "I didn't do it" or "Tom did it." He frequently tattled on Tom and often made up stories about Tom that were designed to get Tom into trouble.

Andrew had a way of putting a mask on his face to conceal his thoughts, feelings, and emotions. It had been functional for him for a long time. Sometimes if Andrew was asked a question too threatening for him, his face would set. It was as though the question triggered a button and his face froze into an expressionless mask that implied, "Who, me? Don't ask me. Don't look at me. I'm retarded. I'm not responsible. I don't have to be responsible for any of that behavior. How can I be accountable, don't you see that I'm a dum-dum?" These were the messages we received from the mask that Andrew put on his face. It was an amazing performance. His eyes would not blink, his lips and cheeks would not twitch.

In general, Andrew had good eating habits. However, he was

extremely noisy at the table; he smacked his lips and chewed his food very loudly in a way that we found offensive. I'm glad that the institution had not stated in writing that Andrew was toilet trained. When Andrew came to live with us he was completely toilet trained as far as sleeping overnight in his bed. There has never been an incident of Andrew wetting or soiling his bed or pajamas during the night. During the daytime it was another story. Andrew frequently soiled his underclothes, sometimes two or three times a day. He never wet his underclothes as such but he soiled them. We thought perhaps he had not learned to use toilet paper and wasn't wiping himself thoroughly after bowel movements.

Andrew had little sense of ownership, boundaries, or territories when he first came to live with us. He was curious about everything and was apt to pick up and walk off with anything. He was fascinated by light switches and took several of our table lamps apart before we were able to redirect his interest. We found Andrew's language difficult to understand. We thought that it would help to ask him to speak slowly so we could understand some of what he was saying. It was amazing how clearly he could speak when he was trying to get Tom into trouble and how garbled his speech was when a person was trying to help him take responsibility for his own behavior. Andrew often carried around a deck of playing cards and liked to sort them and shuffle them, over and over again. It seemed to us that Andrew had good things going for him and that we needed to give him support to continue his interest in his own grooming and appearance. We wanted to help him develop a wide range of athletic interests because he had such a strong body. We hoped to help him expand his vocabulary and improve his speech.

In terms of surviving in the family there were three things that we had to focus on in order to make living together immediately comfortable and in order to maximize the living experience for Andrew in the future. He needed to control all behaviors having to do with toileting, and we viewed that as a priority for him in our home. Second, we wanted Andy to learn to take responsibility for his own behavior, not anyone else's. He needed to stop tattling on others and begin to take responsibility for his inappropriate as well as appropriate behaviors. The third concern was to help him learn to keep his hands off people and things. He needed to learn appropriate touching and discrimination about touching. Of all the boys Andy initially gave the appearance of being the most like "other people." Because of his excellent mimicry skills he was an extremely passable person until he began to converse. At that point his speech betrayed his minimal functioning.

When Phillip joined the family a year later, the following letter was sent to us:

> Phil is a fine, good-looking 15-year-old boy, usually good natured, with an infectious sense of humor. He is reasonably obedient and cooperative, loves attention, and thrives on affection. He is extremely neat in his dress and in general appearance, a fact which brings to mind one of his several faults—if he is given an article of clothing which does not suit his fancy he is quite liable to create some damage to the particular item, such as destroying the catch on the fly of his trousers or ridding a shirt of its buttons, so that the item will not be wearable. In fairness to Phil, however, I should say that this has become less and less of a problem as he has matured.
>
> He enjoys music, crafts, outdoor play, all sorts of mechanical toys and is imaginative and a self-starter in all his play. He plays well with his peers but does not necessarily need a group to enjoy himself. Which brings us to a second fault. In competition of any sort with other boys he resents losing and will sulk, not to any serious extent, and can be easily talked out of his depression.
>
> Phillip's medication consists of half a grain of phenobarbital, TID. This medication is in no way prescribed for convulsive disorder but rather to assist in the control of his hyperactivity and occasional depression. While on the subject we could also remind you that Phillip has slight hyperflexia in both knees scarcely noticeable in his normal gait but sometimes evident when he climbs or descends stairs which appears, in small measure, to disturb his balance.
>
> Phillip is completely continent, dresses himself, brushes his own teeth, combs his hair, has good eating habits and use of all eating utensils. He can bathe himself with some supervision required in making preparations and temperature control of his bath water.
>
> Phillip attends Woodside School, a special education institution of the Lapeer Public School system and is enrolled in the trainable group of the school. The school reports on his progress, interest, and deportment have thus far been excellent. There is no reason to believe that he will not continue to make good progress in this area.

This was the way Phil was described to us. Phil *is* an attractive person. He held himself tall and held his head proudly. One of the first things we noticed about him was that in spite of his good posture he was poorly coordinated. He was extremely clumsy and conscious of every step he took. If he possibly could he would find something to hold onto, a railing or a person. He could not swim, play basketball, ride a bicycle, or run when he came to us. He was extremely loud. He talked frequently but except for two words, it was generally unintelligible. He called himself and everybody else "Perry." The gibberish that he spouted was always shouted. Very early we realized that Phillip had no comprehension of privacy or the need to close doors. Evidently he had been used to toileting, bathing, sleeping, and all other activities with large groups of people and did not recognize the need for boundaries, territories, or privacy. Phil responded quickly and joyously to any kind of praise, affection, or positive attention. When he was corrected he was prone to sulk, pout, and act in a stubborn manner. Sometimes he would stand rigidly still and refuse to move as he was being confronted over an inappropriate action.

It seemed to Wade and me that there were three things that Phil needed to control in order to become an acceptable member in our family and, eventually, an acceptable person in a larger situation. First, Phil needed to learn to respect and honor privacy. He needed to learn to knock on doors and wait until he had been invited to enter. He needed to learn to use a bathroom alone with the door closed. We realized that the fact that Phil was going to be in a bedroom by himself was going to enhance and ease this learning to some extent.

Second, we believed that Phil needed to learn that every individual has his or her own name and identity. We saw as the second task the need to help Phil learn to own his name and to recognize that other people had their own names. We decided that he would need to learn Wade, Martha, Tom, and Andrew as individuals separate and apart from Phil and that he would need to learn to call them by their correct names instead of calling everyone, "Hey, Perry."

The third big task was to help Phil decrease his loud obnoxious language. He needed to learn that people were turned off by his screaming in a voice remindful of an Alaskan bull moose. We wanted to give him support, praise, and affirmation as he continued to maintain himself in terms of toileting, bathing, and dressing. We hoped to introduce him to sports that would improve his large muscle coordination.

As a result of foster parenting for three years, we began to feel that we were ready to have a fourth boy and we let it be known to MORC that we were ready. Wade and I innocently and arrogantly thought that after Tom we could handle practically any boy. We did not believe that there could be another boy who would put such a demand upon us. Because of this attitude, Wade said to the agency, select a boy that you feel would grow in our home. Consequently, he was told by the agency that they wanted to place Mark in our home.

We were not provided a letter as with the other three boys, but we were told that Mark, age fifteen, had lived in many different foster settings and that he was functioning at a higher level than the other three boys. He had epilepsy with frequent seizures, but he also faked numerous seizures. He was a fighter who had a reputation for doing mean, ugly things to the children in the homes where he had lived. We agreed to have him come and visit for a weekend.

Mark was on his best behavior the entire weekend. He was so helpful that we were constantly tripping over him. He repeatedly made complimentary remarks about us and our home. He pleaded to live with us. At the end of the visit Wade told him that as far as we were concerned he was welcome to come back and live with us if it could be worked out by the social workers. Wade told him that he would not be able to come back for several weeks because we were going on a lengthy vacation; he could not move in until after that. Three weeks later Mark moved into our home, and, once again, our family was tossed into a tailspin. For the umpteenth time I found myself looking at Wade with a combination of respect, bewilderment, and annoyance. I was pleased with him that he felt confident to take on a boy who had such a complex behavioral problem. On the other hand, I frequently thought, "Why us? Don't we have enough working with Tom?"

Things started out smoothly enough with Mark. He was a well-mannered boy and knew how to take care of himself. After three or four days of finding his place in our home we began to see how Mark needed us. At the outset Mark appeared to be much brighter than the other three children. He did function at a higher level, and his conversation was more sophisticated. He could read simple words, print, answer the telephone, play cards, and generally function at the level that the school classifies as educable. But he needed us, or rather I should say, he needed Wade. He needed the firmness of a father. Mark was a manipulator with a capital M. He had three techniques he used to try to get his own way. First, he wheedled and whined. Second, he had seizures to get sympathy. Third, he got very physical and used his fists or anything he could get into his hand. He used the wheedling and whining approach with the children and adults alike. The fake seizures were directed at grown-ups primarily. The pugilistic style was reserved for his foster brothers.

We decided that we needed to work on the fake seizures first. The first challenge to us was to become familiar enough with Mark's seizures so that we could tell a real one from a fake one. For the first three or four weeks we just let life flow and watched things as they happened. Every time there was any seizure activity we asked the other children to move out of the way and we made sure that Mark would not hurt himself by hitting any sharp object. Other than helping him avoid injury we attempted to give him no kind of positive feedback or attention as a result of a seizure.

There were three important learning goals for Mark. First, he needed to stop faking seizures. Second, he needed to learn to recognize and heed any warnings of impending seizures. And last, he needed to cut down on his fighting with the other boys.

We made the first year of foster parenting even more demanding by adding the responsibilities of house renovation and moving. Now that the year is a memory, I am glad we subjected ourselves to such a series of challenges—new life experiences and situation for Tom and Andrew, new parenting responsibilities for Wade and me, new job for me, *and* a house to renovate. Somehow we all survived, with some organization and a lot of help from our friends.

4

The First Few Months

FOR THE FIRST FIVE MONTHS that Tom and Andrew lived with us they were caught up in the whole experience of renovating the house and planning to move into it. The house we were renovating was located across the street and down four lots from the old one, with a wider lot that went all the way through the main street to a secondary street in the rear. In terms of play area, there was more land over which to roam. The property was fenced and there was a three-car garage on the land, as well as the big old house. From the very beginning the boys played at the new house after school every day. Wade would meet the school bus at the old house. The boys would change their clothes, have a snack, and then the three of them would go down the street to take part in the renovation process.

This put the boys into a situation where they had the opportunity to know the carpenter, his assistant, the roofer, and the painters. They began to know the different jobs that different people did. They learned about the different tools that people used. Wade permitted them to play freely in and out of the house. The interior was almost gutted in order to renovate the old house from top to bottom: new roof, new wiring, new plumbing, new stairways. Every inch of the old oak woodwork was stripped and brought back to its natural condition. There was hardly a day that the children went down to the house to play that there were not several men working around the house. Always Wade and Frosty would be there and usually the carpenter and his assistant. As the boys learned about the different types of equipment and tools people were using, they began to respect them and leave them alone. The adults began to give the children simple errands to accomplish. "Take this tool to Wade," or "Go get a hammer."

I went near the renovation project only on weekends when I would go down to see the progress that had been made during the week. Often the boys would be able to report to me about the interesting things that were taking place. Wade and I spent all of our free time away from the boys doing necessary errands: selecting fixtures, fabrics for drapes, carpeting for floors, dining room furniture, dishwasher, and on and on and on. The children were very excited as each new thing was delivered and installed. Early in January of '74 Wade and I took the boys shopping for five new single beds and mattresses. We permitted the boys to pick out headboards. Later I sat down with the boys and went through a catalog to choose bedspreads and linens for the new beds. We designated the particular rooms that they would have in the house and they began to talk about them. "That's going to be my room. That's where we're going to have a pool table. That's going to be Magoo's room." Tom's name for me was Magoo, and he called Wade "Big Stuff."

Early in March the second floor was in reasonable order and the boys' excitement began to increase. One day they came home to tell me that the carpeting had been installed in their bedrooms and their beds had been delivered. That weekend the boys and I went down and made up all the new beds with the new linens and bedspreads. A few days later a man came to set up the pool table in the playroom. Day by day the boys could see their new home nearing completion.

Early in April there was a day of great activity. Suddenly everything was nearing completion. The carpeting had been installed downstairs, the drapes were hung, and moving day had arrived. I attempted to ease some of the pains of moving by helping the boys move parts of their new life with us over a few days. We moved all the game equipment and playthings one day. Another day we moved all of the clothing that went into the closets. Another day we moved all of the things that went in bureau drawers. A young friend helped us with much of the moving. He was about seventeen or eighteen years old at the time. The children liked him and followed after him. He was patient with them and gave them a lot of attention as he helped them move and settle their things in their parts of the household. Suddenly we were moved.

At the new house the children were to sleep upstairs, while we as parents would be sleeping on the first floor. Our bedroom door in the old house had been six feet from their bedroom door. I was apprehensive about the fact that the boys would be out of earshot and we would be unable to hear them during the night. I was so concerned that I had convinced my husband that we needed an intercom system. Frosty installed a two-way system through the entire house so that we would be able to tune in on the children and make sure that they were safe and so they would be able to call us at any time if there was an emergency. It turned out to be a complete waste of money. By the time we moved into the new home the boys had lived with us six or seven months and they were trusting about going to bed and getting up. In two and a half years Wade and I never used the intercom system to monitor the children or to have them call us. The system was used a great deal to pipe music through the house, which was delightful, but we never used the system for its original purpose.

One feature in the new house needs to be described in detail. Off the kitchen was a large closet area that ran the length of the hallway. One could pass through the hallway to go down to the cellar or out the back grade-level door to the yard. Frosty had divided this closet into six cubbies. Each cubby had a lower compartment with a clothes pole large enough to store five or six articles of clothing on coat hangers. There was adequate space at the bottom to store such things as boots, playshoes, etc. and above the coat area was a shelf that was adequate to store lunchboxes, hats, mittens, etc. The six-compartment closet was one of the best renovations that we introduced into the house. It proved to be an excellent device in teaching the children where to put their things in relation to someone else's. There was a kind of security for the boys to know that everyone had a winter coat. Each person had his own and his own hung in a particular cubby, but everyone else also had his own. With the addition of the individual cubby for outside clothing and game equipment, the boys had adequate storage areas all around the house. Each boy had bureau, closet, cubby, and a certain section of the garage in which to store big equipment. The careful attention to assigning territorial places for each child helped a great deal to introduce the concept of ownership, the responsibilities of ownership, and the respect for another person's ownership.

During the process of developing a new home and preparing to move into it we had not been able to spend much time with friends and acquaintances. It was heartwarming to experience the love and affection that came to us from unexpected sources during that process. People who through the years had been casual acquaintances suddenly became supportive in many interesting ways. In the process of renovating our house we had a call one night from a young man who said, "I would like to do all of the interior painting that you need to have done in your house." I said, "What do you mean?" He said, "Well, I know that you're going to have to paint many of the rooms in your house and I would like to do that for you. I would like to give that to you as a gift, as a way of honoring and respecting what you are doing." To make a long story short he and another man, both of them full-time social workers and part-time house painters, painted the entire interior of the house because they wanted to show us in a concrete way that they supported what we were doing. Two other friends organized a garage sale for us to help us unload a surplus of furniture. Two other friends came out the weekend before we moved into the house and scrubbed out closets and cupboards, lined bureau drawers, and washed windows. Another friend cooked meals all day long for the two weekends of the garage sale so that those of us who were doing many different tasks would not need to attend to that. One friend designed and executed the invitations we used for our open house. We had not expected such an outpouring of support.

The same kind of support came from a private clinic where I had done a small amount of private practice. The pediatrician, psychiatrist, psychologist, and chief social worker let it be known that the clinic was there to provide our home with service at no cost to us. What a gesture of support! And how gratefully I used it. Three of those people consulted with us about managing Tom's behavior. There is no question that Tom's successful adjustment to our home was partly a result of those three clinicians' taking a Saturday afternoon to brainstorm the entire intervention strategy with us. They helped us think through the implications of each step of the initial management plan. Three other professional men mentioned to us that any time we were caught short or in a crisis they would be available to come and stay with the children to help us out.

However, there were instances of lack of understanding from people in the community who were fearful about what we were doing and were apprehensive as to the effect retarded children would have upon the street. Wade convinced me that we should ignore all comments and just sail along. He believed that we should demonstrate to the community a way of life and trust the community to judge our actions after some experience. We had every intention of improving the property at the renovated house and did so in a way that reflected positively the interests of the Historical Commission which was concerned about old properties in the community. We intended to maintain our home well and to raise children who would learn to be respectful of other people and their property. Wade convinced me that over a period of months and years we could demonstrate to the community that we were contributing to the neighborhood in a positive manner.

There were instances of people being outright curious about "those crazy retards" that we had brought home from the institution, but we were not aware of anyone saying anything directly to either of the boys in a hostile or hateful way. It may have happened and the children did not know how to tell us. In a couple of instances we were disappointed in not getting support from people from whom we had expected it. This has been hard to understand and we never discussed it with the people involved. It seemed to us that some acquaintances felt that our course of action was ridiculous and I resented that they did not care enough to discuss with us why we were interested in what we were doing.

The most blatant example of lack of understanding came from a man in the community who held a position of some status. He was a resident of long standing and the community looked to him as a model. He was considered to be an educated, professional person and had achieved a fair amount of success in terms of worldly acquisitions. It happened that there was a public meeting regarding rezoning a piece of property on the street. The rezoning had nothing to do with our house, but it had to do with property that this man was interested in. At the meeting he made some derogatory remarks about the children living in our home. That was a disappointment for we had assumed that with education and position went intelligence, acceptance, and understanding. Once again, of course, we learned that this was not necessarily true.

In the process of our being licensed as foster parents, our house was inspected for fire safety and rechecked on an annual basis. With fire inspectors and building inspectors, we had several different public servants in our home. They inspected the home from top to bottom to make sure that it met health and safety standards. This was a good thing because in each instance the inspectors were persons with a certain amount of informal power in the community structure. They were impressed with what we were doing. On one occasion the inspector was a man who lived in the neighborhood. He had children who had been playing with our boys. He was more than cordial as he did his job. When he and the other inspectors made favorable observations in public about our home and what was happening within it, we experienced a subtle change toward full acceptance within the community.

After we accomplished the move with the help of many people, we prepared an open house to celebrate the new home and to introduce our son-in-law to friends. The boys had new clothes to wear and they had practiced for the experience so they were gracious and delightful. We were fortunate, too, in that most of the friends who were with us that evening were people who are in the helping professions. Perhaps more than most people in the community, they were accustomed to relating to people sometimes viewed as different by the rest of us. It was a good time for Tom and Andrew.

Even though we moved in April of '74, the work was far from done. The house was functional, but it would be many months before the third bathroom would be finished and the radiators reinstalled. From April of '74 until fall of '74 all of our energies were directed toward completing the outdoor area. Wade arranged to have an in-ground swimming pool installed. This was a very interesting project for the boys to observe. From the arrival of the earth mover to the final step of filling the pool with water was a ten-day process. The pool was filled just in time for Tom's birthday, and of course he claimed the pool as his birthday present. And why not!

The backyard, however, was still a shambles. The pool was in and the cement deck around it, but all of the rest of the yard was torn up. It was a laborious summer of trying to remember to take off outdoor shoes before entering the house. Gradually through the course of the summer, the lawn was graded and seeded, new cement sidewalks were laid, and finally the parking lot was resurfaced. The parking area was adjacent to the garage and was arranged similarly to half of a basketball court. In addition to basketball, the boys had a tether ball and punching bag in that area. Finally by autumn the backyard, the swimming pool, and the play area were tidy places in which to play.

Part of the backyard had been fenced off to provide a running area for the Siberian huskies. The only way a person could walk from the front of the property to the back of the property was to pass through that section of the yard fenced off for the dogs. Since Tom and Andrew got off the school bus in front, it meant that they needed to learn to open the gate into the dogyard, close and latch it, and pass through the dogyard in order to reach the major part of the yard. It was a big accomplishment for Tom to learn to handle in a responsible manner. We were worried that the boys might be careless and not latch the gate and let our dogs get away. This never happened. The boys were responsible about making sure that the gates were latched. It was fortunate that they learned to be so comfortable with this procedure, since it is not uncommon for footballs, basketballs, and frisbees to end up in the dogyard and the boys were able to go in and retrieve their playthings.

The swimming pool made our home the center of interest for all the children in the neighborhood. All of the children were given the same message: "When the pool is finished you will be able to swim in it anytime your father or mother brings you over to swim in it. We will not be responsible for your being in the pool." This message served two purposes: it let the neighborhood children know they were welcome to come and play. It also clearly stated that the use of the pool could only be under their parents' supervision. Wade and I believed that we were going to have our hands full just taking care of Tom and Andrew when they were swimming without supervising other children at the same time.

During that first summer a young couple with a toddler lived next door. On the other side of our property lived a widow whose grandson was visiting her for the summer. The grandson, a boy of eight or nine, could swim very well and came frequently to swim with the boys. The young parents brought the toddler to the pool just once, but they came by themselves several times. The young father was especially gracious to the two boys, visiting with them often. He was never impatient with their questions of "Where have you been? Where are you going? What did you have for supper? When are you going to come back?" He was able to handle all of these questions comfortably and easily. Down the street about three houses lived a family with a twelve-year-old daughter and an eight-year-old son who came frequently to visit with our boys. During the entire summer of '74 the boys rarely played outside our own yard. Occasionally, with express permission, they were allowed to visit in a neighbor's backyard. During that summer the boys began to be comfortable with going in and out of the house at their own choosing. The only restriction on such traffic was that they had to take their playshoes off before they went into the house.

During the summer we decided it was time to have a third boy come to live with us, and we discussed the idea of having their former friend join us. Early in August of '74 Phillip came to visit.

Phillip was a very pleasant young man to meet. He was capable of taking care of his own needs. Although he was afraid of many things that were new and strange to him, he would attempt a new thing if he realized than an adult was with him. The entire weekend of his visit was spent at home. We saw this as an opportunity for Phillip to demonstrate his degree of comfort in our home, with the dogs, the swimming pool, and the play area. We were anxious to see whether or not the three boys would re-establish the relationship they had at the state institution. Tom was gracious with Phillip. Andrew was noncommittal. Wade and I felt that Phillip should join our family.

When the social worker returned after the forty-eight-hour visit to take Phillip back to the institution, we had an interesting conversation. The early part of the conversation had to do with working out the particulars of Phillip's coming to live in our home. Then as the young social worker drank his coffee and watched Tom and Andrew swimming in the pool, he made some surprising observations. He told Wade, "You should know, Mr. Dickerson, that at the institution we never believed Tom would be able to make it in the community. In fact we had a pool going and people were betting as to how long it would take for him to bounce back to the institution. None of us believed that Tom could make it in the community. It's hard for me to believe that this is the same boy that we sent to you last fall. It's clear that Tom will never have to come back to the institution again."

Of course Wade and I were pleased to think that Tom had made so much progress in our home, but at the same time we did have some feelings of anger. We had gone through so much hell with Tom for the last several months that we thought that it could have helped had we known his behavior was of long standing. However, as we talked about our anger we began to realize that it was a good thing we had not known the low expectancy the institutional workers had for Tom because we might have accepted that attitude. As it was, Wade had expected Tom to perform and the boy had responded to Wade's high expectation. So perhaps it was just as well we did not know what a tremendous challenge we had taken on when we agreed to work with Tom.

In any event, we agreed to take Phillip, too. A week later his mother and stepfather came to visit us on a Sunday afternoon. They were also pleasant to meet. They drank coffee and watched the two boys in the pool. They were anxious for their son to have a good home to live in since it was not possible for them to have him in their own home. They appeared to be comfortable with us and pleased with the home where Phillip would live. We talked about how much they would want to see their son. It was agreed that once Phil moved in, they would not ask him to come to visit at home for two or three months in order to allow him ample time to get used to his new home. But after that Phil would go home frequently for weekends, for holidays, and for other family occasions.

In mid-August Phil arrived. He had been completely outfitted with new clothes and had had a complete physical. He was in good health and ready for community placement. I had arranged to take my vacation during the month of August in '74 so that I would be able to be with the family as it added a new member. Wade and I had thought that Phil, the newcomer, needed to have some special time in order to be absorbed into the family and its routine. It would be equally important for Tom and Andrew to have some special support to help them to permit Phil to come into their world.

Phil was given a bedroom by himself, a large room with twin beds and two big closets and dressers. He was told he could choose whichever bed he wanted to sleep in. Phil came with boxes and boxes of paraphernalia. He had collected all kinds of things and discarded nothing. As he settled in, we found that closets, bureau, nightstand, and extra bed were piled high. Much of it was trashy junk—crumpled papers and wadded, soiled tissues. We decided to ignore it for a few days until Phil had settled into our home. But I decided that before I would finish vacation and before the boys went to school, Phil and I would have a cleaning day when he would determine the kinds of things that were appropriate to keep and what things should be discarded.

Wade and I had quite a discussion about this. On the one hand we did believe that a person should have the right to save, treasure, protect, and take care of those things he wanted to have. On the other hand, when we considered a long-range goal for Phil it would be unfair to allow him to continue in this kind of pack-rat behavior. Probably Phil would live in a group home eventually. Wherever Phil would live in the future he would be expected to share a room with one, two, or three other persons. He would be expected to keep his belongings in such a way that his messiness did not spill over and become offensive to other people.

Phil was capable of performing many different tasks including running the vacuum cleaner and setting the table. He was anxious to prove himself and be accepted into the family, and we were anxious to help him do so. Tom and Andrew resented the help that Phil contributed to the household because Phil could do tasks very well that they were just learning. He could vacuum the dining room without monitoring, he knew to move out all the chairs and vacuum under the table and put the chairs back and vacuum the outer part of the room without any reminding through the whole process. Tom and Andrew were not able to complete a task with as much independence. Initially, Andrew was very resentful of Phil's skills and abilities. Initially, Tom and Andrew both had difficulty recognizing that Phil needed to learn about other areas that were important for his growth.

When Phil came to live with us, I doubt that he had any sense of who other persons were except himself. He called himself and everybody else by his own last name, Perry. It was the one word that we always understood, Perry. He called everyone Perry: Wade, Tom, Andrew, me, himself, and any stranger. He would mouth a series of incoherent phrases that obviously had something to do with Perry. Occasionally we would be able to understand what he was saying by reading the gestures that accompanied the sounds. The only other word that we could always understand was *no*.

After two or three weeks we began to realize that an interesting thing had happened to one of the other boys. Although Andrew's garbled speech had been understandable to us, and we had learned to understand him somewhat, he was now motivated to speak with more clarity than ever before. He was in the position of translating and interpreting Phil's gibberish to the rest of the family and in the process of doing so his own speech became much clearer.

Phil quickly got into the routine of the family. He was an obedient boy and seemed to understand most things asked of him, trying to follow any directions or guidance that were given to him. He seemed to have a delightful sense of humor. It was not at all uncommon for him to laugh and giggle and otherwise respond joyously and freely to any humorous thing that happened. In many ways he was a very pleasant person to be around. Tom's method of acting out his resentment of Phil's presence was to be overtly hostile; Andrew was more devious. On several occasions he destroyed some article of Phil's clothing or a piece of his equipment or one of his favorite toys. When confronted with this kind of behavior Andrew acknowledged it but did not appear penitent.

When fall came the children were assigned to different schools. Phil and Andrew were both enrolled in a training program in a community some distance from our home town. This, in essence, meant a promotion for Andrew because he had turned fourteen. Phil had not attended any school before. Tom, however, continued on in the special class provided for him in our local school district. This meant that Tom went to school for a shorter day. Tom was away from home fewer hours every day than the older boys because they had a lengthy ride before and after the school session. Tom was not entirely pleased about the fact that the two older boys were going to Oakland Training Institute while he had to continue going to Fairview School. He felt their attendance at OTI meant they were big boys, and he did not like being a little boy at all. However, he did enjoy the extra hours he had with Wade.

5

Others Joined Us

WHEN WE RETURNED from Alaska in September of '73 Wade and I started to locate people to help us with the children. A very fine young man, John, was known to us because he had been placed with me for one of his practicum experiences when he was in the school of social work. He and his wife, Noni, agreed to be available to us about once every four or five weeks for a concentrated period of time so that Wade and I could get away for a weekend. We were delighted to make contact with such a fine responsible couple. I was familiar with John's style of work. His first year of practice as a student had been in the field of retardation, working with adults. I had been impressed with his sensitivity, honesty, and sincere acceptance of the clients with whom he worked. Wade and I were pleased to have John and Noni make this kind of commitment to us. He was not in a position, however, to work more frequently than that, and, of course, it was out of the question that he could ever become a live-in worker. So we started to look for such a person.

Through our contacts at the school of social work we heard of a first-year graduate student who was interested in working. This was the Frank who was later to give the boys a hairdryer as a welcome present. Frank came to us highly recommended, and he, too, had experience working with adults with mental retardation. We had several conversations with Frank during the months of September and October and arranged for him to be involved with every step of the process as the boys were introduced in our home. Frank agreed to use the same techniques of managing the boys' behavior that Wade, as the fathering person, would use so the boys would feel consistency in the way they were being treated. We knew the supplementary parenting people would come and go in their lives but we still wanted as much consistency and constancy for them as possible. It was agreed that Frank would work a minimum of ten hours a week, generally over the weekend in two units of time. Sometimes there would be occasions during the week when he might be asked to work additional hours. Since Frank was living at home it was agreed that once we had moved into the larger home he would come to live with our family and be the live-in worker. We felt quite secure about the arrangements we had made to provide for supervision and training for the two boys.

The last piece that fell into place for us was when a former colleague offered to be a cleaning person for us. This fine woman had worked in a building where I had my office a year before. She had been aware that my reason for terminating from civil service was to become a foster mother, and she wanted, in some way, to support that decision. She told me that she had never done day work, for her usual job was maintenance work in a big city building, but that she was willing to work for us. We accepted her offer and she filled a necessary role in our home.

When we moved we had expected that Frank was going to move in with us. However, there were changes in the demands upon Frank, partly as a result of the death of his father, and he told us in May that it would not be possible for him to move in with us. While we were disappointed at this turn of events, a new person appeared.

Jane, a twenty-one-year-old friend of ours who was between her junior and senior year of college, needed a summer job. We asked Jane to work the craziest of schedules the summer of '74. Several mornings a week Jane came to work at 8:00 in the morning and stayed until 11:30 or 12:00. She usually arrived just as the boys had finished breakfast, and she would monitor play time during the morning. This allowed Wade, who is an avid golfer, to spend several mornings a week at his favorite sport. I do not believe that Wade could have survived as a foster father and maintained his patience if he had not been able to indulge his passion for golf. Even Wade knew his own limits just as at the beginning he made the pronouncement that he could not tolerate children who did not tolerate animals.

As the summer wore on we realized that we needed to find a replacement for Frank. I contacted the two schools of social work that were within twenty-five miles of our home and asked to have the job listed. We interviewed two fine candidates in September of '74. Each of the men was very interested in the job and either would have been a superb addition to our home. Unfortunately for us, or so it seemed initially, it turned out for both men that to take the job with us would jeopardize a scholarship loan that they were receiving from the university. Wade and I could not put up the kind of money that would compensate for this large tuition grant, so with much self-pity we had to accept their decisions not to work for us.

However, a little later a young man, Dwight, returned to Michigan to go to graduate school at the University of Michigan. He and his wife had been friends of our son and thus of our family for many many years. Dwight had worked for a summer in a coeducational camp for teenagers and had worked for two years in a residential program for difficult youth in California. When he expressed an interest in working with and for us we were overjoyed. So again we had excellent helpers. They grew accustomed to the boys at the right time because our friends, John and Noni, needed to stop working to raise their own family. So as John and Noni and Frank needed to become less involved, Dwight and his wife, Cindy, became more involved in our lives.

For the next year and a half our major source of help came from this young couple, with Dwight carrying the major responsibility. Dwight worked many hours each week doing all kinds of things with the children. Frequently he and Cindy worked for twenty-four or thirty-six hours so Wade and I could take some time off. The boys had learned the house routines and assumed responsibility for their own self-care and we did not need as much help. We made the decision in January of '75 to cease looking for a live-in person. A few months later, our cleaning woman had a family emergency and needed to stop working in order to attend to the crisis. We assumed that her absence would be temporary, but as the weeks turned into months we recognized that her leaving was permanent. During her absence the boys had learned how to take care of their own rooms and their playroom and to help with family chores. We no longer needed a regular cleaning person. We shifted to a different plan and arranged to have seasonal help. Two or three times a year we arranged to have someone come to work in our home for several days to do the heavy cleaning, such as washing walls, ceilings, and windows, and other chores that needed to be done periodically.

Eventually it was possible for Wade and me to consider a lengthy vacation. We needed to find an additional source of help because it was not convenient for Dwight and Cindy to spend extended periods of time in our home. Again, we had good fortune in finding a person to work with us. Through a mutual friend we heard of Bill.

Bill was a man in his late twenties who had had much experience working in the field of retardation. He had been a recreational worker in a state institution and later a teacher in a special school for retarded children. At the time we made his acquaintance he was searching for a new field to conquer and new interests to develop. It was our good fortune that he was able to help us. Bill provided live-in help for the family on two different occasions so that we could take two-week holidays away from the children.

Another person who became involved with our children was Michael, a social work student at the institute I had supervised during the academic year of 1975–76. When I learned that he intended to stay in the field of retardation and needed supplementary income during his second year of graduate school it seemed only natural that he should join us. Every person that worked with the boys had a background in social work and/or special education and this enhanced the contributions they were able to make to the child rearing that took place at our home.

As each person came to work in our home there was an introductory period. Wade and I spent several hours talking with the young people about the boys, our goals for them, and some of the techniques that we had found worked well for managing behavior. We discussed in detail, step by step, the routines that we had developed for the boys in order to provide the structure that ensured the greatest security for each of them, and especially for Tom. In some instances we wrote down the particular steps of a routine so that the worker could follow it exactly. In some instances we wrote out the specifics of a growth-producing contract that had been made with a particular boy. We asked the young people to accept Wade's patterns and routines and follow them. We asked them to ignore the behaviors that Wade ignored and to expect performance of behaviors exactly as he expected. We felt it was necessary to do this in order to allow for the easiest changeover of responsibility among the adults involved. Some of the people who worked with us were able to do this better than others.

We were concerned on those occasions when we realized that food was being used too frequently as a reward for Tom. There were instances when we left our home in the afternoon expecting Frank to spend time with the boys. We returned to find that Frank was watching a football game and the boys were being boisterous with minimal supervision. It took us longer than it should have to recognize the implications of Frank's inconsistent manner. When we talked with Frank, he agreed to do all of the things that Wade wanted to have done and in the ways he wanted them done and indicated his willingness to follow our recommendations. We had been pleased with the thoughtful gifts that he had given the children: a hairdryer to encourage hair grooming and personalized T-shirts to develop pride in clothing. He had taken the children on some of their initial shopping expeditions for their clothes and had been helpful to them in selecting nice clothing and good equipment that was highly individual. However, when it came to the day-to-day, hour-to-hour management of the boys, Frank was too permissive, and we began to realize that his permissiveness was contributing to Tom's confusion about house rules and expected behaviors. The whole issue of territory was an example.

The children were learning to respect places and properties that were off limits to them. They knew that they were not to be in our private sitting room unless invited there by us. It was distressing for the boys and for us when they reported to us that on one occasion they had spent several hours in our sitting room so that Frank could watch the football game. They reported that they had their dinner on trays in that room during the football game. The boys were distressed because they had broken two limits. They had not eaten their meal at the dining room table as was expected, and they had been in a part of the house where they were not supposed to have been. I was distressed for them because Frank had understood the boundaries which we had discussed with him. For him to invite the boys to break rules was not in the best interest of their growth and learning at that time. Such adherence to structure would not have been necessary with children who had larger repertoires of functional behaviors. But considering that our boys needed to learn basic rules, it was far too soon to put them in a situation where they had to handle exceptions to rules and their feelings about the exceptions.

Once when Frank had the boys for a Saturday outing I was appalled to see the receipts for the day's expenses, documenting the tremendous amount of junk food that had been consumed that afternoon. The boys had gone to the cider mill for cider and doughnuts. On the way home from the cider mill they purchased ice cream and a pizza. When I asked Frank why they had spent so much of their time eating junk food he explained that Tom was so high that the only thing that he could do to contain him was to provide him with treats. We did not know it at the time but have since learned that large amounts of over-processed food with additives contribute to Tom's highs. It was discouraging to learn that Frank was relying so much on junk food to ensure desired behaviors when all the rest of the week we were working hard to give other kinds of support, reinforcement, and rewards.

It was a different experience to observe John and Noni as they worked with the children. They moved into our home, stepped into our shoes, and the routine continued. Noni seemed to take the same responsibilities toward the children as I did, and John picked up where Wade left off. One might expect that part-time workers in our home would have been more tolerant or more permissive, but this was certainly not the case with John and Noni. Noni expected good manners and did not permit Tom's disruptive table behavior. She refused to have it. She was an attractive personable woman and it was important to Tom to have her approval. She was straight with him and told him, "You are displeasing me. I do not like what you are doing." He tried very hard to behave well around John and Noni, and they did some lovely things with the children, taking them on picnics and out for walks. There was only one episode that was troublesome during their many months of working with the children. Noni had some medication that she was taking during the early months of her pregnancy. It was in a bottle in her suitcase, and Tom got into her suitcase and took some of the pills. Tom was not hurt by the medicine, but we were disturbed by the fact that he had gone off limits into someone else's bedroom and into someone's suitcase.

It was a bonus for the children that John and Noni were expecting a baby and that they were able to discuss the pregnancy with the boys in a wholesome manner. Tom was innocently and lovingly curious. Andrew did not seem to respond at all to the news. John and Noni were able to come and stay a couple of times with the boys after their daughter was born. By this time the boys had learned to respect space and time. They were able to realize that certain adjustments needed to be made around the house because of the infant's presence. John and Noni worked as a team with the children. They did not take care of the boys at all, but rather they instructed, supported, helped, and monitored. For example, Noni did not comb

Tom's hair, but she did remind him that it needed to be done, stood beside him while he looked in the mirror to comb his hair, and then praised his efforts. John and Noni explained to the boys ahead of time what was expected of them for a particular experience. They practiced with them so that the boys could approach something new with some comfort. If they did not act appropriately then they would receive one warning, and after the warning if the behavior continued they were removed from the situation. Tom and Andrew felt very secure with John and Noni. They knew what to expect and how things were going to be.

They did not have the open affection for John and Noni that they did for Frank. All three young people were working for us at the same time. The boys experienced Frank as the indulger, because he let them have their own way, and John and Noni as the stern ones. At that particular period of time Tom and Andrew might have favored Frank in terms of affection, but in terms of security, they favored John and Noni. As the time passed and none of the three young people were able to continue working in our home, it was Big John and Noni who remained in the conversation.

Jane was a competent girl who had grown up with three brothers and had learned to survive with them. She was able to be strong and mischievous. I think of her as having a good head set around children. She worked many summer mornings with the boys. She always had a pleasant time with Andrew but needed to demonstrate to Tom that in spite of her obvious youth she was a responsible adult, in charge of the situation. She was able to handle his roughhousing with ease, having been well trained by three brothers. After a few run-ins with Tom she was able to convince him that because she was a woman did not mean that she was fragile, nor did it give him the right to rule the roost when she was taking care of them.

Jane played games with the children and taught them a simplified version of Old Maid. She talked at length with Andrew, who adored her, but Tom's relationship with Jane was guarded at best. Perhaps after Tom realized he could not abuse her, he became wary of her and did not quite know what to do. She was an effective person with children and we would still have her working with us except that her life took her to California. Jane was the one exception to the plan to always have male workers. Fortunately for us Jane came to the children at the right time. Frank needed to stop working because of a time conflict and John and Noni needed to spend more time at home with their new baby. About the time Jane needed to move on because of her personal commitments, Dwight and Cindy came on the scene.

Dwight and Cindy brought strengths into our home comparable to those that John and Noni had possessed. Dwight's extensive experience in other settings with children had convinced him that consistent, constant management was basic to building relationships with children. Therefore, Dwight had no difficulty accepting the regime as it was laid out. He was a thoughtful man and frequently he wanted to discuss with Wade and me the rationale for doing something as we were doing it. In every instance he accepted the plan after it was discussed with him. His observations were welcome and accepted, and frequently his suggestions resulted in some change in the way we were managing a particular situation.

Dwight and Cindy were individually and together stern with the boys. They put down firm limits and there was no negotiating. Each of them approached a new task, situation, or new behavior with one or all of the boys by explaining it step-by-step, giving the boys the opportunity to ask questions, practice, and perform. Dwight and Cindy were generous with encouragement and provided some room for mistakes. They took the boys to many different places—parks, lakes, swimming—and in every instance their method worked well. If Tom was not able to accept the limits they set he was removed. The children felt safe with them, although they were not indulged by either of them.

All of the planning was done with Dwight, and most of the time he worked alone with the boys. There were occasions when he and Cindy worked together over a weekend. Sometimes Cindy chose to come along with Dwight when he came to work for a few hours. This kind of natural involvement on Cindy's part was an enriching experience for the boys, for they experienced Dwight and Cindy as an older brother and sister. Dwight and Cindy lived about fifteen miles from our home on some acreage where they raised a garden, and they entertained us as an entire family on occasion.

One of the most special times for Tom was when Dwight hired him to help clean up his garden, and Tom was the guest of Dwight and Cindy in their home overnight. Tom worked diligently all the next day with Dwight cleaning the garden, gathering produce, and preparing the area for fall. A few days later Dwight and Cindy asked us to supper, and as a family we went. Most of the food that we ate that evening came from their garden. Tom was proud because he could identify the various vegetables that he had helped gather and now were served on the table.

Because of Dwight's schedule at the school of social work and Cindy's full-time employment elsewhere, they were not able to give us more than three days at a time for most of the period they worked with us. We felt the need for a longer vacation and in the spring of 1976 decided that the boys were secure enough for us to be away for a couple of weeks. Since Dwight and Cindy could not come for such a long period of time, we recruited Bill.

Bill was as competent as anyone else and brought into the situation some new dimensions that were delightful. Bill took the boys to visit his family and they accepted the children graciously. During the two weeks we were away, the boys were guests in Bill's home for dinner and an evening of fun on two different occasions. Bill and one of his friends took the boys to a public park for a bicycle trip. He introduced them to a fish pond where it was guaranteed they could catch fish. Not only did they catch the fish, but they came home and cooked them for dinner. During his stay with the boys Bill helped them build a go-kart. Bill was able to control the boys' behavior and help them adhere to the sustaining routines that they knew, and, in addition, he provided them with some exciting recreational experiences.

Dwight's commitments were taking him across the state, and

he had fewer and fewer hours to give to us and the boys. Even as he was needing to move on, Michael was needing part-time employment. Once again, we met the right person at the right time. Michael, in a very different way, brought some experiences to the boys that were appropriate for their ages and skills. He was a soft-spoken man and had a reasonable approach. After a couple of weeks the boys responded well to Mike's style, except for Tom who, once again, needed to test and retest. He attempted to manipulate Michael. The other boys appreciated Michael's reasonable approach and his efforts to involve them in decision making. Tom, on the other hand, saw Michael's style as vulnerable and attempted to challenge it. He did everything imaginable to test Michael, including things that he had not done for months. Riding down the street in the car, he rolled down the car windows and screamed out the windows. He defied Michael and broke the boundaries, took his bicycle and went around the block. Michael realized belatedly that he needed to take a different tack with Tom than he did with the others. Tom still needed a firm approach. After a few days of struggle, Michael got the controls back in his hands, and then the situation ran smoothly. Michael was a very sensitive person, cognizant of the kinds of things that young teenagers should learn. He was able to handle their discussions about feelings and some of their curiosities that were beginning to emerge about sexuality.

We were fortunate that the people who worked with us were all from helping professions, people who were able to accept all ranges of disabilities as part of the human experience. Some of them were skillful in knowing how to manage behavior and some of them were exceptional in knowing how to maximize the opportunity for good performance from low achievers.

As Wade and I worked with the young adults who assisted us, we shared with them our ideas about child rearing. We expected them to accept our ideas about supervision, routines, rules, and limits. We saw it as the adult's responsibility to establish the tone, atmosphere, feelings, mood, and morale of the home. It was our responsibility to create an atmosphere conducive to the boys' growing. We were the ones who needed to model, as well as teach, the attitudes that we wished to have the boys incorporate into themselves. It was expected in our home that everyone would try to do as well each day as he did the day before and a little bit better. The attitude held in our home was that everyone had a right to be and everyone had a right to become.

We also tried to create an atmosphere of fun in our home. Generally we were not disturbed by noise or roughhousing, although we preferred the physical activities to be outdoors. With few exceptions we did not worry too much about things the boys said or how they said them. We were more interested in helping them experience our home as a safe place where they could try many different behaviors and discard the ones that proved to be unworkable for them. Pervading the entire experience of living together was Wade's and my acceptance of the responsibility of maintaining a home atmosphere and that the boys would be supervised at all times. At no time in our home was an adult not present. At no time did they leave our home without adult supervision. Within the home territory there was ample opportunity for free play, and the boys had maximum opportunity to select and determine what they did and how they did it with two exceptions. The boys were never permitted to be in the swimming pool without poolside supervision from an adult, and they were never permitted to be in an automobile without an adult in the vehicle with them. We saw supervision as a responsibility that rested upon us and an expectancy that we put upon ourselves. We expected there would be no deviance from this.

In the process of developing and creating a comfortable, warm home for all, routines were established in order to get the most out of home with a minimal amount of dissonance, disruption, and discord. Obviously, a person did not get punished for not adhering to a routine. Rather, parenting people took the position that they would monitor, remind, support, model, teach, discuss, and negotiate the maintenance of routines. There were of course some permissible exceptions to maintaining the routine. Routines were not carved in granite. They existed only for the good and welfare of the family. If a routine was not functional for the family, it was changed. For example, there was a routine for mealtime in our home. It was expected that everyone would be home for dinner. Obviously, there were permissible exceptions. Sometimes I worked late and I did not get home for dinner. Sometimes a boy was going to be doing something special such as attend the Teen Club, and he needed to have his dinner early, but more on routines later. One mealtime routine that was accepted by all of us was that the table was set and that every placemat had a knife, fork, spoon, and napkin. That was the procedure or "way of doing it." It really did not matter whether the napkin was folded and placed underneath the spoon or whether it was placed between the fork and the knife on the center of the placemat. That was a matter of preference of the person carrying out the procedure for the family's convenience. I made a big point of this because we have tried not to allow ourselves to get confused. Often the boys chose not to cooperate with any routine, and that was aggravating when we parents were tired. It would have been easy on these occasions to slip into a posture of being a punishing person, but punishing was not appropriate when we were talking about maintaining routines. Periodically we had to stop and remind ourselves that rigidity was getting in our way. A little later I will describe some of the routines and procedures that helped make our home secure.

We saw rules as highly individualized and negotiable. Rules were intended to be guideposts to help a person experience, grow, develop, and change. Hence, rules developed and changed depending on the particular needs of the boy at that particular time. Here again, as parents we tried to remember that rules were there to guide the boy to achieve what he could do best. It became very clear to us that we should not punish one who did not adhere to his guideposts. We taught how to follow the guideposts. We modeled, supported, encouraged with praise, and we rewarded accomplishment. We admonished and corrected the failures.

This is not to say that as parents we did not expect adherence to rules or guideposts that had been negotiated. In our home one such rule was that beds were to be made before breakfast. Some mornings Tom decided to be stubborn; he refused to make his bed and the situation developed like this. Wade would say, "Tom, why don't you want to make your bed? Are you sick?"

"No."

"Well, if you're not sick, make your bed so you can get dressed, have breakfast, and go to school."

"I don't want to go to school."

"If you don't want to go to school you will spend the day in bed because the only reason children don't go to school is that they are sick. If they're sick they stay in bed."

Tom would attempt to wheedle.

"You want breakfast, you want to do many different things, but the rule stands. Until you make your bed, the other things do not happen."

On two or three occasions Tom refused to make his bed. Therefore, he did not proceed on to dressing or having breakfast or catching the school bus. After this happened a few times Tom accepted the fact that making his bed was expected of him. It was a rule he had negotiated with Wade, a guidepost that he knew he must follow or other things did not happen.

As foster parents Wade and I had lengthy discussions about managing the boys. It was difficult to walk the thin line between fair and firm. We examined how strict we should be in establishing rules of behavior for each boy. Fortunately for Wade and me we were able to talk about this at great length and we usually reached an acceptable resolution.

When we thought it through, there were only three absolute limits that were maintained in our home and they could be simply stated. One, no one hurt anybody, including himself. Two, no one damaged property, including his own. Three, no one exploited another person's weaknesses or strengths. In our home we viewed the three limits as not negotiable. They were limits for everybody, and any infraction of the limits immediately brought a response from parents and other members of the family of instant disapproval and possible punishment. In our house Wade did not hurt me, and I did not hurt him. We did not hurt the dogs. We did not hurt the boys, and they did not hurt us. I was not permitted to throw dishes, smash glasses, kick out window panes because my day had not gone well. Wade was not permitted to smash his tools and slash his tires because his day had been a disaster. The same limits applied to every member of the family. The first two limits were rather clearly understood by the boys. The third limit was more subtle and difficult for them to understand. An example of exploiting another person's strengths was that Andrew was extremely competent with many tasks, and unless carefully monitored, Tom was apt to coerce Andy into doing his work for him. To permit this to happen accomplished no good for either boy; Tom was not learning his task or responsibility for himself, and Andrew was developing a type of behavior that only made him increasingly vulnerable to exploitation by others.

Infractions of limits called for immediate action. Wherever and whenever the behavior occurred it was addressed as soon as possible by the adult involved. The boy was given a verbal message of disapproval immediately. "That is not allowed. You will stop it now." The boy was removed from the situation immediately and he was informed of some loss of privilege or denial of some special treat. Immediately and instantly the child felt some discomfort as a result of his infraction.

We had learned, being parents of Jori and Frosty, that there were several units of time within each day that could be made stable, safe, and secure for them and us by making clear what behavior we expected during those periods of time. Wake up, bedtime, meals, and after school were times during the day when each family member had individual tasks or behaviors for which he had to be accountable. In addition, there were expected patterns of behavior among all of the family members during each of those time periods.

As parents we tried to teach, model, and praise the procedures that made these times harmonious and least burdensome. We established the routines and attempted to teach adherence to routine within reason. Therefore, it seemed to us that one of the first responsibilities we had as foster parents was to introduce the boys to routines and to the procedures necessary to maintain a routine. We believed that this would play a large part in establishing an atmosphere of safety and security. As we established and maintained the routines common to every member of the family, it provided us with the time we needed to become familiar with how we could respond to each boy's unique needs.

6

Introducing Routines

Fᴵᴿˢᵀ, the routine of wake-up. As with all other tasks, Wade and I tried to consider the way we wished the boys to function when they would leave our home to live in a placement setting for adults with retardation. Therefore, in terms of morning routines, we tried to identify the kinds of behaviors that would be functional for a man living in a group home. We then identified the first things a boy should learn in order to prepare himself to accomplish those future behaviors. We considered what particular tasks each boy could already perform.

We decided that the first thing they needed to learn about wake-up was to dress themselves independently. For each boy there were parts of the dressing procedure that were difficult. Two of the boys had difficulty telling front from back when putting on underclothes and shirts. One of the boys had difficulty matching socks. Another had difficulty learning how to tie shoes. We were tempted to take the easy way out and buy loafers. We decided that was not going to be the best thing for him because he really needed to learn how to tie his shoes.

So the procedure for the routine gradually developed. We supervised the actual putting on of clothing and prompted the boy by saying, "Turn the shirt around" or "Those socks don't match" or "Find the socks that look alike." We relied on verbal prompting a great deal. We also took time to teach tasks such as shoe tying.

Once the boy was dressed we moved him to the next task, which was to make his bed. At first we did the chore, allowing the boy to help to the extent that he was able. When a boy had learned a par-

67

ticular piece of behavior, he was always expected to do it. For example, once he learned to button his shirt, he always buttoned his shirt. A boy was never allowed to manipulate us with statements such as, "I don't know how" or "Help me" or "Do it for me." Once he could do it, he had to do it. Gradually, over weeks and weeks of time, the boys learned the entire wake-up routine of dressing, bed making, hair combing, lunch preparation, eating breakfast and toothbrushing. As parenting people, Wade and I spent an hour to an hour and a half a day in the boys' bedrooms with them teaching them step-by-step and monitoring them step-by-step until the learning had all taken place. As we developed the morning routine, we tried to help them learn the best use of the bathroom, how to use the bathroom quickly, how to use the bathroom only for toileting and washing, and dressing in bedrooms. For our home, at least, it was more functional to have showers as part of the evening routine which I will describe later. After two years, Tom, Andrew, and Phillip had demonstrated that they could do every single one of the morning tasks. They had to do all of them and we never made an exception. Every day started the same way in our home.

After that, for two of the boys, the sequence of behaviors clicked off every morning like clockwork, but frequently Tom refused to do an expected behavior. He was not allowed to go on to the next step if he had not completed the first one. After the first year, he missed the school bus about ten times because of balking at one of the morning behavioral tasks. For example, if he had not made his bed, he was not allowed to get dressed. If he had not combed his hair, he was not allowed to pack his school lunch. If he had not packed his lunch, he was not allowed to eat breakfast. Tom had demonstrated that he could do the entire morning routine, and he did do it most of the time. Ten misses in two years is not bad.

We found that performing the tasks in a routine manner removed anxiety and apprehension from the morning. In every instance when Tom had difficulty proceeding through the routine, there was something happening that morning that caused him to be anxious. For example, Tom had difficulty with the morning routine the first day after Christmas vacation. It was clear he was anxious about going back to school. He was frightened all over again. It was as though he had to act this anxiety out during the whole waking up and preparation process. Our expectation is that over the next several years, Tom will become more trusting in this area and we will see less and less balking around the morning routines.

On weekends the boys were encouraged to sleep late. They knew

that they could either get up in the morning whenever they wished
or they could stay in bed. If they chose to get up, they could go to
the playroom, talk, play with their toys, or watch television. In any
case, they learned to be quiet so other people could sleep late. It was
gratifying to us when we realized that they were able to do this.
After that it was usual on weekends for the boys to be quiet until
9:30 or 10:00 in the morning. They were apt to go into the playroom
and turn on the television or play pool. Once the household was
awake, we moved into the routine of the day. Then the routine was
similar to the other five days of the week: dressing for the day's activity, bed making, hair combing, breakfast, and toothbrushing.
The routine varied little, but the starting time of the routine
changed depending on the day of the week. We thought that it was
important for the boys to learn weekend routines and weekday routines. In a group home for adults the routine would also vary on Saturday and Sunday from workdays. We believed that our boys needed
to learn to respect sleeping privileges. They finally learned that to
stay in bed late was enjoyable if the rest of the household was also
reasonably quiet. "I've got to be quiet so other people can sleep;
then they will be quiet so that I can sleep."

The same pattern carried on through the summer routine. The
test really came the first summer. Wade likes to get up at the crack
of dawn to play golf. I did not want to get up and go through morning routine just because Wade was going off to the golf course at
6:00 in the morning. The boys learned to accept this unusual summer schedule. Until they could hear me around the house they were
very quiet. When I called, "Good morning," someone would say to
me, "Wade has gone to play golf." Later we had a new signal in the
house. When the parents got up and turned the music on, the boys
knew they could begin to make noise and talk loudly to each other.
This adjustment to morning routine was a sign of the boys' growth;
they woke up easily and respected others' needs. In the beginning
we were dealing with boys who woke up frightened and had to check
immediately as to where the parenting people were; later that did
not have to be done. They knew that the place was safe. They knew
that they could get up and go to the toilet and go back to bed, go to
the playroom, turn on television or play pool, and be quiet. That was
an indication of how trusting they were in this situation and how
sure of themselves in their home. After they knew that breakfast
would come, that the day would be all right, wake-up became a
pleasant time.

Wade and I decided that in our home the children would shower in the evening before they went to bed. We wanted them to enjoy a routine that could be functional for a lifetime. We agreed on these steps: stripping clothes off, showering, putting on pajamas, putting soiled clothes in hamper, toileting, and going to bed. As needed a boy would include other grooming tasks such as washing his hair. From the beginning, Wade and I agreed that all supervision of toileting and bathing would be provided by Wade or the male staff who worked for us. We wanted to help the boys learn appropriate behaviors from other men. During the years in the institution their needs had been attended primarily by female staff and we chose to broaden their experiences to include greater contact with men. Since the institution had provided for group bathing in a large shower room, the boys had no experience with faucets and the need to regulate water flow and temperature. The use of faucets required monitoring for a long time.

The boys enjoyed lathering themselves. It was fun to take soap and rub it all over their bodies, but each boy needed to learn how to rinse his body thoroughly so that he would not itch afterwards. They needed to be reminded to rinse in all the crease places—under arms and between legs. We were not too sure how thoroughly they learned to dry themselves because it was so easy to crawl into flannel pajamas and have the dampness absorbed. For weeks and weeks and weeks Wade helped them bathe. He never did get in the shower with them, although that might have been a good idea. He stood beside the shower and reached in and helped. He was there to supervise, remind, encourage, and give directions as they proceeded through the showering. After months and years the boys were responsible for themselves. Wade spent some time with each boy at bedtime. He might shoot pool, watch television, or have a conversation. He was available while the boys showered.

Hair washing was still a problem. Periodically I felt the need to wash their hair over the washbasin so that I was certain it was really clean. Wade teased me and reminded me that I must let the boys grow up and take care of that themselves. "If they can't learn to wash their hair, they'd better have it cut." Trimming fingernails was still difficult for the boys. The chores of maintaining clean bodies that needed to be done the most often were learned by all of the boys. They were proud to take care of themselves. They were proud of their bodies. They knew that the more they took care of themselves, the more they were like the other children they met on the street.

As the two older boys moved through adolescence they had problems with their skin and were reminded to wash thoroughly. It helped them for me to check their faces two or three times a week. It gave me an opportunity to treat pimples that might be surfacing on their skin. I use medicated pads to wipe over their skin and if the pads were soiled afterward I showed them to the boys and said, "Look, you didn't do a very good job of washing your face." At the same time I had the opportunity of cleaning their faces for them.

Preparing for bed was not difficult for any of the boys to learn. Andrew and Phillip quickly accepted our home and the security of our presence. They trusted the new situation and experiences, but going to bed was extremely difficult for Tom. Tom was still a very anxious boy. His anxiety was never more apparent than at bedtime. He dreaded the risk of going to sleep. The first several weeks of bed-down were a nightly experience in pain for Tom and me.

Wade and I decided that I would be responsible for teaching Tom to go to sleep. It seemed to be a legitimate distribution of labor because I was away most of the time and Wade had the responsibility of supervising the boys through the entire day. It would relieve Wade if I were responsible to teach Tom to go to sleep and it was an opportunity for me to try some ideas about teaching. I was convinced Tom as a boy had been harshly treated at bedtime. I was tempted, even though he was eleven, to provide him with a loving, mothering, nurturing type of experience that would include everything short of suckling. I talked with three of my professional colleagues about my concerns and tentative plan for Tom. After this consultation I decided that there would be little gained by perpetuating the infantilization that Tom had experienced because of his retardation. I decided that I was going to try to treat him in a way that would be more appropriate to age eleven. I told Tom that I would spend several nights with him until he learned to go to sleep in a happy fashion. I explained that I was not going to play with him, but I was going to be with him until he could fall asleep comfortably.

Wade supervised the boys' bathing, had a quiet conversation with them as they got into bed, and said goodnight. He left the bedroom and went downstairs. I sat at the side of Tom's bed and talked quietly to him. There were times when he screamed, yelled, jumped up and down on his bed, and asked for toys. I responded with "Tom, you *will* go to sleep. You *will* lie down. I will stay here with you until you go to sleep. I will put my hand on your back so that you can feel that I am here." It was difficult for me but I did resist his pleas. Most of the time I was able to get him to lie still. I soon learned that he liked to lie on his stomach. I found that I could place my hand between his shoulders and remain motionless. The warmth of my hand and my constant soft conversation was soothing to him. Gradually, over the weeks, he began to accept this and his approach to sleeptime was quieter. After several weeks I moved to a chair at the foot of his bed where he could see me. I would sit there and do nothing until he had drifted off to sleep. After a couple of weeks I said to him, "Tom, I really would like to be able to read my paper while you go to sleep. I'm going to sit out in the hall where there is a light and read until you are fast asleep." I sat in the hallway nightly for several weeks. Sometimes he called out to me and I went in and placed my hand on his back to soothe him. I talked to him for 20 or 30 seconds and reminded him that I was going back to the hall and read. Finally, one night I told him, "Tonight, Tom, I'm going to go halfway down the stairs and read my paper. You are such a big boy I believe that you will be able to go to sleep knowing that I'm down there." The timing was right. He was able to accept that. After a couple more weeks of sitting on the landing, I was able to tell him goodnight and go downstairs to join Wade for the evening.

There were two important considerations in this plan that should be emphasized. Wade and I had agreed that during the time it would take Tom to learn to go to bed there would be no other demands upon my time. Every single evening for several weeks, I did not take a phone call or answer the door. I did not go downstairs until Tom was asleep. In retrospect that was extremely important. Tom intuitively got the message that he was so important to me that nothing was going to interrupt my attending to him. He was able to learn to go to sleep with trust. There were testing times after that, as with any other child, when Tom resisted going to bed and he raised hell. In every instance he responded to me when I walked into his room and said in an extremely firm voice, "Tom you *will* go to bed now. You are safe. You don't need anything else now. I will see you in the morning."

In addition to this consistent, constant attention from a parent, there were other things that we did to make bedtime attractive. Tom went shopping to get Disneyland sheets and a new bedspread. He was allowed to have soft music in his bedroom, but no toys. We insisted that his shade be drawn so as to eliminate distraction from outside.

Through all this, Andrew never gave any indication of jealousy about the attention Tom was receiving. Since Andrew and Tom shared a bedroom it was important that whatever I did with Tom had to be viewed by Andrew as helpful and reassuring. The boys did well with the routine of bedtime after that.

Generally, we did not have a scheduled bedtime on nights preceding a free day. However, if the children were going to go to school the following morning, bedtime was established at 10:00. It was not unusual for Tom to choose to go to bed early. He did this happily and contentedly. If he wanted to stay up he knew that he could. I was pleased that Tom learned to make bedtime a good time for him. I believe that it was critical to have done so since he would spend a third of his lifetime in bed, and it would be better if he could do so trustingly. As he learned to trust going to bed, his anxiety diminished and he learned to trust other things in his world. After two years I no longer needed to give Tom support in going to bed and was not part of his bedtime experience at all. He looked for me every evening to tell me good-night and he went off to take care of himself. He became so comfortable with bedtime procedure that he did not resent Wade's waking him later in the evening in order to avoid bedwetting. He was able to go to the bathroom and back to bed without problems.

All of the boys slept well. We had no need to be quiet around the house after the boys had gone to bed. We did not hesitate to go upstairs or turn on lights, and when there were guests in our home, the additional traffic did not appear to disturb the children. The children learned to respect the guestroom areas and did not intrude upon our guests. The men who worked in our home kept the bedtime constant and functional in our absence, the children accepted this routine, and it became comfortable for them to follow.

We recognized that mealtimes were an important part of the day for the boys. We wanted mealtimes to provide an opportunity to learn social skills such as table manners and appropriate ways of conducting conversation, in addition to having healthful food. We decided to provide many different types of mealtime experiences. We knew the boys had experienced a limited diet prior to coming to us. We expected there might be some resistance about accepting new foods, but we expected the boys to try different kinds of meats, fish, cheeses, and vegetables. We wanted the children to learn how to prepare meals for themselves for we believed this would be useful for them as adults in a different living situation.

The procedures for each of the three meals varied because the time allotted for each meal was different. Breakfast was our most informal meal. It worked out well in our home for the boys to take responsibility for setting their own places for breakfast. Wade served each boy individually from the kitchen. As soon as a boy completed the task of packing his lunch, Wade told him what he needed for dishes and silverware for that particular breakfast. The boy got his own silverware, dishes, and napkin, prepared his place at the table, and returned to the kitchen where Wade served him. All food was served to the child individually in the kitchen and the boy carried it into the dining room and ate his breakfast. Tom was usually the last one served. Then Wade carried in his breakfast and joined the boys at the table.

On school days, lunch was out of a lunchbox at school. Dinner was the most structured meal in our home, where the entire family ate together at dinner time in the dining room. When dinner was ready, everyone prepared themselves for the meal and sat at the table. The food was brought to the table in serving dishes. When everyone had assembled, Wade served.

It has been a procedure in our family for thirty years that when three people have been served, they may start eating their dinner. I do not know where the procedure came from, but it has been functional down through the years. It was usual for us to have a number of people at dinner, and food did get cold if people waited for everyone to be served. The boys learned that when three people had their plates, they could start eating even though Wade was still serving any adults that were at the table. From the beginning there were two expectations. The boys were to wash their hands before the meal, and they were to wait until all members of the family were at the table.

For three years, the list of expectations about table behavior grew longer and longer. The boys were expected to close their mouths while chewing. This was difficult to learn and persisted as a problem for Tom. We found that it helped Tom to take small mouthfuls when we gave him a small fork and spoon to use for a few days. We explained to him that he was using the smaller fork and spoon in order to learn to take smaller amounts.

We tried to help the boys learn that they talked or they ate, but they did not do both at the same time. They learned not to lean on their elbows with their heads drooping into their plates. Sometimes Wade would say to one of the boys, "Are you tired? If you're not tired, sit up." Sometimes the remark would be, "Look at all the camels at the table with their humps." These kinds of remarks were experienced as teasing, and the boys began to remind each other. They began to learn to keep napkins in their laps and how to use them. They tried to do what the adults at the table were doing. Occasionally we needed to say to a boy, "Are you a napkin holder?" Now they remind us if we are tardy about placing our napkins in our laps. I do not remember that Wade and I ever talked to the children about asking to be excused from the table, but they learned to do that by watching the adults. Of all the boys, Andrew was the most courtly. He was anxious to act appropriately. He quickly imitated such things as how to use his knife and butter his bread. We did not make a big issue about the refinements of eating, but rather we concentrated on trying to help the children learn to eat quietly and unobtrusively. Gradually, they began to learn to cut and spread with their knives. Tom was the only one who had difficulty with cutting. The boys learned by observation to carry their dishes to the kitchen. They put their soiled napkins in the clothes hamper or waste basket, depending on what kind of napkin had been used. It was an achievement for them to learn the difference between disposable paper napkins and washable fabric napkins.

The more the boys learned about appropriate mealtime behavior, the more we demanded of them. They learned that they were ready for a meal when they had washed their hands and faces and combed their hair. They knew that when there was company for dinner they were expected to make a special effort to be tidy, perhaps changing their clothes. They began to learn the special ways we treat friends in our home as contrasted to the casualness permitted to family.

Wade and I had a difference of opinion as to how a dining room should be furnished. When we renovated the house we knew that we would have retarded boys living with us. I am embarrassed to admit I thought we should take preventative steps so there would be minimal accidents or damage to property. I really was tempted to go the plastic route; store the good dishes, have a linoleum floor and, as Wade said, "Make *another* damn institution." Wade would have none of it. He took the position that we would be using the dining room for the rest of our lives and he wanted a dining room the way he would enjoy it as head of the family. We had long and heated discussions about the dining room and its furnishings. Wade asserted that he knew that children, given an opportunity, would respond to beautiful things by taking care of them. He convinced me that it would be done his way and insisted upon placing an oriental rug, a family treasure, in the dining room. I was certain he was insane. Now, I have to admit I was the one who was rigid and limiting. The boys took very good care of the beautiful old maroon rug that was under the dining room table. We used china, pottery, crystal, sterling silver, stainless steel, paper napkins, linen napkins, plastic placemats, and woven placemats. There was no breakage. There were no ruinous spills.

The boys learned to clean off their chairs and wash their own placemats. There was little discussion about the need to "take care of anything." The boys realized that these things were there to use, enjoy, and care for. They came to expect certain dishes, silver, napkins, placemats, and candles to be used when we had company. We entertained frequently, and the boys enjoyed helping put the best things out for company. Early in Tom's and Andrew's experience with us we had company for dinner. Andrew had observed me getting silver from a particular drawer to set the table. The following Sunday Frosty brought a guest home for dinner and Andrew was upset because I was setting the table with the knives and forks from the kitchen drawer. He reminded me that I should get the silver from the drawer in the dining room.

The boys enjoyed the many different patterns and colors of paper napkins that we purchased at different times. Summer meals were enhanced by using paper products that matched: plates, cups, napkins. The boys experienced this as something special.

Mealtimes became a pleasant time in the family. The routine was different on weekends in that one meal was generally eaten in a restaurant. It was an expected event each weekend. One meal during the weekend was usually prepared by one of the boys. By turns, one boy worked with me to prepare a meal. This meal consisted of a casserole, salad, and dessert. There were many reasons that this became a part of our weekend. It provided a time for one boy to have time alone with mother. It also gave the boy and me an opportunity to work on some skills in food preparation. Wade and I wanted each of the boys to be able to prepare a simple breakfast, dinner, and pack a lunch before they left our home. With this in mind, I selected simple menus for the boys to prepare with me. Phillip had a specialty—he learned to make clam chowder. The other boys learned to make casseroles. Each of the children learned to make a special salad—cole slaw, waldorf salad, or tossed salad.

There were many different kitchen tasks that needed to be learned in order to prepare these dishes: how to chop, cut, slice, stir, open a can, and turn on the stove. In every instance I selected a recipe that did not call for measurements, for none of the boys was able to read or identify a measure. Each of the recipes allowed for a good result even though something might be left out or the quantities might vary. For example, in the clam chowder, it really did not matter if there were three cups of milk instead of two.

The boys took a great deal of pride in being totally responsible for an entire meal. To prepare a hot dish, salad, and dessert, and to serve food at mealtime was a source of great pride. They learned best by starting with the task closest to the finished product. The first time we made chowder, Phillip had the task of opening the cans and putting the contents into the kettle. I had the responsibility of cutting up the potato, the onions, the bacon. Phillip had the responsibility of stirring the ingredients as they cooked in the kettle. I had the responsibility for seasoning. Every time Phillip and I made clam chowder he did more and I did less. Eventually Phillip was able to make chowder by himself. I found that I could hold a boy's interest in the task by allowing him to be involved in those steps which were closest to the finished product. Andrew and I made a casserole together involving cooked rice, cream of mushroom soup, cashew nuts, chicken, and black olives. It worked well for Andrew to open all the cans and stir everything together in a casserole. I do not believe he would have been interested in the process if he had had to stay in the kitchen while the rice cooked for 45 minutes. After he was able to see and eat his finished product, he could stay with the process for the entire time. It took five different meals for Andrew to learn all of the steps in making the casserole. Each time he started closer to the beginning. When he could say, "I can make a chicken rice casserole," it meant that he knew all the ingredients, the kind of saucepan and casserole dish needed to cook rice, and how to mix it and put it into the oven. The dishes we cooked together were the kinds of recipes that were not damaged if they were cooked at high, medium, or low heat.

We provided the children with an opportunity to cook breakfast which involved pouring milk, using the toaster, buttering toast and cutting it, using a can opener, and counting three cans of water for one can of frozen juice.

The more we worked with the boys, the more they taught us about attending to the minute particulars of a larger task. Wade and I could talk about making a casserole for dinner, assuming complete understanding between us of all the specific things that needed to be attended to in order to accomplish the larger task. We learned that when we communicated with the boys, we needed to help them see the minute particulars. As they experienced enough of those particulars, they were able to understand the totality of the experience. Later, it was my responsibility on the weekend to spend two or three hours with one boy for one meal. That included preparing, serving, and cleaning up after one meal. We believed everyone should clean up after himself so we allowed time for it.

Packing lunches was a part of the mealtime routine. The first task they learned to do independently was the task closest to the completed product. The boys learned to do things in this order: first, get lunchbox from the storage place. Wade put the prepared lunch in the box for them. Second, get a napkin and put it in the lunchbox. Third, place the prepared lunch items in the lunchbox. Four, select the fruit for lunch. Five, wrap cookies. Six, wrap sandwiches. Seven, make sandwiches. This proved to be a very effective teaching technique for these three boys.

Tom, especially, had a very short attention span. Initially he was not able to complete the task of packing his lunchbox. He tried. His lunchbox looked as though a hamster had nested in it. But turning the procedure around, reversing it, worked extremely well. After three years, I could say to any of the boys, "It's time to pack your lunch. These are the things that you can make into a lunch today." I knew that each of the boys could make sandwiches, cut them into parts, put them in sandwich bags, select dessert and fruit, wrap it, get a paper napkin, and put the meal in the lunchbox.

It was fun to introduce the boys to new and different foods. When they came to live with us they could name very few foods. They called all meat "ham" or "chicken." They did not recognize eggs unless they were scrambled. Lettuce was the only vegetable they recognized uncooked. They were accustomed to carrots, peas, potatoes, bananas, oranges, and apples. As the months and years went by the boys learned to eat many different kinds of meat, fish, and poultry in our home. They came to enjoy cheese—the sharper the better. They enjoyed a variety of fresh fruits and vegetables, cooked and raw. One might have called them salad freaks.

During the first several weeks of living with us, the boys had a lot of dessert type foods. Every weekend I baked a double batch of toll house cookies and a couple of pies. We served many pastry-type desserts and puddings with whipped cream for we knew they were familiar foods for the boys. We were anxious to make the transition from institution to home as easy as possible and believed that familiar foods would be helpful. As the weeks and months went by we began to cut down on the number of pastries and puddings. Three years later, we had one rich dessert a week. The boys were content with meals where desserts consisted of fruit or ice cream. Many meals included no dessert. However, the boys were at the point where they did not believe they had been well served unless they had a salad. In our home it was customary to start dinner with a large salad, followed by the hot part of the meal which consisted of meat or fish, and vegetables. Occasionally, we chose to eliminate the salad as a first course because of the nature of the main dish. Usually one of the boys said, "Where's the salad?" I knew that we had taught enjoyment of salad when one of the kids ordered a salad in a restaurant instead of the usual fries and hamburger.

When we went out to eat, the boys were allowed to have what they chose. They were not very adventurous in restaurants. They were apt to choose a hamburger, fries, pizza, or pancakes. That was typical teenage behavior! I seem to recall our natural son doing the same thing. The boys also learned to enjoy varied things at home— sour cream, yogurt, granola, nuts, raisins, and celery. And peanut butter! It was usual for us to consume four pounds of peanut butter a week. Tom chose peanut butter over anything else for a sandwich. The boys also learned to eat eggplant, zucchini, mushrooms, avocado, cantaloupe, plums, and shrimp. Liver was the least favorite food.

We found that one of the best ways of introducing a new food was not to make it available. The first time Tom ate mushrooms, he said, "Yuck, what's that?" Wade's response was: "Mushrooms. It's just as well you don't like them, Tom; they're for grown-ups." Tom immediately wanted some, but Wade did not serve him any. A few nights later we had mushrooms again. This time Wade said, "Mushrooms are grown-up food. You may have a little taste, but it is really for grown-ups." That was all that was needed to make them want them in great quantities. That approach worked with mushrooms, egglants, roquefort cheese, chowder, fondue, and all other kinds of foods that the boys had not seen in the institution. The children ate well. They ate what they were served and almost always wanted second helpings.

Wade and I tried to help the children learn the relationship between good meals and good health. We talked about the fact that milk was good for bones and teeth. We talked about how fruit and fruit juices helped protect us from colds. We gradually reduced the amount of sugar that was used in our home. Occasionally, the boys suffered from an attack of "sweet tooth." Wade and I tried to help them understand that too much pastry and candy was not good for them.

Tom and Phillip were bottomless pits. They needed guidance from grown-ups as to how much they should eat. Otherwise, I think they might have eaten until they burst. Andrew was thoughtful about his eating. He enjoyed a particular part of a meal but did not glut himself. I never knew him to overeat. But if there was something for dinner that Phillip particularly liked, he was apt to eat quickly to make sure to have a second helping. Wade always reminded him, "Slow down Phillip. There will be another helping for you." It was Wade's habit to allow for second servings for everyone at the table. Phillip responded to an occasional reminder, but Tom was a different story.

We found that one of the best ways of helping Tom slow down and chew his food was by providing him with an egg timer. Since Tom did not understand how to count beyond two, we served him the amount of food that appropriately could be eaten during two turns of the timer, or six minutes. This served to slow Tom down, but his anxiety continued to be apparent at mealtime.

We found that it was just as important to have a secure routine for after-school activities. Again, we tried to look at the most important behavior an adult would need in order to move successfully from work to leisure time. Even for some adults, the transition from the structure of a work day to unstructured leisure time is difficult to handle. We decided that we wanted to help the boys learn to make the transition from their school into late day activities with a feeling of security and serenity about themselves. We felt that there were tasks that we could teach the boys that would insure this security for them. For example, most adults need to put away the equipment or clothing necessary for the work day and move into a different kind of clothing and equipment for after work experiences. We decided that we wanted the boys to learn to come home from school, take off their school clothes, and put on play clothes in order to relax and play. We wanted them to learn that this was a time of day for relaxation, not a chore time. It was time where they had a right to expect to wind down, to shift gears, and we wanted to help them learn to do that. Changing clothes was the first task and a difficult one for the boys to learn. They came to us with little perception that different clothes served different needs. In our home they had expanded wardrobes and for several days they felt that it was some kind of punishment to have to put their school clothes aside and put on clothes appropriate for hard play in the out-of-doors. It was difficult for them to accept that they needed to preserve their school clothes so that they could enjoy them longer. One of the ways we got around this distrust of changing clothes was to provide treats. "When you have changed your clothes you may have a treat." After the play clothes had been put on, the children were allowed to choose a particular treat. The choices usually included a couple of kinds of fruit, raisins, or perhaps a peanut butter sandwich. This provided another opportunity for learning. The children could have any one thing they wanted from a selection. Sometimes it took a long time to make the choice. Once the choice was made and the snack eaten, the boys could move on to the play activity of their choice. Weather permitting, they were free to go out or stay indoors.

As time went on and the boys began to acquire appropriate play clothing and equipment, changing clothes after school was no longer burdensome. For example, snowmobile boots were fun to have and put on. They felt important coming home in the wintertime and putting on a special kind of jacket, boots, and heavy gloves in order to go out and play. No longer was there an argument about changing clothes. No longer was there a feeling of being deprived of not being able to wear school clothes to play. "When I play I wear one kind of clothes, when I go to school I wear something else."

We used two or three techniques to help the boys learn acceptable after-school behaviors. Initially, the treat was the big factor. Later the treat was not so important. There were times when the two older boys decided they did not wish to have a treat. Sometimes Wade would say to them, "Dinner will be early tonight fellas, so I don't think you need to have a treat." They accepted this statement graciously and went on to change clothes and play. They accepted the responsibility for changing clothes as part of the routine. Having their own cubbies in which to store their equipment made this task considerably easier.

The boys had to learn how to play out-of-doors. Initially, each boy was afraid of some aspect of playing outside. Phillip was very clumsy and had poor muscle coordination. He did not like to go outdoors because he did everything so poorly. That changed when Wade got him a bicycle. As he became competent on the bicycle, he also began to learn how to throw basketballs into a hoop. Eventually, Phillip learned to swim. As his play skills improved, it was easier for him to use leisure time outdoors. Andrew was always athletic. He was always adventurous about trying new activities and especially in the out-of-doors.

The whole idea of going outdoors to play was very frightening for Tom initially. When Tom came to live with us he could not tolerate being outdoors without an adult being with him. The way we induced Tom to go out-of-doors without an adult sounds cruel, but months and years later, I am convinced it was the appropriate step to have taken. Every day we insisted that Tom get dressed and go out to play. Initially he was required to stay out three minutes. As the days and weeks went on, the time periods became longer. At first, Tom would scream and yell most of the time he was outdoors. Gradually he began to learn that there were fun things to do. He began to learn that some of the things that had been put out there for him to use were exciting. After many months of this kind of conditioning, Tom was given a bicycle for a Christmas gift. It was the most important gift he ever received from Wade. It was important for a great many reasons but in terms of helping him enjoy the out-of-doors and playtime in the immediate surroundings of our home, there could not have been a better gift.

The after-school routines were not as structured as morning or bedtime routines. After-school time was leisure time, a free-choice time. We felt minimal constraints should be put upon each boy as he chose to do the things of interest to him. The boys had the option of playing at whatever they wished until 20 minutes before supper time. The options varied. Outdoors, they could play basketball, tetherball, baseball, football; they could ride their bicycles or swim. Inside, they could play pool, hook their rugs, play with toys, or watch television. Twenty minutes before mealtime the boys were expected to put their toys away and prepare for dinner. It was not unusual for a boy to ask Wade if he could help with preparation of the meal, and frequently one of the boys did. Two or three times a week the boys went with Wade to do errands, to a market, hardware store, or on other shopping trips.

Rules or directions were few during playtime, but the limits remained constant. No one hurt anybody. No one hurt anybody else's playthings. No one exploited another's strengths or weaknesses. Generally, the boys did very well with the after-school time, but occasionally there was some limit infraction and some behavior that called for a correction, reminder, or admonition from Wade or from me.

This may be the most difficult time of the day for parents of children with developmental disabilities. It was very difficult for children to learn to live with minimal structure, and these were the hours of the day when we expected the unpleasant, unwanted behaviors to occur. Wade showed some of his greatest patience during these hours. He developed the habit of planning his day so that his work activities had him unobtrusively around the area where he expected the children would be playing. For example, he might be working in the garage, mowing the lawn, cleaning the pool, or reading on the back porch. He skillfully figured out ways he could be near them without appearing to be in a position of supervising the play activity. He consciously ignored many infractions and deliberately allowed the children to test their wills against each other up to the point of its becoming dangerous, seeing this as a way for the boys to learn responsibility and independence. The mischief or misdemeanors that occurred usually were appropriate for the boy's age. We tried not to overreact, but I tended to want to protect the boys from injury, and thus I did not allow them to take risks. Wade was more able to act upon the statement, "Let boys be boys. Let them grow up to be men." During the playtime hours, I had a tendency to think about retardation first and normal growth and development of boys second. The reverse was true for Wade. It appeared to me that Wade seldom thought about the children as being disabled kids but rather as boys who needed to learn.

During the time we were establishing routines for our new family, we were also gathering first-hand information about each child. We began to be involved in the long process of "raising the boys."

7

The Goal—To Raise Men

WE HAD ONE LONG-RANGE GOAL for the boys: to help them minimize the limitations of retardation so that the world would make the retardation less of a handicap. Wade and I had worked with persons with retardation long enough to learn that everyone with whom we had worked had given evidence of being capable of functioning with more independence than they had achieved at the moment and they gave every indication of being anxious to do that. During the long months of planning for the boys we talked about how we would help them achieve the best growth with us. Wade made one very strong statement. "We are going to raise men, not children. If these children are as limited as all the tests indicate, then we had better be concentrating on helping them learn the behavior now that will be necessary for them as adult men in the community. If we keep reminding ourselves that we are raising men and not children perhaps we will avoid spending time on developing skills and expertise of little practical consequence."

The first several weeks the boys lived in our home was a getting-to-know-you time. We observed their behaviors that were already basic and appropriate to achieving maturity and determined their strengths and their weaknesses. We realized that even as we got to know the boys as individuals, we needed to spend an equal amount of time learning how they related to their new physical environment. It was not enough to know as much as we could about the strengths and weaknesses of each boy. We needed to look critically at our home and identify those things that were too stimulating, too tantalizing, too unsafe to provide the best growth experiences for them.

The first step in the process of getting to know the boys was when Wade went to the institution and observed them in the classroom and in the dormitory. We learned a great deal about the boys as he visited with their teacher and the institutional social worker. The contacts with Andrew's family were helpful, and the social worker from the agency added information. We were both able to observe some situations that caused stress and strain for Tom and Andrew during their brief visit with us prior to confirmation of their placement. Even with this preparation we still needed to learn a great deal about each boy, and we spent many weeks doing that.

The first goal was to assure Tom and Andrew that they had a secure, safe home where they were accepted. For the boys to accept the security and safety of our home meant that they had accepted the routines, procedures, limits, and rules. During the first several weeks we allowed, urged, and assisted the boys to do anything and everything. This was a time for us to learn how well they could use their hands and how well they could speak. Could they write, could they color and stay within the lines? Did they recognize one playing card from another? Did they know how to answer a telephone, flush the toilet? Handle the cat, speak to strangers, cross the street, stay in the car? Use the safety belt, use scissors, pick up a sharp knife, use the vacuum cleaner?

In the process of living together, going through a thousand and one minute tasks of daily living, we began to learn the strengths and weaknesses of each of the boys. We considered the behavioral strengths and weaknesses of each of the boys in five general categories. First, how did he present himself? Second, how did he walk and manage his body? Third, how did he communicate? Fourth, how did he use his neighborhood and community to build relationships? Fifth, what evidence did he give that he could assume responsibility for himself?

We considered how each boy attended to his clothing. Was he able to dress himself, button his clothes, zip his clothes, get front to front and back to back? Was he clean, tidy, free of odor? Could he comb his hair, brush his teeth? Did he wear clothes that matched? Did he have some sense of the right kind of clothes to wear for the right situation, such as a warm jacket to play outdoors in winter time? Did he show any pride in the care of his hands or in having his face clean? Did he walk tall with his head high, shoulders back?

How did he look? Were there any unusual negative things in the boy's appearance that would cause outsiders or strangers to view him with curiosity or negativism?

I already mentioned that Tom's mouth was always open. Usually it was in action because he talked or babbled almost without ceasing. When he was quiet his mouth was open and his tongue protruded slightly. Tom had bald spots all over his head where he had pulled out his hair. There were many noticeable bruises on his body, especially on his lower arms, the results of his self-abusive behavior. Andrew generally made a fine presentation. He was a handsome boy and took a great deal of pride in his personal appearance. Both of the boys proved to be quite odorous at times because of toileting behaviors. Frequently they had sour breaths because they did not know how to care for their mouths.

Phillip generally looked neat and attended to his clothing, although we learned that he disliked changing his underclothes, which caused a problem of body odor.

Fortunately Mark, upon his arrival, gave every indication of knowing how to present himself in a neat fashion.

We looked at how the boys stood, moved, sat in a chair, sat at the table, sat in the car, used the steps. Were they able to use equipment such as bicycles, basketballs, skates, sleds? Were they able to carry things in their arms without tripping and falling? Could they reach over their heads without losing their balance? Could they walk between two points without direction or assistance from another person? Could they open doors? How did they perform tasks that demanded a great deal of manual dexterity, such as the use of their knives, forks, and spoons at table? Could they pour without spilling? Could they stir without slopping?

Generally the boys had more strengths than weaknesses in this area. Andrew was a well-coordinated child, but his lack of confidence showed up whenever he needed to rely on his body in a public place. For example, simply walking down the street Andrew needed to hold onto me in order to maintain any sense of direction. Andrew could not simply walk beside me down the street. He wanted to hold my hand. If this was not permitted, Andy's way of walking down the street was to walk in front of me down the street and cover the ground on both sides of the sidewalk up to 15 feet in each direction. It was as though I was walking down the street with a human mine sweeper. He walked back and forth, back and forth, in order to reach the corner with me. This was an extremely disrupting behavior if we were in a situation where the sidewalk had some constrictions such as fences or buildings that made barriers for this activity, to say nothing about how this behavior impeded the mobility of other pedestrians who were trying to use the same pathway.

Tom was continuously in motion. He never walked, he ran. He never went down or upstairs without running, skipping three of four steps by jumping them. Tom continuously rocked when he was in a chair. If he was expected to stay in one place for whatever reason he hopped up and down on one foot or jumped up and down on both feet. His body was constantly in motion, usually accompanied by his mouth.

When Phillip joined us he had an extremely awkward, clumsy gait. Wade had a hunch, subsequently proven true, that Phillip's lack of regular exercise was a factor in his clumsiness.

Mark managed his body well, and when he came to us he had already learned many sports.

We wanted to know what the boys knew about using language and about relating to other people through language. We listened to them carefully for the first several weeks to determine whether they knew their own names, addresses, and phone numbers. How accurately did they know the names of other people? How many objects could they identify correctly? How many objects did they know how to use and could they describe their function? How many command words did they understand and respond to appropriately, words such as *yes, no, stop, take it easy, hurry up*? How sensitive were they to recognizing a tone of voice? Could they detect from a tone of voice anger, displeasure, teasing, and affection? How capable were they in following directions: one-step directions, two-step directions, three-step directions? Could they make sentences, and of how many words? Could they relay a message accurately? Could they answer accurately a sequence of questions such as, "where is it, where does it go, where does it belong, who does it belong to?" Did they recognize colors and numbers? Did they recognize their body parts and their body functions? Did they have the correct words for toileting? What survival words did they know? Could they recognize written survival words? Words such as *stop, go, walk, danger, men, women*? What did they understand of time? Did they differentiate between tomorrow, today, yesterday, next week, next year? What was their range of understanding about qualitative and quantitative words? Did they understand "not so much, not so fast, take a little more, or put some back?" Did they have a sense of knowing how to ask for help, how to ask for directions? Did they appropriately use courtesy words such as *please* and *thank you*? Did they know how to describe their feelings: I'm angry, I like, I'm hurt, I'm sad, I love? It seemed to Wade and me that the more the boys knew of language, both in understanding it and in using it, the more capable they would be in relating to the larger parts of their world.

Immediately we recognized some challenges with our boys. Tom had the most extensive vocabulary. He had an amazing understanding and command of words and could make sentences very well. He could follow directions and frequently his bodily gestures were consistent with his spoken messages. But he could not identify colors and his concept of numbers went no farther than two. He had little understanding of time. Everything merged together for him. He did have a good sense of individuals and their names. Tom also had an extremely complete vocabulary of foul words—obscenities and profanities. He was in the habit of using these words when he was frustrated, angry, anxious, or apprehensive. Since those were the feelings that he entertained most of the time, most of the time he was using foul language. He had a tendency to repeat the same story over and over again, day in and day out, week in and week out. It took us a while to realize that when Tom said, "I don't want," most of the time that meant "I want very much." "I don't want a dessert" meant "I want it so much I can hardly wait for it."

Andy, on the other hand, had a minimal vocabulary. He made a lot of sounds, but we didn't understand many of them. Tom seemed to have some ability to communicate with him. Andrew understood a great deal and was extremely responsive. Wade could ask him to make his bed and he would do the task immediately. If you were to ask him what he was doing you would not understand from his speech what he was up to. We had a hard time getting used to the way Andrew confused opposites. Like Tom, he frequently said *no* when he meant *yes*.

Phillip came to us with the least language of all the boys. He had one tone, loud. He had an emphatic *No* which was always used to indicate *no*. When he said this word, it was a stubborn, emphatic statement accompanied by a deep scowl. His other word, actually two slurred together, was *Heyperry*. This was an incorporation of *Hey* and his last name, *Perry*. As explained earlier, he used this word to make demands, to call attention to himself, and to express all of his needs where *no* was inappropriate. Usually he accompanied

Heyperry with some definite body gestures. He would pantomime what he needed or what he wanted to do. Usually the other boys, Wade, and I would respond to his gesturing.

Mark brought an extremely sophisticated style of communication as compared with the other boys. He was able to use words that expressed a wide range of feelings, and he could understand and talk about things in terms of time and space. Frequently, however, he would attempt to get his way or otherwise influence adults in our home by talking in a manner more typical of a three year old. Unfortunately for Mark, Wade and I were not impressed by this performance and experienced it as unpleasant as well as inappropriate.

We tried to determine exactly how much each of the boys understood about ways to act in different places. Did they know that the way to act at a swimming pool was different from the way to dress and act at the circus? We tried to determine to what extent each boy knew how to take turns, to wait, to share. We tried to assess how far they could go away from home by themselves. How far could they be permitted to go down the street without wandering out into the road? To what extent were they able to cope with new experiences?

Andrew and Phillip, when they joined us, were able to trust Wade to introduce them to situations that were safe because he, or some other responsible adult, took them. Andrew and Phillip could cope with any new experience with adult sponsorship. Andrew would move into the new experience with anticipation, interest, willingness to try, and the desire to communicate about it. Phillip would go into the new experience cautiously but accepting that it was OK because Wade said it was OK. And then there was Tom. Anything new was certain to provoke an attack of anxiety for Tom. It became apparent very early that Tom needed to have a secure adult with him, just for him, in any new experience. The circus, a boat ride, a restaurant, whenever the experience was for the first time, we needed an adult for Tom and an adult for the other boys.

Initially Mark appeared to be knowledgeable about expectations of different behaviors in different places. However, this false impression gave way to the recognition that Mark had had little experience in the community other than to attend church-related functions.

An important idea we wanted to teach in conjunction with using the neighborhood was the whole idea of learning to establish relationships. Appropriate use of the boys' life situation outside of our home required recognition of a wide range of options to interact with other people. They needed to know the difference between a casual contact with a sales person and going to a movie on a date, including all the behaviors that can occur when two people have a meaningful relationship.

When we thought about this area of concern we did not limit it to how each boy with a limitation related to another boy who also had a limitation. How did he relate to a boy of his own age who did not have a comparable limitation? How did he relate to girls and women of any age? How did the individual boy understand his own limitation, compared to the other people he experienced in his world? How did he respond to authority figures such as the doctor, the dentist, the policeman, and the teacher? To the regular limit-setters such as adults with whom he lived in the house? How did the boy initiate contact with new persons?

Each of the boys was very different. Tom was extremely aggressive when he reached out to make friends with other people. He was both physically pushy and verbally abusive. These two characteristics, in addition to his constant motion, resulted in much rejection from others. Nevertheless, he continued his attempts to interact with other persons. Andrew approached all other persons with confidence in himself. He seemed to expect the other person to accept him. He had a graciousness about him and an ease of manner that made him attractive initially. He was especially attractive in situations where his behavior was contrasted to the other two boys. Phillip approached all new contacts with other persons with extreme caution. He was hesitant and wary, almost distrustful. We realized immediately that we would have concerns about Andrew's not knowing how to protect himself from exploitation. His attractive good looks in addition to his comfortable trusting acceptance of other people would make him vulnerable to enticement by an unscrupulous older person. Tom, too, was vulnerable to enticement, but for a different reason. His desperate need for acceptance and affection led him toward any person who offered him this type of experience no matter how fleeting it might be. Wade and I had very little worry about Phillip because he was so reclusive and exclusive about himself. We did not believe that he would ever go to another person for any reason without first checking it out with a responsible adult such as Wade or myself. Mark had a tendency to be overly aggressive in some situations and withdrawn and shy in others. There seemed to be no reasonable explanation for this inconsistency.

To what extent were the boys able to choose and be content with the choice about clothing, food, activities? Were they able to choose between two articles of clothing without regretting that they did not have both? Were they able to consider the advantages of two things and decide upon one? To what extent were they able to plan for an activity, an experience, or a happening? To what extent did they recognize what needed to be done, by whom, and how long it might take? To what extent could they participate in preparation? Could they be accountable for their own belongings, their own time, their own space, and their own behavior, good or bad?

Of all the children Andrew was most able to choose and be content with the choice. He seemed to have a sense of ownership of his clothing and his toys. However, he didn't seem to understand another person's ownership, or at least if he understood it he didn't act upon it. Tom and Phillip gave little evidence of self-responsibility. They appeared to need constant monitoring and direction. None of the children could own their behavior. If any one of the boys was asked a direct question, "Did you do ____?" whether the behavior was a good behavior or not, their immediate response was, "I didn't do it, he did it." Later, I began to recognize this as a behavior functional for an institution. It was as though the best way to protect oneself was to not own anything and let it belong to the other guy all the time.

Mark was able to assume responsibility for certain aspects of his behavior. However, he exploited his epilepsy by pretending to have seizures when it suited him, and then denying it when confronted.

As we thought about the boys' behaviors in these categories we began to realize that we could not change every behavior that needed change. We needed to figure out the most critical behavior in each area. We began to ask ourselves some questions. If an adult could do only one thing about "presentation of self," what would be the most functional thing for him to do for himself? That question could be followed by a second one. What would most people in the community *least* prefer to do for an adult man living in the community? It didn't take much discussion for us to agree that if an adult could only be responsible for one behavior, he had better know how to toilet independently. Most people do not care to assist an adult with toileting. We asked these same two questions over and over under each of the five categories of behaviors.

Under "Walking and Managing the Body," we believed that the most functional behavior for a person would be to attain composure of his body. It would guarantee the most acceptance for him in the larger community. To learn to be composed, quiet, and serene when your body was in a resting state would serve to help you be less of an irritation or aggravation to other people in the community.

When we considered "Communication," the first thing that each of the boys should know by the time he achieved manhood was to be able to identify himself. It was most important to know, "I am Tom," "I am Phillip," or "I am Andrew." A person needs to own his name, respond to his name, and recognize the wonder of his own self-hood through the ownership of that name. By the same token we needed to help these boys who were becoming men to eliminate from their vocabulary the words that cut off the great majority of people. The words that they were using were used in a rhythmical, sing-song, self-entertaining way. The result of the words being used repeatedly, offensively, and loudly was to alienate the very persons with whom they wished to establish communication.

When we considered the most important skill in terms of "getting along with other people" we began to think that if the boys could learn as men to smile, to listen, to attend, that that would open them up to be participants in a two-way communication. They should eliminate from their behavior the pushing, shoving, demanding, screeching overtures that were viewed as offensive by the great majority of the uninitiated. In terms of "Using the Neighborhood," the boys about to be men needed to learn to respect their own territory and things, and they needed to respect the territory and things that belonged to other people. To assume "Responsibility for Self," Wade and I believed that if we could help these boys to own their behavior responsibly, it would do much to insure their experiencing their humanity, their humanness, with dignity. They needed to decrease their tattling and blaming other people. They needed to learn the joy of owning that which was good, that which was so-so, and that which was not so good about themselves, about each other, and about adults.

We spent weeks getting to know the boys and learning to be objective about them by sorting their behaviors into classifications and clusters so that we could be helpful parents. At the same time we were critically looking at our home, our neighborhood, and our styles of parenting to see what changes needed to be made in order to insure the best experience for all of us. As we learned about the boys we needed to think in terms of each boy and his unique needs as to what were safe and unsafe areas in our house. We needed to identify the places in our home and our yard for free play. What parts of our home should be off limits to children always? What parts of our home were for use under supervision? We thought about our home, room by room, and considered the things that were in them. We wanted to help the boys feel secure by making the home child-safe. What do you put away? What do you teach to use?

Wade and I had many many heated discussions, if not arguments, about the kinds of things to put away and the kinds of things to be left out. After long discussions I finally gave in and accepted Wade's meager list of things that needed to be inaccessible to children. It seemed to me that many other things should have been included. But time was to prove him totally right, and I, if not totally wrong, was at least inappropriately anxious. The kinds of things that were put away and have remained so are the following: valuable papers, keys, money, first aid kit, and all medications except the boys' prescriptions. It was very easy to arrange to have papers, keys, and money kept in the rooms that were our personal territory anyway. The first aid kit was kept in our bathroom which the boys viewed as our private space. Everything else in our home was kept in its usual place, it was used in the expected manner, and the boys have learned, step by step, how to use them as they are needed. The list included such common items as scissors, knives, tools, kitchen appliances, washing machine, electric can opener, coffee maker, garbage disposal, and power lawn mower. Over time the boys were given the opportunity to learn the names of all these items and their uses, where they were kept, and the responsible persons who could use them. Because of Wade's firm position they were never stored away.

Wade took another position which I later came to accept: if the boys who were to be men were to live in the community, they had to be able to live with all kinds of attractive, dangerous, hazardous, potentially injurious equipment, toys, tools, and situations around them. They needed to learn to live among them and not be possessed by them, not be limited by them, and not have their handicapped condition exaggerated by them. We even considered the kinds of things that we would need to avoid or let pass by, such as strange animals, hornets, mosquitos, spiders. What would be the way to go around these creatures when you lived with a child as anxious and as fearful as Tom?

We began to look critically at our routines and the boys' use of them in terms of individual growth. Our home provided security and had routines whereby the chores of daily living for each person and the common chores were done. There was opportunity to learn, opportunity for play, opportunity for companionship, and parenting alone and in groups. Our experiences were causing us to be even more committed to the idea of regular routines. We knew that this depended upon a parenting person's availability to the children consistently during the routine. As we lived with the children and tested the routines we learned that we had needs, too, and they needed to be met.

Since our routines divided the school day into four parts (wake-up period, mealtime, after-school time, and bedtime), we began to recognize the challenges, enjoyments, and pitfalls for each one of us, parents as well as boys, in each of those four large periods. We quickly realized that, because of the demands of my work schedule, it was not possible for me to be involved in mealtimes. At the same time, we recognized that Wade was tired and running out of patience by bedtime and that that was a good time for me to be involved. We began to recognize the particular thing that went best for each boy and we learned what was upsetting for each boy in each time unit. We began to realize that as parents we needed to do everything we could to stabilize each unit of the routine. We needed to remove as much disturbance and disruption from the experience as possible, and we needed to put in as much patient, parental involvement as we could manage. It was amazing how much smoother the household ran when we worked to minimize disruption and maximize parental input.

We began to identify the three or four behaviors for each boy to learn that would enhance his personhood as a man. As much as possible we attempted to identify behaviors that seemed to be apparent in two or more periods of the day. Once we had identified three or four behaviors for each child to focus upon, we moved to analyze that behavior, to determine what was the particular factor in the behavior that needed to be learned, to be changed, or to be stopped. For example, we realized that we had to help Tom and Andrew achieve total independence in toileting.

When we thought about "total independence of toileting," it was overwhelming, but as we analyzed the skill and began to realize that the first thing that Tom and Andrew needed to learn was the use of toilet paper, the task was less awesome. We were on the way because we were teaching the boys a specific action that they needed in order to learn other actions, so they could achieve independence of toileting. They gave ample evidence that they knew when to go to the toilet, that they knew how to prepare to go to the toilet, but they still did not know how to clean themselves after bowel movements. Tom and Andrew needed help. They could not accomplish independent toileting until someone taught them to use toilet paper.

It was our plan to give all kinds of praise to each boy as he learned a new action. Once he had learned a new task, he was never allowed not to do it. He was held responsible and accountable for it from then on. For example, as soon as we were sure that a boy had learned a particular task, he was allowed to proceed to learn the next one. Initially Wade prepared the snacks for the boys. Step by step they learned the specifics of snack preparation until finally they learned the whole sequence of the task. Much later, the boys came home from school, made their own sandwiches, and got their own fruit for the after-school snack. The entire snack preparation was done independently without supervision. Much time and experience passed in order for this to happen.

As we worked with the boys to train them it was important to maintain accurate records. This was necessary in order to give the boy and the parenting person accurate goal achievement feedback. Each boy enjoyed being reminded frequently of all the things that he could now do that were so "grown-up." They needed to be reminded of such things. "Tom, I can hardly remember when you used to do that. You've grown up so much. You used to do that when you were younger, but you know better now." It was helpful to us as parents to monitor, to follow the growth of the children, and to record the milestones that had been attained. It was one of the best encouragements to us as parenting people. There were times during the three years when Wade and I were filled with despair and dismay because it seemed as though it was taking devilishly long for the children to learn certain things. When we sat down and reviewed the log notes from the earlier days, they always served to refresh us and to renew our commitment to the boys.

The sponsoring agency required maintenance of records, and they provided a form that was helpful to us. This form was completed every month and required particular information, such as a weight check and a place to record any professional contacts the child had other than school: doctor, dentist, speech therapist, etc. The form had a space to record any visits the boy might have had with his natural parents. A record was kept of all social and recreational contacts the boy had outside his home. Finally, and most important, a record was kept of the specific goals for training the individual boy and the progress observed toward achieving that goal. As foster parents we were asked to record the methods we used to achieve the goal. We indicated any problems or concerns we were having in helping the child reach his goal. This monthly report form was invaluable to Wade and me. It became routine that the last day of every month I spent four or five hours doing all the financial records for the house and bringing the boys' logs up to date. In January of 1974 and again in 1975 we were asked to complete the American Association for Mental Deficiency Behavioral Scale on each of the children. This instrument was designed to help responsible adults look at the progress a child is making on an annual basis.

The entire process of setting goals for the boys was well worth the time it took. Once a person has determined the goals, he has accepted for himself, he has also recognized that there are some things about which he will *not* be concerned for a period of time. If I decide to work for a period of time on a particular task, then I do not have to worry about learning anything else and I do not have to feel guilty about it, because I have made a decision about my own tasks or goals. I think it was freeing for the children in our home to have a few set goals to work on. It was freeing for us as parents. All those weeks and months that we worked with the boys on achieving the goal of independent toileting, we spent no time on helping the child achieve excellent dental hygiene. We helped, supported, and supervised them as they brushed their teeth, but independent toileting was the main goal in our home from which we would not deviate. By determining realistic goals and adhering to them, a person can feel achievement and know success. The more success a person experiences the better a person feels about himself.

In those first three years, Tom learned to do many things, and for every thing he learned he has liked himself better. The more he liked himself, the more comfortable he became about taking risks to try to learn something else. It was as though one goal achieved set a strong base for the next goal to be achieved. Through all of our work with the children, our striving to help them become more attractive, more acceptable, more likeable, and more normalized (whatever that means), we were kept on course by remembering Wade's statement: "It is unfortunate these boys have so little time to be children. It is unfortunate that they need so much time to prepare to be grownups. But that's the way it is and they must accept that. We are going to adultize them. We are not going to infantilize them." We tried to help them achieve behaviors consistent with the size of their bodies. We tried to help them become acceptable within their chronological age group. We were not going to permit them to be patronized and infantilized and kept forever unaccountable.

As we considered the boys and their individual growth needs, their acceptance of us as foster parents, and the uniqueness of our home, we began to develop strategies for working on the short-term goals that we had identified for each boy.

As we had examined the five behavior categories, we had identified concerns for each of the children that were impediments in terms of their "making the most of themselves in the community." For each boy, we selected the impediments that were the most frequent in occurrence, and the most alienating to others and proceeded to focus on them. Thus, short-term goals for learning were identified. As indicated in the earlier descriptions of the boys: Tom needed to learn all aspects of independent toileting, cease his foul speech, and stop having tantrums. Andrew needed to learn toilet management, stop his tattling on others, and learn to keep his hands off people and things.

When Phillip arrived he had different immediate needs. He had to learn respect for privacy, names of individuals, and cease shouting.

When Mark arrived, we identified a unique set of short-term goals. He needed to eliminate the faking of seizures, stop fighting with other children, and learn to talk about his concerns with an adult.

We checked these short-term goals against the five categories of behaviors: presentation of self, managing the boys, ability to communicate, use of community to build relationships, and responsibility for self. It seemed that the short-term goals were reasonable.

If we continued to adhere to our routines, we could develop a positive approach to teaching new preferred behaviors to substitute for the inappropriate, infantile habits that the boys possessed. The next chapter describes some of the techniques we used to assist the boys in their efforts to become more socially acceptable.

8

Learning to Be a Family Member

THE FIRST TIME the children took baths in our home, we checked their bodies over thoroughly. We were satisfied that there were no sores or anything to indicate infection. Tom had a history of self-abuse, and he came with many bruises all over his body which were undoubtedly self-inflicted. There were scars on his hands where he had bitten himself. There were spots on his head where he had pulled out patches of hair. All of the boys came to us with very short hair, almost as though their heads had been shaved a month or so before.

Wade and I agreed that a good self-image was important for the children and good health would help to develop this. There were three basic regimes we wanted to incorporate into their daily living as a way of helping to develop their responsibility for themselves and thus enhance their feeling of worth about themselves. We believed that the boys needed to develop habits for sleeping and exercise, for toileting and cleanliness, and they needed to have regular, nutritionally balanced meals. In terms of health and our initial impression as described earlier they needed to achieve good habits in these areas. In terms of how they would feel about themselves, they needed to develop pride and independence in self-care, and particularly toileting.

When two of the boys came to live with us, they were not completely toilet trained. They soiled their underclothes, Tom more often than Andrew. Tom frequently wet his bed. Both needed to learn independent toileting in every aspect. Wade's rationale was simply stated. He could not imagine a thirty-five-year-old man functioning in the community with smelly, soiled underwear. It was common for the children not to recognize the need to go to the toilet for a bowel movement. They did not wet themselves during the day, seeming to recognize their need to urinate and anticipate the need in time, but responsibility for their bowel movements was difficult for them. I think it was because they could not tell the difference between wanting to pass gas and wanting to have a bowel movement. Wade took the position that the boys would be responsible for cleaning up any mess that they made. There was no punishment put upon them by the parent, but the boy was responsible for his own behavior. If he messed his own clothes, then he had to clean them up. We also put them onto a behavior reward program where they earned part of the following meal by being clean.

It became apparent that Tom and Andrew usually had a bowel movement in the middle of the afternoon. We started to remind the boys that there was a certain way to behave when they toileted. My husband taught and monitored each specific task in private toileting, beginning with closing the bathroom door for privacy and ending with hand washing. The boys were made responsible for the entire toileting process. If a boy had soiled his underclothes before a meal, he had to wash out his soiled clothes, put on clean clothes, wash his hands, and join the family at the table. For that meal the boy could have two slices of homemade bread and butter and a glass of milk. I emphasize the homemade bread for I had difficulty denying the children food for whatever reason. So I comforted myself by knowing the bread was homemade. This proved to be a very good plan since the boys enjoyed eating.

Our table had many interesting foods of different textures, colors, and tastes which provided the kinds of experiences boys enjoy. I had learned early that one of their favorite foods was whipped cream. For the first several weeks that the boys lived with us, they had more whipped cream than they had ever had before or since. I made puddings with mounds of whipped cream on top. It was very painful for a boy not to have a yummy dessert when everybody else was having it, especially because he had been careless about soiling. Not to have the same meal as other people proved to be an effective method to help the children learn. There were times when it was difficult for me to cooperate in adhering to this rule. The most difficult time for me was the first Christmas dinner the boys shared with us. Andrew did soil his underpants. I wanted to relent because it was a holiday, but my husband said, "No! It is more important for Andrew to grow up learning to be a clean adult than it is for him to eat Christmas dinner in 1973." He reminded me of our contract that he could make all crisis decisions. I was furious with his unreasonableness, but I did follow his suggestion that I have a drink and let him handle Andrew. It proved to be the right decision, for after Christmas 1973 there was only one other instance of soiling on Andrew's part. To salve my own conscience, I saved tastes of everything from that Christmas dinner and let Andrew have it the next evening. That was the first of many instances where I felt the need to let the boy have the rule eased a little bit. I guess I was really the one who needed to be placated.

Tom tested us in many ways. One day when he was sliding he soiled himself. He came home, changed his pants, and hid them. Subsequently we found them and knew they were his because his underclothes had been marked when he had left the institution. Initially he denied that he had soiled himself but eventually explained how he thought the soiling accident had happened. In any event, Wade enforced the rule and was especially firm with him. He insisted that Tom take a shower to clean himself thoroughly for his buttocks were caked with dried feces. It was a firm stand on Wade's part and Tom, of course, resisted. He fought like a tiger, kicking, biting, swearing, and screaming. Tom took the shower and learned that the rules were for real.

We had some of the usual difficulties. The children used too much toilet paper, stuffed up the toilet, and did not flush it. Of all the difficulties, stuffing too much paper into the toilet causing it to be plugged was the worst. After four or five times of using the plunger, Wade became annoyed with this procedure and made a drastic move. Initially I was distressed by his action, but it turned out to be exactly what was needed. As usual, it was Tom who had glutted the toilet bowl. Wade insisted that Tom put his hand into the toilet and pull out all the toilet paper and put it into a mop pail. He had to clean the toilet until it could flush in the usual manner. This was a revolting task and Tom screamed, swore, and protested that he would not do it. Wade stood behind him with his hands on his shoulders insisting and forcing him to clean up the mess. Tom cleaned up the mess and there was no recurrence of that activity. Again, Wade demonstrated clearly for me that regardless of Tom's level of functioning, he could learn to be responsible for his own actions.

It was always difficult for Tom to learn. No matter what the plan was to help him learn a task in our home, we realized that Tom would test and retest, every step of the way. There came a time when Tom had a very loose bowel movement when he was playing outdoors. It was clear that he knew exactly what was happening because he danced around in front of Wade and made several remarks indicating that he knew that he had to go to the bathroom. When Wade reminded him to do so, he looked him right in the face and deliberately soiled himself. Wade took him by the arm, led him into the bathroom where Tom had to strip himself. He was filthy. Wade insisted that Tom take a shower and wash all of his clothes and himself. The whole procedure was done with cold water. Wade made it as unattractive a task as possible. For 20 minutes Tom was in the bathroom screaming at the top of his lungs. Wade stood in the doorway and insisted that Tom would not leave the bathroom until his underclothes, bluejeans, and socks were washed, as well as the bathtub and himself. On this occasion and every other time Wade enforced a rule, Tom's reaction was physical and verbal. As mentioned before, Tom had a colorful vocabulary. Any confrontation between Tom and Wade about a piece of behavior would result in Tom's screaming all of his derogatory phrases at the top of his lungs. For Tom to call Wade a bastard was one of the most benign remarks he threw at him. During those early months when Wade was concentrating on helping Tom learn to control himself in toileting behavior, Wade chose to ignore the language that came out of Tom's mouth.

There was one final smearing incident with Tom shortly after we had moved into our new home. On a Saturday afternoon everyone was busily doing things around the house. Wade and I became aware that Tom was missing and had been for 5 or 10 minutes. Wade went looking for him and found that Tom was in the downstairs bathroom. He had smeared feces all over the fixtures, the mirror, the walls as high as he could reach, and all over himself. Wade was furious! He came storming out of the bathroom, through the kitchen, and into the dining room where I happened to be and said, "*You* do something! I cannot do anything with him now, I may hurt him!" I don't recall ever seeing Wade as angry. It was good for the situation that I saw his anger and knew it for what it was, for it gave me what I needed in order to remain calm in the situation. It took a lot to remain calm. When I walked into the bathroom, Tom by this time was screaming and swearing as though in anticipation of a confrontation with Wade. I walked into the bathroom, took him by his shoulders and shook him and told him that he would stop instantly and clean up the mess. *"You will do it now."* He was so startled by my involvement in the intervention that he started to obey me. I had him get into the bathtub and strip. I told him to fill the bathtub with cold water and wash out his clothes. I told him, "When those are clean, you will wash the walls." At this point he screamed at me that he was going to have a seizure. "You can't make me or I'll have a seizure." At that challenge I stared him straight in the face, clenched my teeth, and in my most firm voice told him, "You go right ahead!" I guess my eyes were flashing fire for I will never forget the effect upon Tom. He stopped dead and said to me, "You're not afraid?" I answered him, "Hell no, I'm not afraid. I've seen a lot of people have seizures so you just go right ahead and have one." To tell the truth I was scared to death, for I was well aware that Tom took medication for seizure control, and though he had never had a seizure in our home, I was braced for the first one. I suddenly realized that Tom had probably been using that threat for years in the institution in order to get his way. Fortunately for me and Tom, I had my back up just about far enough so he was not going to win with me. When he realized that I was not intimidated by his threat, he calmed down completely. He stopped his tantrum and began to cry. He wept gently and softly for the half hour that it took him to clean the bathroom. I stood in the bathroom door and kept giving him directions and encouragement, telling him that he could go right on crying but he would clean up the mess at the same time. The tantrum passed. After that day he has not threatened either one of us with having a seizure. Nor has he smeared feces. Two things that had worked for him in the institution suddenly and dramatically proved not to work with people on the outside. He learned there were people who were not afraid of seizures and who would not clean up after him when he smeared. In retrospect, Wade and I realized that that whole experience was the turning point for gaining Tom's respect and helping Tom gain control of himself, for until that point in our relationship, Tom had felt he was always going to be able to manipulate the situation. Afterwards, he knew better.

Bed wetting was not a problem for Andrew, who always was able to recognize his need to toilet during the night and took great pride in the fact that he did not have a rubber sheet on his bed. He took good care of his bed, he was clean with his bed, and never gave us a concern.

And then there was Tom. Wade and I believed that bed wetting for Tom might occur through puberty and on into adult life due to his possible seizure activity. We also felt, however, that he should take responsibility for cleaning up after himself. Tom, someday, would live in a group home where he would be expected to take care of himself and his bed. Even though bed wetting might occur through a seizure pattern, it did not take away Tom's responsibility for taking care of his bed.

There were two or three times during the first year that we believed that Tom soaked his bed to punish us. One time I heard a ruckus and went out into the hall. Tom's bedroom door was open and he was standing on his bed urinating. I believe he knew what he was doing, and I could see no reason why he could not have walked to the bathroom. He seemed to be trying to get even with us. By the third year Tom no longer acted that way. He understood that if he messed his bed he had to clean it up. He understood that the chore of cleaning up his bed was an interruption in the daily routine and could be very costly. There were Saturday mornings, for example, when because of his bed cleaning chore he was not able to go on an outing with the other boys.

The procedure for cleaning up bed wetting was this. Tom immediately stripped his bed and took all the dirty linens to the basement, washed and dried all the clothing, and changed his bed. This whole process took two to two and a half hours. We did make arrangements for a spare rubber sheet, but all the other bedding—sheets, blanket, spread, and pillow cases—had to be washed, dried, and put back on his bed *before* any other thing could happen. That meant before getting dressed, having breakfast, going to school, or going to play. Of course Tom had to test this. He did not believe that we would let him miss the school bus. After he had missed the bus a couple of times, he realized that Wade really did mean it. So over a period of several months, the bed wetting ceased to be a big problem in our home. Gradually, the bed wetting incidents decreased.

Wade gave Tom some additional support about bed wetting. Every night before Wade went to bed he got Tom up to toilet. Of course this cut down on the number of bed wetting incidents. The rule still stood: if you wet your bed, you washed it and you changed it.

Tom made great progress in acquiring independence and responsibility in every aspect of toileting. There were times at the beginning when Tom threatened us by saying, "I'll shit the bed" or "I'll mess my drawers." Three years later he no longer needed to taunt us in this way. He no longer needed to test the rules. He learned and he achieved a sense of pride because he could, in most instances, attend to himself in toileting. There were still some things to learn. On the two occasions that he went to camp, there was nightly bed wetting. We realized that this could have happened because Tom was in a new situation, under new pressures. However, we told him that he could not have a sleeping bag until he came home from a visit with his sheets and bedding dry.

Bathing and dressing were not too difficult for the boys. They enjoyed the comfort and good appearance they experienced as a result of attending to their grooming, with the notable exception of caring for their teeth.

Teaching our boys to brush their teeth was a huge challenge. We felt a great deal of support from the school about toothbrushing, for toothbrush drill was part of the school day. We concentrated on toothbrush routines after breakfast and after dinner. One time Andrew was observed squeezing the toothpaste out of the tube and into his mouth. For a period of time, the boys used electric toothbrushes, but this novelty wore off. Each of the boys learned that toothbrushing followed meals. Even so after three years none of the boys did a thorough job without a great deal of prodding from grown-ups.

All of the boys received regular dental attention and support for good dental hygiene in the dental clinic. The decreased use of sweets in their diets had a good effect as well.

We knew that it was a big change for the boys to leave a situation where they lived with thirty other boys to come and live with a foster father and mother. This was never more apparent than around play time. The boys did not know how to use their bodies or how to do some of the simple sport-type activities most boys enjoy. They did not know how to play together, demanding, rather, to play with an adult. Tom could play with me and he could allow Andrew to play with me, but he would scream, yell, and physically interfere if Wade played with Andrew.

Four days after Tom and Andrew moved in with us, we took them to a neighborhood park to play touch football. We intended to use one football and play two against two. Wade and Tom were a team, and Andrew and I were a team. It seemed to us that this type of teaming would make for the fairest balance of skill. The game was a total fiasco. Every time Tom got his hands on the ball, he ran out of the boundaries designated for the game. Wade would follow him and bring him back. In our nervousness about this new boy and our responsibility, we did not see that we were tricked right into Tom's game. By taking the football and running off the playfield he forced Wade to run after him. It resulted in Tom's having Wade's full attention. When Wade overtook him and admonished him that he had to return to the playing area, the admonition appeared to roll off Tom's back. He was pleased because of the attention that he was getting. That was the first of many incidents that helped us realize how Tom had been affected because of so little contact with men for so many years. We had a challenge facing us as we introduced the boys to leisure time activities. When the boys came to live with us, Andrew was adventurous, fearless, quiet, and careless. He would try anything. He was quiet about it and often oblivious to the hazard of the situation. Tom, on the other hand, was an anxious, apprehensive child who was afraid of everything—afraid to go outdoors, afraid of weather, and afraid of animals. In his fear he acted out in a boisterous, noisy manner, screaming and yelling at the top of his lungs and usually jumping up and down. For the first several weeks, the priorities were to keep Andrew from injuring himself and to help Tom take the risk of new experiences. These tasks were further complicated by the short attention span which each boy manifested. We learned that a grown-up needed to be involved in every leisure time situation or the boys would go and find the grown-up wherever the grown-up happened to be. Since Wade and I had decided that the children would never be left unattended in our home, it meant that for the first many months of the boys' living with us, they stuck to us like glue.

We wished to have the children learn to experience a play time, an activity, an outing without physically hanging onto father or mother. For the first six months, it was usual for the situation to be two on two: two parents to two boys doing any activity.

After eight weeks the boys were able to be in our den, a room about 9' x 12', with two parents and their toys. Wade could watch a football game and I could read a book while the boys played on the floor with their toys—on the floor because when they first came to us they were very unfamiliar with the different types of furniture present in a home. Tom, especially, needed to learn that chairs, lamps, tables, desks, radio, television, and all the other pieces of furniture in a home were not to be attacked. His original way of approaching a piece of furniture was to run and slam into it. Since that was the case, playthings were on the floor and boys were on the floor playing with them. They were sprawled out pushing and pulling toys and building with blocks. They enjoyed toys generally used by children eighteen months to two years of age. In that small room with low-key activity, the boys could play contentedly for as much as an hour. Every few minutes Wade or I would give some sort of verbal support or demonstrate some interest in what they were doing in order for them to sustain the play activity. Neither boy had any interest in books, television, or music. In other situations, they wanted to do what the grown-up was doing, but they never imitated adult behavior by playing with books, listening to the radio, or watching television.

After we had lived with Tom and Andrew for a few weeks, we began to realize how much they needed to develop their bodies. They needed to learn how to move with ease. Wade began to think about the long-range plan for helping these boys develop themselves to the fullest capacity as men. One night he told me his decision to concentrate on teaching the boys activities they would be able to use as adults. He wanted them to learn the kind of sports which they could do independently or with other people so that their deficits would be minimally noticed. He decided to teach the boys to play pool, basketball, swimming, and bicycle riding. Over the months and years, these four activities became very important aspects of the boys' lives. Wade decided that the first activity to learn would be pool because it is a game that can be played the year round in spite of the weather. It is a game that can be played by one, two, three, or four people. Six months after Tom and Andrew came to live with us, Wade ordered a full-size pool table. I considered this purchase just another of Dickerson's insanities; I had assumed he would start the children on a bumper pool table. When I made such a comment Wade emphatically said, "They will be men soon. They will learn to play on a full-size pool table so that they will play like men. They might as well start learning now because it is going to take them longer to learn."

Wade made no attempt to teach the children the intricacies of the game. Rather he insisted that they practice learning how to hold the cue in the proper fashion, how to line up the ball, and how to hit the ball so that it could hit against another one. He designed all kinds of simple games to help pool become interesting. The main drawing card to the pool table was the fact that "Big Stuff" spent time with the boys over the activity. Each boy had his own pool cue with his name on it. There was a reason for this. In the early stages of learning to play pool, the tips easily came off the cues. Wade wanted each boy to be responsible for his own cue and felt that a boy should not be hampered in playing just because a tip had come off due to someone else's carelessness. So the rule was, "Andrew, play with your own cue and if your tip comes off I will repair it. Until it's repaired you will keep your hands off of Tom's cue."

Andrew and Phillip did very well learning to play the game. They stood and carefully lined up the cue stick with the ball and hit the ball. Soon they were aiming balls into pockets that they had designated. Not so Tom. Tom was a slam-banger. He would approach the ball with an impulsive poke, then scream, yell, and swear when the ball did not go where he had intended it to. It was difficult for Tom to take his turn, but Wade insisted upon it. So slowly, slowly over the weeks, Tom began to accept the fact that when playing pool he would play in rotation with the other persons playing. Gradually he accepted this behavior. This was never a problem for Andrew and Phillip. They could accept sharing as part of the game.

Fortunately for the family, Mark was familiar with pool when he joined the family.

Swimming was the next activity we introduced to the boys. Here again, Wade thought of the expected behavior from grown-ups that he wanted the boys to learn as he introduced them to the use of the swimming pool. Wade took the position that "when grown men swim, they do not wear life jackets in a swimming pool; they learn to swim and take care of themselves in the water. There will be no life jackets." I remember that summer as a summer of great fun for all of us and much satisfaction for me because I did teach the boys to swim.

Each boy was initially afraid of the water. We started wading in the shallow end, which was divided from the deep end by a heavy rope with floats. Above this rope we installed a water badminton set. For several weeks Wade and I swam in the deep end and tossed balls over the net to the boys in the shallow end. Gradually they became comfortable with the water being splashed on their faces. Occasionally they would lose their balance and fall down and get their heads wet. Day after day for at least two half-hour periods, Wade and I would toss balls back and forth over this net toward Tom and Andrew in the shallow end. Increasingly they became so involved in the game that they began to overlook the fact that they were in the water. It splashed on their faces, ran down their necks, and they grew more comfortable.

They were envious that they could not go off the diving board as Wade and I did. They pleaded with Wade to let them jump off the board and repeatedly they were given the same message, "No one goes off the diving board if they do not swim. When you have learned how to swim, we will teach you." Many times this statement was made with no response of interest from the children. Wade and I recognized though that this was a good way to motivate them so we went off the board many more times than we really cared to just to make it look inviting. We kept talking to each other about how well we were doing with our dives. We deliberately ignored the boys. They were dying to go off that board. They kept asking for the life jackets because they believed that if they had them they could go off the diving board. Wade kept stating, "No jackets and no diving board until you can swim." Daily Tom bragged, "I can swim, I can swim, I can swim," but when we gave him an opportunity to demonstrate swimming the width of the shallow end, he would, to use his words, "turn chicken."

Andrew was the first one to decide that he was going to take the big risk. We noticed that he would imitate what we were doing and use his arms in a stroke with his feet on the bottom. I asked him if he would like some help. He was ready and I started to teach him how to swim and take care of himself in the water. We reinforced Andrew's efforts to learn how to swim by letting him jump into the pool on the shallow end. This was great fun and gave him the experience of having his head wet. Tom could not stand being bested by Andrew's accomplishment so soon he too was thrashing around in the water with a dog paddle.

Late in August we asked a family to come and swim with us. There were four children in the family ranging in age from nine to thirteen who could swim like turtles. Tom and Andrew were dismayed. The other four kids could swim and they could not. The other children went off the board and they could not, and had privileges in their pool which they did not. It became very important to catch up with the other kids. They began to ask, "Show me how, show me how." I was impressed when Andrew demonstrated that he could swim the width of the pool. I said to him, "Andrew, you can swim the right distance. Now it's time you learned to swim in water over your head." He trusted me, and so when he asked the question, "Can I do it?" I said, "Yes you can," and he did. He swam from the shallow end to the deep end. It was wonderful, he got all kinds of praise, and he did it over and over again. Wade and I took turns swimming beside him. After three more swim periods he was ready to go off the board.

Meanwhile, Tom was at the other end of the pool, green with envy. He could not stand it. Andrew was swimming and was getting all this attention from "Big Stuff" and "Magoo." He started to dare himself. He was frightened, but he dared himself to swim. Wade and I swam on each side of him close enough to touch at any time. We swam that pool back and forth, back and forth, and eventually Tom was comfortable. One day he went off the board. Oh, how he crowed that day! That chicken had turned into a rooster.

Shortly after Tom had become a swimmer, Phillip, our third foster son, came to live with us. Phillip was frightened of the water and viewed the swimming pool as an oversized bathtub. He sat on the bottom step in the shallow end and washed the water over his arms and shoulders and face as though he was taking a bath. It seemed important to take a whole different approach to teach Phillip. The swim period took on a different format. Wade monitored the two Johnny Weismullers that were swimming around in the pool, learning to dive, while I took the responsibility of introducing Phillip to our family fun. He enjoyed having me pull him through the water. I put my arm around his chest and dragged him through the shallow end so he could get the feeling of being horizontal. On other occasions, I sat with him on the side of the pool as we splashed water with our feet. Gradually, I was able to get him to sit on the bottom of the pool, hold onto the side with his arms, and kick his feet. It was difficult for Phillip to trust his body to float. Finally he got it. He turned out to be the strongest swimmer of the three of them. Perhaps because he was bigger-bodied, perhaps because he was older, or perhaps because he wanted to be as grown-up as the other two boys. Phillip learned to swim before we closed the pool on the first of October. He was anxious to go off the diving board before we closed the pool, and I wanted him to do that.

The boys learned to jump off the diving board by first jumping in the pool at the shallowest spot and kept moving around the rim so that they gradually were jumping into deeper and deeper water. Finally they were standing right beside the diving board to jump and then on the board itself. Many, many times Phillip walked out to the end of the board and then backed off the board again; he could not take that last jump. After countless times of backing off the board, Wade became very annoyed and said to him harshly, "You are going to go off the board into the water. That is the only way you're going to get off the board. You are not going to back off." I felt that it was a very hard position to take but Wade said later, "If you continue to let him back away from that because it's hard, he isn't going to learn a damn thing." Phillip stood on the edge of the board for 35 minutes by the clock, but finally he went in. We insisted that he do it again. He did it ten more times that day and achieved complete comfort.

When Mark joined us he could swim. However, he was overly aggressive and "pushy" in the pool. He needed to learn pool manners.

All of the boys were comfortable in the water after that and swam very frequently. For the next two school years they went swimming twice a month through the school program and they went to Family Swim at the YMCA on Friday nights. We were proud of this accomplishment; it meant they had learned a sport they could do the rest of their lives. They had learned appropriate pool behavior. They knew that they must look before they jumped in the pool or dived off the board. Their pool behavior was exemplary. They did not splash people or jump and grab people in the water. They swam in the YMCA Olympic size pool with as many as a hundred persons of all ages from all over our community. Our boys were never asked to leave the pool by the lifeguard. There were times when the boys left the pool because we did not like their behavior. We felt justifiable pride when we took the three boys on a trip and stayed in a motel for two nights. Both nights we took the boys swimming in the pool. The boys behaved beautifully. They were courteous to the other motel patrons and at the same time had a good time.

Tom still had some trouble with squealing. He would get so excited playing in the pool that he squealed or pretended to be hurt or injured. Fortunately, he did not do this in public swimming areas, only at home in our pool. I think this was part of his old act of wanting to insure his place as a center of attention in my world or Wade's world.

In the fall of '74 when the cover went on the pool the children had to accept that swimming at home was discontinued for a few months. Their disappointment was eased by the installation of a basketball hoop on the side of the garage toward the parking area. This area was comparable to half a basketball court and was a nice place to play. When the basketball hoop was installed we realized again that the boys needed to learn an activity individually before it could be shared. The boys could not take turns shooting baskets so Wade got a basketball for each of the boys. During fall of 1974, outdoor play time was used by the boys to develop their skills shooting baskets. Andrew, the athlete, showed amazing prowess. He was able to sink a basket from almost any place on the court and even do fancy shots. It was more luck than skill for Tom and Phillip, but they had fun in the effort. Finally, Andrew and Phillip learned to take turns on one ball. Tom still had difficulty with this. Often Tom took the ball and ran away when it was his turn. Phillip and Andrew were able to take care of this interference by themselves. Wade and I did not interfere when this happened. If Andrew and Phillip were playing basketball together and Tom tried to disrupt the game, Phillip was very capable of telling Tom to "butt out" and enforcing that if he had to. Since Phillip could manage Tom's behavior, we followed his suggestions and minded our own business too.

Mark was not interested in playing basketball. He seemed to have trouble with the spontaneous movement and change of balance. Perhaps this was related to his epilepsy.

When Tom came to live with us he talked a great deal about a bicycle that he had ridden at the institution. We checked on this and learned that he had been permitted to ride a bike around the grounds. For fourteen months Tom nagged us about wanting to have a new bicycle, but there were things Tom had to learn before he could receive a bicycle. Tom was afraid of the outdoors when he came to live with us. Initially, Tom only wanted to go outdoors in the warm weather and with an adult. He was afraid of the snow. He was afraid of the rain. He was afraid of the cold and he was afraid of the thunder. Mostly he was afraid to be out if we were in.

Andrew did not have these fears. He enjoyed being out in all kinds of weather. He enjoyed exploring his territory to the limits of its boundary. Andrew's adventuresome nature only aggravated the situation for Tom. He wanted to do everything Andrew did. He was aware of the praise that Andrew received from us for his activities outdoors, but he was afraid. Tom needed to overcome his fear of the outdoors in order to get a bike.

In the early months we had a particular pattern we followed with Tom. Tom asked to go out to play and we responded, "Are you sure you want to go out to play now?" He would say, "Yes." "If you go out to play, Tom, you must stay five minutes." As time went on, the five minutes became ten, fifteen, and so on. Initially we went through many instances of Tom's getting his clothes all on—boots, hat, and gloves. He went outdoors only to decide that he wanted to come right back in. We would say to him, "Tom, you said you wanted to go out. Now you must stay out for that amount of time." Gradually he did achieve this. However, there were times we wondered if he would ever learn. He stood on the porch and screamed.

After three years of living with us, Tom became as comfortable outdoors as the other boys. In good weather he would go out to play the first thing in the morning and play until he was called in for lunch. He no longer needed to stay close to the backdoor for security. He could play up and down the back street and in the neighbors' yards. He knew how to watch for cars and he could ride his bicycle. So, he was able to conquer many of the things that had been frightening for him. I think acquiring the bicycle was the turning point for Tom in learning to play outdoors. Tom received his bike as a Christmas present in 1974. Wade purchased the bicycle weeks in advance and stored it in the basement. He had not assembled it because he wanted it to be a surprise. Christmas morning came and all of the gifts were unwrapped. Wade said, "Tom, there's one more present for you down in the basement." They went down and found that there was a part missing in the box holding the bicycle. Tom was so excited about truly owning a bicycle that he was not upset that it could not be put together until we could get the part. Wade was aggravated because he had planned so long for this day for Tom. There was no way of solving the problem on Christmas as all the stores were closed. We had expected that Tom would be actively excited with his gift, but he just sat and looked at his bike. He had his very own bicycle. Occasionally he would touch it, to know that he really owned it.

The next day Wade took Tom to the store to get the necessary parts. That afternoon Tom rode his bicycle up and down the plowed street even though the snow drifts were two feet high. He felt very proud and important because the other boys did not have bicycles yet. The other boys were not in his league. He had something special and different. The fact that the other boys could not ride a bicycle did not matter. Tom owned a bike! Friends brought pennants and streamers to put on it.

As the winter went on Andrew and Phillip showed much curiosity about Tom's bicycle and they wanted to join in the fun. They were anxious to learn to ride. In June 1975, Wade bought the other two boys bicycles. Phillip immediately learned to ride, but Andrew, the athlete, could not coordinate himself. For weeks he straddled it and walked with his feet on the pavement. Eventually he got to the point where he could coast on it. Finally he learned to ride.

Three boys on wheels reopened the issue of boundaries since it was not much fun riding the width of one house lot. Gradually Wade extended the distance they could go up and down the back street until they could go up and down the entire block. There was little traffic so they were able to do all kinds of stunts like riding with no hands and riding standing up. Tom wanted to carry one of the neighborhood children on his handlebars. Although there was no question of his ability to do it we refused and insisted that it was unsafe.

As Phillip and Andrew became more skillful on their bicycles, Tom began to be bored. Instead of riding his bicycle, he began to take it apart. He let the air out of his tires, reinflated the tires, and so on. There were weeks and weeks of flat tires, inflated tires, deflated tires, new inner tubes, new tires. Belatedly we realized that Tom was jealous of the fact that Andrew and Phillip had bicycles that were taller than his. Tom had decided that he should have a new bicycle. He began to tell everyone who would listen, "I'm going to get a new bicycle for Christmas. I'm going to get a new bicycle." Two or three times Wade and I told him, "No, you are not going to get a new bicycle." Finally we ignored all of his conversation about it, thinking that it was one of his perseverations that would go away.

But Tom had a master plan. He took the bicycle completely apart. At other times Tom had taken his bicycle partially to pieces and put it back together again, but he had never totally dismantled it. When Wade asked him why he had taken it apart, Tom said, "I'm getting a new bicycle for Christmas." Wade answered, "No way. You are not getting a new bicycle this Christmas." Tom retorted by saying, "Well, Mike will get me a new bicycle for Christmas." Wade repeated, "No, he will not." "My grandma will get me a new bicycle for Christmas." "No, she will not." Wade gathered up all the parts of the bicycle and put them in a bucket and said to Tom, "You will put the bicycle back together." Tom kept saying, "I'm going to get a new bicycle." Everyone ignored him.

One day in desperation he said to me, "Magoo, I'm going to get me a new bicycle for Christmas." At this point I sat him down and said, "You listen to me." I insisted that he look straight at me and hold his hands to his sides and concentrate. I said, "Tom, you listen.

I am not going to get you a bicycle for Christmas. Wade is not going to get you a bicycle for Christmas. Grandma isn't. No one is going to get you a bicycle for Christmas." I made him repeat that back to me. With a great deal of pain and eventual tears he said it back. "You're not going to get me a new bike." And I said, "That is right." He put that idea away. He knew then there was to be no bicycle that Christmas.

Wade had told him that if he was going to ride a bicycle again, it would be his own for he could not ride the other boys' bikes. He would have to put his bike back together. Then began the struggle between Wade and Tom. After four or five days, Tom did get the bicycle back together but he was missing a bolt. Wade was able to find a new one in a repair shop. Wade gave Tom the new bolt and a wrench. He explained that he expected him to put the bolt on. Tom was equally adamant that this would not be so. He sat on the garage step screaming and swearing at the top of his lungs as he tried to put the bolt back on the bicycle. He became so angry that he picked up the bolt and threw it into the swimming pool. Fortunately, the top was already on the pool for the winter. The bolt was retrieved and Tom was told that he needed to take care of the bolt because Wade did not intend to buy another. Wade told Tom that he had to be responsible for the bolt because if it was lost so was the bicycle. He explained to Tom that the bolt was necessary to make the bicycle work and that Tom had to assume the responsibility for putting it on. For several days Tom dismantled the bicycle and put it back together again repeatedly, but refused to put the bolt on. He stamped his feet, swore, and did not even try to do the task. One day, Wade had had enough. He could not endure one more day with the bicycle game. He told Tom he could not go out to play until the bike was done. He could go to the garage and work on his bicycle, but he could not do anything else outside of the house. Three days went by with Tom refusing to put his bike together. On Saturday we decided to make it unpleasant to be indoors. There was a full day of outside activities, down to the park, washing the car, and out to lunch. Tom missed all of the fun because he had decided not to put the bike together. Tom lasted until 5:00 Saturday afternoon. At that time Phillip, Andrew, and Wade returned from the ice cream shop with cones for everyone. Since Tom's bicycle was not together he was not permitted to have the ice cream cone. Finally, he got the message. In less than fifteen minutes he put the bicycle together and decided to join the rest of the family.

Once again, Wade was right. I had protested all along that the task was beyond Tom, and Wade was insistent that it was not. Wade believed that since Tom had done all parts of the task before, he could do that last part. This proved to be true.

As the boys learned to use their bicycles and accept the boundaries within which to ride them, it made it possible for them to begin to enjoy playmates. Frequently three or four different children from two different families joined the boys in play on the back street, riding their bicycles, playing basketball, kicking the football, and playing with the tether ball. The neighbors accepted the boys' boundaries and did not pressure them to overstep. The boys felt accepted because they were able to go out to play with other children from the community. They enjoyed having their friends come up on the porch to call for them and ask them to come out to ride bikes or play ball. Their increased skill with sports equipment had made it possible for them to communicate over play with children who were more mature than they in many ways.

Their boundaries permitted them to visit the man at the end of the street. He lived alone and spent a great amount of time in his garden. He was gracious to our boys. For the boys to learn to ride a bicycle and to use the extended boundary within which to ride a bicycle resulted in their making one more friend. The neighbor never made an effort to come down the street to meet the boys, but responded to them when they began to ride their bicycles up to his end of the street.

Mark brought a bicycle with him when he came to live with us. He introduced competition and so the four boys enjoyed racing on their bikes. This was a worry for us, because sometimes Mark was too involved for too long and the activity was followed by a seizure, but he gradually began to manage this.

Wade's decision to help the children learn grown-up activities or activities appropriate to their age rather than their level of functioning proved to be wise. The children achieved more than they dreamed they would, and were challenged beyond their own expectancies. They were proud of their accomplishments. There was not the same success in introducing the boys to things they could do within the house alone or together other than pool. It was very difficult to find appropriate toys, games, and equipment within their range of abilities that would not be infantilizing to them. Andrew was fascinated by the types of blocks that an 18-month-old child would enjoy. Wade and I experienced it as a failure on our part to give Andrew such infantile toys. We searched and searched to find toys that would be more appropriate. We tried tinker toys, but they were too difficult for him and caused frustration. Finally we compromised and provided huge kindergarten blocks. He had a lot of fun with them. He built towers, bridges, and buildings. Phillip enjoyed the blocks also and created even more complex designs. Tom wanted no part of the blocks, except to knock down what someone else had built. He was bored silly with their play.

Andrew, Phillip, and Mark had record players and enjoyed playing records alone or together on occasion. Tom was not interested in this activity except to disrupt it. In the summer of 1976, at age fourteen, the best he could do was to keep his hands off the records and record players that belonged to the others. Phillip and Andrew also enjoyed viewmasters. They were able to operate them, change reels, and talk about what they had seen. We think the boys got more enjoyment out of working the lever than the pictures they observed. Tom received a viewmaster at the same time as the other boys, but he destroyed his within a day.

The most successful toy that we introduced was a flashlight. The boys were beginning to have an interest in the kinds of activities that would help them develop eye-hand coordination. We also provided each boy with a slate that was bordered by a margin that demonstrated numbers and letters of the alphabet. It helped Phillip and Andrew to look at the big block letters as they copied them onto the slate. They were able to write their complete name and all of their numbers. They learned this at school and practiced at home by the hour. Phillip learned to write his address and phone number.

Phillip had learned how to make cord in a spool while living in the institution. He enjoyed this activity very much. I was able to help him make a simple mat by sewing the coil together and he was proud of the product. We used lengths of his woven rope to hang bells and mobiles on our porch. It gave Phillip pleasure to contribute to the decorations of our home.

In 1976 he learned to use a latch hook and completed two rugs. He was proud of this craft. We learned that Phillip learns best tasks that he has observed someone else doing over a long period of time. That was the case in terms of learning to use a latch hook. During 1975 I frequently worked with a latch hook in Phillip's presence. He was fascinated. He never asked to learn how to use it, and I never volunteered the information. At Christmas time I gave him a kit. It did not take him fifteen minutes to learn to use the tool. Within a half hour he understood how to use a particular color within particular lines. He completed two rugs that he gave to his mother. Usually Phillip spent an hour and a half a day sitting at the table working on his rug and listening to the radio. When Mark came to live with us, he became interested in making rugs, too. Now he and Phillip share this interest. We hoped that before the boys left our home they would each learn a craft or hobby that was adult in appearance and product. We saw this as one more way of helping the boys join the mainstream and function with their chronological peers. We had not yet figured out or discovered the craft or hobby that would appeal to Andrew or Tom, but we were hopeful.

9

The Wonder of Words

THE DEVELOPMENT OF LANGUAGE, and the acquisition of new words was fun to observe in the boys. I guess we took that all for granted with Jori and Frosty.

It was difficult for us to understand Andrew although he seemed to understand us quite well. He responded to his name and to words such as *stop, that's enough,* and *take it easy.* He knew the names of many objects and their correct use. Andrew could follow simple directions having no more than two parts. For example, when directed he could go to the kitchen and get a cup for a drink of water. Andrew often confused yes and no. We were never sure whether it was an honest confusion or whether he was searching for the correct answer. We could ask a particular question and he would answer "Yes" with a question mark, or he could answer "No" with a question mark. This was confusing for us, for often when we expected a yes he would give us a no. For example, if asked, "Would you like another cookie?" his answer would be "No" with a question mark.

Andrew quickly understood the names of the persons who were frequently in our home. He might not be able to explain what foster mother or foster father meant, but he understood the difference between who we were to him in contrast to his biological parents. He certainly understood the difference between Wade and his father. He never wanted to call us by such parenting names as mom and dad. Occasionally Andy made his wants known clearly, but it was many weeks before Wade and I began to realize that it was functional for Andy to have such garbled speech, that it was a protection

119

for him. We began to realize that the challenge for us was to help Andrew trust his environment enough so that he would want to relate to it openly, clearly, and without the need for a protective shield. We began to realize that his failure, resistance, or unwillingness to communicate was similar to his relying upon his mask of stupidity to avoid situations that were unpleasant for him. We began to recognize this discrepancy in Andy's behavior as we observed situations where he would react with complete abandon and his speech would be easily understood.

Tom's speech was clearly understood. He had a large vocabulary of acceptable words and a rich collection of obscenities and profanities that he used with great frequency. To use obscenities, profanities, and the accompanying gestures was part of Tom's behavior when he was frightened, excited, worried, frustrated, disillusioned, or despairing. In fact, any kind of situation Tom experienced as stressful was the time for him to use his "pirate's" vocabulary. If Tom knew any of the socially acceptable words for bodily parts and functions, he certainly never used them.

Tom could correctly identify and name numerous objects, and he understood their functions. It was possible for Tom to follow two- and three-part commands. He quickly learned where things belonged and soon had the responsibility of knowing where everything was in the house. Many times we said, "Tom, do you know where such and such is?" and he could find it.

Neither of the children had much understanding of colors other than black or white. They differentiated between night and day but did not understand the concepts of morning and afternoon. Days of the week, months, seasons—all were unknown concepts to them. Andrew could count to ten with some reasonable accuracy. Tom always floundered beyond two. Early we recognized that we could say to Andrew, "Please get four spoons," and he could do that. Tom was not able to follow such a command. However, if I asked Tom to set the table for Wade, Andy, Tom, and Martha, he would do it. He would name the forks: a fork for Wade, a fork for Andy, a fork for Tom, and a fork for Martha.

Tom's mouth was always involved. For the first many weeks and months of living with us it seemed to us his mouth was usually involved in a negative way. Either his verbalizations were part of a tantrum or else he repeated in a sing-song manner over and over again, "I want, I want, I want" or "Andrew did it, Wade. Andrew did it, Wade. Andrew did it, Wade." Tom, like Andy, frequently confused yes and no. Additionally, Tom had the habit of making the statement exactly contrary to what he really intended to say. For example, "I don't want to go to school. I don't want to go to school. I don't want to go to school." It took us many weeks to understand that frequently his repetition of a negative statement was prompted by his anxiety about going to school or his apprehension that perhaps he would not be permitted to go to school when actually the last thing he wanted was to be kept home from school.

Tom's mouth was initially so foul that we recognized that he needed to clean up his language in order to achieve some social acceptance. The language Tom used was so offensive that it turned people away from him, and yet we knew that Tom's best learning was going to come from his wider and wider exposure to the community. One of Tom's rhymes was very lengthy and started out with "Pantyhose, pantyhose, pussy, prick." He repeated this rhyme frequently when he wanted to annoy people or when he had nothing else to do at the moment. We found this particular rhyme very offensive, so we determined to extinguish it from Tom's speech pattern. We told Tom that we did not like the rhyme and we did not want him saying it. We explained that whenever he did use the rhyme we were not going to have anything to do with him. We would not answer him or acknowledge in any way that he was talking. This ploy did not work. After two or three days we began to realize that it was unfair for us to say to Tom that he could *never* say his rhymes—more to the point he could not say it in front of other people. "If you want to talk like that, you may talk like that in your bedroom or in the playroom, but don't say that in front of us." This served to curb his language. He needed and wanted to be with us so much of the time that he could not stand the thought that he would need to be removed from us if he talked in a certain way.

For two or three weeks he tried very hard not to use the rhyme. Whenever he started "Pantyhose" he responded to a glare from Wade or me and ceased. It was true that during that time we occasionally heard him by himself, ostensibly out of earshot, saying the rhyme. We felt good about it, felt that we *were* going to clean up Tom's language.

About a week before the boys' first Christmas with us Frank took the boys shopping. As the three of them entered the store the store manager was announcing over the public announcement system that there was a special on hosiery that day. According to Frank, the announcement went something like this. "A free pair of pantyhose for every three pairs of pantyhose that you purchase today." The announcement triggered Tom, and he ran the length of the store screaming at the top of his lungs, "Pantyhouse, pantyhose, pussy, and prick," and the rest of the rhyme. Andrew, not to be outdone, took off in another direction in the store, screaming the identical rhyme with superb enunciation. This from Andrew! Until that day, Frank had not understood one word that Andy had said. Frank told how he ran down the middle aisle of the store and intercepted the boys at the back. He took them by their arms and instantly removed them from the store. On the way home he let the children know that he was furious with them because he had not liked the way they had acted in the store and because other people had been turned off by them. He brought the children home immediately and told them that they would not go out again that day. They were very disappointed.

The next day Frank came to work and told the children that he would take them shopping. Before they left the house they sat down and talked about what they would and would not do as they went shopping. One of the things that they would not do was scream the rhyme. The boys promised they would not do this. On that basis Frank took them shopping, and there was no incidence or poor language. Over the weeks, with this kind of reaction from the adults, Tom used the rhyme less and less. By the following summer the rhyme was heard occasionally when Tom was, in fact, in a private place.

One day a group of us were swimming. Tom was in the pool watching one of the guests standing on the side of the pool, preparing to dive in. She was a very beautiful woman, prompting comments from other guests such as "Wow, is she pretty," or "What she does to that bathing suit," and "Isn't she a lovely looking woman!" Tom started on his rhyme. "Pantyhose, pantyhose." I screamed at him, "Tom!" He ducked. The amused comments from a couple of the men were "He certainly has good taste" or "He certainly can pick them." I did not think much more about the incident that day. A few days later we had four women as guests. Once again Tom was in the pool when the women walked toward the pool side preparing to swim. Once again Tom said "Pantyhose" and instantly submerged himself without my prompting. Suddenly I had an idea.

Without any anger I asked Tom to come out of the pool and said to him that I wanted to talk with him. I took him off by himself and said, "Do you think those ladies have pretty legs?" He answered,

"Yes." I said, "Do you think those ladies have pretty breasts?" Again he said, "Yes." We began to talk about the fact that they were very pretty women and it was really nice to think so. I suddenly realized that Tom had never learned the appropriate way to talk about or to an attractive woman. I suddenly realized that for him to say "Pantyhose, pantyhose, pussy, and prick" should be translated to mean, "She's a pretty woman, she turns me on." I suddenly remembered the comments that had been made a few days earlier. No one had been shocked when our friend, the Methodist minister, had said, "Is she ever an attractive woman!" because that was an acceptable statement from him. Tom was trying to say the same acceptable thing with his rhyme, but the rest of us considered it obscene. It seemed to me that we needed to authenticate for Tom that it was permissible to admire the attractiveness of another person's body. We needed to help him learn new ways to talk about his feelings so that others would find him acceptable. I had the idea that he might accept some of the things that I was saying to him if I encouraged him to share his observations about pretty women with Wade. I suggested to him that he call Wade's attention to good-looking women when he was riding in the car. I told Tom that he should say quietly to Wade and Andrew, "Look at that pretty lady. Isn't she pretty!" I talked with him about the fact that if he learned to say that, he would never need to say "Pantyhose, pantyhose, pussy, and prick." He understood what I was saying to him. During the rest of the conversation with Tom I used short and simple statements. I repeated them. I had him repeat them back to me and I believed that he understood. A couple of days later I selected a television program that I knew had a lot of girls dancing. I thought this was an opportunity for me to sit down with Tom and watch the girls dance and discuss with him how nice they looked. How they had pretty breasts and pretty legs, and how their costumes made their legs look prettier. I was anxious for him to realize that I also thought it was acceptable to talk about attractive women and I wanted him to have ample opportunity to do this in a way that was permitted by most other people.

It worked better than I ever dreamed. After that Tom talked appropriately about attractive women, and he did not use his vulgar phrases. He taught me a lesson that I later applied to other areas with the children. I learned that frequently when they were trying to communicate something that was an acceptable thought, they did not have the language with which to do it. They had not learned the language that permitted them to talk acceptably about feelings of anxiety, trust, ownership, love, displeasure, and hate.

I should not have been surprised that the children did not have the words to discuss feelings. They even had a limited vocabulary for food. As a way of helping the children learn more words, as well as develop a broader interest in foods, we took them frequently to the Farmers' Market. They began to learn the differences between the many fruits and vegetables that were displayed there. They began to learn to differentiate between chicken and ham, hamburger and fish, salad and vegetables, breads and rolls, cakes and dough-nuts. The identification of foods expanded.

The process of renovating a house and moving into the house exposed the children to many new words. They learned words such as *hammer, nail, roof, carpenter, electrician, boards, cement,* and *wire.* They learned relationships between words: paintbrushes to paint to turpentine, wire to plug to electricity. Their experience in the institution had not allowed this kind of exposure. Soon the boys knew the names of hundreds of objects and began to understand the purpose of the objects.

More slowly they began to learn action words. The children began to report actions such as "Frosty left the hammer in the barn." As they learned the appropriate places for things we were able to say to them, "Take the hammer downstairs and put it on the shelf near the washing machine." The children seemed to have diffi-culty with words such as *big, little, tall, short, small,* and *large.* They had difficulty with words that described how they felt. For example, they were apt to say that things were "cute." This meant that the boy liked the object but could not be more precise. A baby was cute, a man was cute, an apple was cute, and a bicycle was cute. We re-alized that adverbs and adjectives were sometimes intangible words and more difficult for the boys to comprehend.

When Phillip came to join our family he added another language challenge. He had no language other than *no* and *Heyperry.* None of us understood anything he said. However, he gave indications that he understood a great deal that was said to him. An interesting thing happened. After Phillip joined the family and we were unable to understand him, suddenly we *were* able to understand Andrew most of the time. Perhaps it was because we were accustomed to Andy's style of phrasing or perhaps because his language had im-proved that much.

The first communication goal we had for Phillip was to help him understand that the different members of the family had their own particular names by which they were called. Wade and I explained to Phil that we would not answer him if he screamed *Heyperry* at us; that he must come to us and call us by name. Phillip obviously was not able to enunciate *Wade* or *Martha* very clearly in the early days so we responded to his attempts. We never responded to *Heyperry*.

As the boys learned the routines of the day and the week they came to understand the concepts of morning, afternoon, and evening because these segments were defined by breakfast, lunch, and dinner which were also routinized. The adherence to weekend routines that were different from the day routines helped the children understand the difference between weekend and weekday. They understood that there was no school on Saturday and Sunday. They understood that on Friday night and Saturday night they could stay up late because there was no school the next day. Although they still confused the sequence of days from Monday through Friday, they recognized Friday as the day they could go swimming or bowling. Later two of the boys joined a Teen Club that met on Wednesday night and they began to understand Wednesday. It appeared that as the routine varied on a particular day, the boys learned that particular day and understood it as different. Months meant nothing to them. They did understand the seasons, winter and summer, but they did not understand spring and fall.

Eventually, each of the boys was able to say his complete name. Each of them understood the difference between several different persons, and they understood the different demands placed upon those different persons. Each of the boys was able to talk about our family members—Wade, Magoo, Frosty, and Jori—and understand their different family roles. We were able to use words such as *father, mother, sister, brother, grandmother, neighbors,* and *playmates* and know that the boys understood what was said. The boys understood the "who" implied by each word, and they also understood some of the privileges and responsibilities that belonged to each of those individuals by virtue of being that person. For example, they knew that there were things that they did with their playmates such as play games and have conversations, but they also understood that playmates were not the persons from whom they might get special gifts or money. They understood that gifts came from grandparents, father, mother, and sister.

They understood words like *angry, happy, love,* and *mad,* and they learned to use them appropriately. They learned to use courtesy

words—*please, thank you, you're welcome*—and permission and re-
questing words such as *may I, can I*. Their nonsensical word pat-
terning was eliminated. After they learned to talk with us and each
other they attempted to use recognizable words. It is true that because of Phillip's severe speech defects, it was sometimes difficult
to understand him, but he tried to use language that he heard
around home. Tom loved to sing and he frequently sang songs that
were popular on television or in school. Usually they were songs
that had a repetitive verse or easy rhyming. Tom had an interesting
inflection in his speech, and sometimes it seemed as though he was
giving a poetry reading. As he talked with us, we got some sense of
his feelings by the way he used words and formed his sentences. Andrew had a tendency to talk in a monotone. Frequently he repeated
exactly what he heard Tom say. There were times when it seemed
we were living with "Pete and Repeat." However, whatever Andrew
repeated was understandable.

During the first three years that they lived with us the children
eliminated the coarse words that they brought with them. However,
they also picked up some of the sloppy language patterns of the
Dickersons. It was not uncommon in our house to use the phrase
"Damn it" when frustrated, and after three years we often heard
Tom using this phrase. He even sounded like Wade when he said it.
Our son, Frosty, also used a particular phrase when he was frustrated. During the many months of renovating the house there were
several occasions when Tom overheard Frosty venting his frustration by using his phrase. One day, months later, while preparing
dinner in the kitchen I heard a voice up in the playroom. I thought it
was Frosty but reminded myself that that was impossible, because
Frosty was in Alaska. It was Tom who had missed a pool shot and
had responded in frustration by saying, "Shee-it!" He sounded exactly like Frosty. So with some chagrin we have to acknowledge
that it has not all been preferred language that the boys have
learned in our home. We did not jump on Tom for language that he
learned from us.

Perhaps we needed to purge our own vocabularies in order to be
better models, but I do know that it was more appropriate for Tom
to be venting his frustration with that one phrase as opposed to the
screaming tantrums that he used to have.

Increasingly the boys tried to talk about feelings with each
other and with us. Occasionally we heard one of the boys say to
another, "I don't like you any more. I'm not going to play with you

today." These statements were in place of the physical rejection that would have taken place many months before. It was not at all uncommon for Tom to say to Wade, "I don't like you today." In every instance Wade said, "That's OK with me Tom, but you are still going to . . . " and then he put down his expectation. Wade constantly gave Tom the message, "Whether you like me or not the expectations about how you will behave are constant. If you don't want to like me and you want to talk about it, that's your privilege, but you will still do what's expected of you."

Of course, in the past Tom had said much worse to Wade. One day when Wade had leaned on him for something, Tom yelled down the stairs to him, "You old bastard." Wade went up the stairs three at a time and said to Tom, "What did you call me?" Tom looked him straight in the eye and said, "Nothing," and Wade said, "Do you think you're going to call me that again." Tom said, "No." Wade said, "Make sure you don't," and went back down the stairs. That was the end of that. Another time Tom threw the obscene finger gesture at Wade. Wade, quick as a flash, reached over and took hold of Tom's extended middle finger with a tight grip. Tom was so surprised he just stood there and jumped up and down. Wade, in his most steely voice, said to him, "Don't you throw the finger at me again," and he did not.

The children clearly understood that there was no removal from our home for anything, there was no threat, worry, or concern about being sent back to the institution for talking out their anger. The boys each understood that it was much better to shout it out than hit it out. They also understood that it was better to talk it out than shout it out. As the boys became more comfortable with the honest use of language they were less manipulative and patterned in their flattery. In the early days, it was very common for Tom to say to me, "I love you a lot. You're very pretty. Please let me." When I would confront him with a piece of behavior or want him to deal with an issue he'd say, "You're a pretty lady." He learned that that kind of manipulation did not pay off. Also, there was a pride in being responsible for his own actions and language. It was more fun, more productive, and more rewarding than being manipulative.

Initially, and occasionally later, we tried storytelling and reading from books to the children. This was not satisfying for them or us. They did not appreciate pictures and they were not interested in being read to. Evidently they had enough of that in school to satisfy them at the time. They did enjoy television and were beginning to be like other teenagers in their viewing habits. "Little House on the Prairie," "Happy Days," and "Six Million Dollar Man" became favorites, and they were able to discuss the story line with some accuracy.

We learned some techniques from the boys that were in turn helpful to them. We found with Andrew, who had a tendency to ramble and evade discussion, that if we slapped our hands together sharply or hit the table, wall, or something close to him so that he heard a sharp sound, and said, "Andrew, listen!" nine times out of ten he would communicate with us responsibly and clearly. Often he needed to be reminded to raise his voice and speak up, for when he was in one of his noncommunicative times he was apt to speak softly. It was as though as he dared to risk being responsible for honest communication he was only able to do it very softly. In Phillip's case we no longer accepted gestures. If Phillip wanted something we insisted that he attempt to tell us what it was. Usually we got the gist of what he was trying to say. We were able to restate it back to him clearly, and he had to repeat his question to us with an attempt to say the words as clearly as possible.

We learned that it helped Tom to assume responsibility for his own statements if we did two things. First, we asked him to assume a position where his body was in control. If he was sitting in the chair, "Tom, put your feet flat on the floor, push down, take your hands, and hold onto the arms of the chair. Pull tight." By doing those things he was in physical control of his body and was able to concentrate. Next we said to him, "What is your name?" and he responded, "Tom." At that point we said to him, "OK, Tom. Don't answer anything until you think it through. Don't say anything." With this preparation, this reminder, we then asked the question or made the statement. Almost all of the time with that type of preparation we were guaranteed an appropriate response. Tom said what he really meant. At that point we praised him verbally: "Tom, that was really good. Thanks for telling it the way it was. It was so good of you to say it that way." The first steps were very important. He needed to be reminded to control his body. Then he needed to remind himself that he was going to be responsible for what he said. Tom was learning to own his behavior and the statements that came from his mouth. It took time, but it saved time, and it helped Tom eliminate all those times when he gave contradictory messages and gave negative answers when he wanted to say the positive.

Formerly when Tom was under pressure he would say he did not want to do something. Perhaps I asked him to comb his hair and I sent him upstairs saying, "Tom, look in the mirror and comb your hair." His response to me at that point would be, "I don't want to go to school." If I did not act immediately, he would repeat that statement over and over again with increasing volume, with increasing anxiety, and lose control of himself entirely. We later recognized those negative statements that were apt to start a series of inappropriate behaviors and knew that we must act immediately. At first we said to him, "Hey, Tom, you're getting high. Let's work on getting it together." Sometimes that's all it took. If that alone did not work, the second statement could be, "Tom, sit on the bottom step and we'll count to three." If that didn't bring him all the way down, the third request was, "Tom, push your feet tight on the floor, hold onto the step, tell me, what's your name." "Tom." "Now, before you do anything else, think carefully, do you want to go to school today?" And the answer invariably was "Yes." At that point he was giving me his total attention. I said to him, "Tom you want to go to school. I know you want to go to school. Before you go to school you must comb your hair. Go do it." And he did. That five-minute experience helped him own his behavior and gain some responsibility and control over his own life space. It avoided a scene where he contaminated himself with his own negative actions.

We learned that one of the ways we could help Tom deal with his anxieties and develop his language in a positive manner was to give him some language and feeling responsibilities. When Wade and I were planning to be away it helped us to take Tom aside a few hours ahead of the other children. We sat down and talked with him. We explained to him simply, step-by-step what was going to happen. "Wade and I are going away. We're going to be gone for several days. Dwight is going to be here to stay with you. We're going to take our car and we're going to Maine to see Jori's family." Then we asked questions. "Where are we going, Tom? Who's going to take care of you, Tom? How long will we be gone? Who are we going to see when we're away? Who's going to take care of you, Tom? When are we going to come back?" After five or ten minutes of this kind of statement, question, and affirmation, Tom really understood what was being said to him. He was prepared to meet the experience as the authority, the person who repeated the message to the other children. This is not to say we did not tell the children our plans. We called the other children together and then told them the same thing. But, instead of Tom's needing to dump his anxiety on us and

Dwight, he was in a position to handle it in a more productive manner. He told the other children what was happening to us, and as he repeated the message, his own anxiety decreased. We learned that when we were having this kind of important sharing with Tom, it helped to sit across the table from him and have him place his hands on the table in front of himself. Wade and I would put our hands on the table too. Sometimes we put our hands on top of his. Again, this was a way of forcing him to concentrate, to listen, to be engaged in the situation of the moment.

Tom was learning to answer the telephone. He was able to do this to the extent that he could say *hello* and wait for the person to say the name of the person with whom they wished to speak. Tom knew then to go find that person. He might scream the person's name before putting the telephone receiver down, but he was making progress. Three of the children were able to answer the door appropriately. They knew to call a grown-up immediately. Andrew was by nature such a cordial, gracious person that he had a tendency to be too quick to invite people into our home. I well remember the day that I was working in the kitchen and the front doorbell rang. I needed to dry my hands so that by the time I turned from the sink and started into the dining room on the way to the front door, I met Andrew in the dining room accompanied by a strange man. The man happened to be a person who was walking down the street looking for a particular family and had stopped at our house for directions. I answered the man's queries and sent him on his way. I found it difficult to explain to Andy why he should not extend such cordiality to most people when they came to the door. It would have been easier to explain had the man done something that was inappropriate, but luckily he had not.

Mark came to our family with highly developed language, as compared to the other boys. He was able to read a few words and was anxious to expand his reading, as well as his speaking vocabulary. Mark was able to use the phone, placing calls as well as receiving them. He could be relied upon to answer the telephone or the door. Mark enjoyed conversation and had a positive effect upon the other boys by providing a peer model for them.

All of the boys were extremely cordial and gracious to guests in our home. It was as though they viewed every person who came as their very special friend. When the man who had helped renovate our home stopped in for a few minutes, the children were delighted. They found it difficult to accept that he had stopped to see us for business reasons. They had experienced him as coming just to see them. Each of the boys made much progress in his desire and ability to communicate with the other persons in his world. It appeared that as they became more sure of themselves, more proud of themselves, more pleased with their accomplishments, the more they wanted to be able to talk about them, to share them. We were hopeful that as we lived together, the boys would begin to be more in touch with their feelings, more able to talk with each other and other people outside of the family about how they feel, about their wishes, and their desires. The more the boys could communicate, the easier it would be for them to establish meaningful relationships with individuals of all ages and both sexes.

10

New Experiences

NOT ALL LEISURE TIME was spent at home or in the neighborhood. The boys went on many kinds of trips. The zoo was the most popular place for us to go. We went to the zoo the first week Tom and Andrew lived with us. For the first several trips, we stayed a short time and visited one section of the zoo. We realized Tom and Andrew could not tolerate longer trips. We had some scary times at the zoo because Tom was frightened of all the animals.

One time we went into a building to see the pigmy hippo. The display was set up so that the observers were on a sloping ramp looking down into a pit area where the animals were displayed. Andrew was with Wade down close to the rail. I had Tom at the top of the sloping ramp, as far back from the exhibit as possible. Tom was trying to contain himself. Andrew had food to feed the baby hippo. He reached over the railing and the animal opened its mouth to accept the food. When Tom saw Andrew reaching toward that open mouth, he began to shriek and thrash. I do not know how I managed, but I carried him from the building. He was terrified.

Gradually, over several trips, Tom overcame his fears about most of the exhibits. On their most recent trip to the zoo, the boys spent the entire day riding the train, walking through the displays, and having a picnic. Each boy recognized favorite animals. Tom watched the bears, lions, and tigers from the open walkways, but he did not walk into the building near their cages. He had learned to enjoy the animals from a distance.

The boys went shopping in all kinds of stores—grocery stores, drug stores, and clothing stores. Many Saturdays we got up early in the morning to take the boys to Detroit's Great Eastern Market. In the early days, Andrew and Tom each carried a canvas bag that could be filled with produce. It was difficult for Tom to look at all the displays before he made a selection. He had the habit of wanting to buy the first thing he saw. Often he wanted to grab, grab, grab. Andrew and Phillip, on the other hand, enjoyed looking at all the merchandise in the various stalls. It was a wonderful way for the children to get to learn about vegetables. During the Saturday morning jaunts to the market, they became familiar with many fruits and vegetables. The boys' enjoyment of salads may be related to the times they went to the market. In the market area was an exciting place to eat. Customers and workers alike lined up to sit on stools at a long counter. It was a hub of activity, and the boys enjoyed it all. One of the stores at Eastern Market had hundreds of jars of different kinds of candies, spices, and nuts in bulk. All the good smells and tastes made it a special place.

Through school, the boys had several opportunities. They went to plays, art shows, farm tours, and the circus. Andrew and Phillip did well on school trips. Tom had some good trips and some bad trips. The first time Tom went with his class on an outing he behaved so poorly that the teacher sent a note home. We were told that Tom could go on no more trips unless one of us accompanied him. Not long after, the circus came to town. We arranged to have Frank accompany Tom to the circus so that he could go with his class. With one-to-one support, Tom survived the circus outing successfully. The teacher reversed her position and Tom was permitted to go on class trips with the understanding that he behave. The teacher and her aides prepared him well for trips by clearly stating the limits before the event took place. Experience and practice resulted in decreased anxiety and improved behavior.

We took Tom, Andrew, and Phillip to a large amusement park. The confusion, noise, crowds, and hoopla of Cedar Point were too stimulating for the boys. Phillip was tired and bored. Tom was overstimulated. Andrew was the least distressed by the unusual situation, but was not in a position to enjoy the experience. Wade and I needed to spend so much time and energy managing Phillip and Tom in the situation that Andrew had to survive by himself. Another time with other people, Andrew would enjoy an amusement park. We selected a boat ride because it seemed to be the least frightening. We rode on a paddleboat that moved slowly down a canal past several exhibits. Tom was very frightened on the boat. I had my arms around him to contain him all the way. Otherwise he might have fallen into the water. We stayed at the amusement park less than two hours.

Everyone was relieved to leave. Wade and I were frustrated by our insensitivity in selecting such a place for the boys and for wasting money for full-day passes for five people. With much frustration we stopped at a pancake house for lunch. The children were enchanted with the pancake house. They thought it was fun to have stacks of pancakes and a wide selection of syrups. After lunch, Phillip said, "Are we going home now?" in the most wistful manner. Wade's answer "Yes" was the best part of the day for Phillip; he wanted to go home.

The best part of the outing had been to stay at a motel and the best part of the motel had been the pool. We talked about our outing frequently afterward. "Can we go to a motel again some time?" "Can we swim in the big pool again someday?"

A three-day experience with the three boys was a little much for two middle-aged parents, but afterward our spirits soared. All of the training, reinforcing, explaining, correcting, modifying, and limit setting seemed to have been worth it when we watched the boys on a family trip.

The boys knew how to behave well. They knew how to do the things that other boys did in such a manner that other people did not look at them. No one stared at them because they were different, their behavior bizarre, or because they were "retards." I believe the waitress at the motel who complimented Wade on his family never recognized that the three young men who behaved so well had once been considered so dysfunctional that they had to live in an institution. Driving up the highway that afternoon we held each other's hands and were smug. We were smug because we knew that the boys had learned to do many things that most people had thought were impossible for them to learn.

Gradually over the weeks and months the boys accepted the routines and procedures of the Dickerson household. They began to act in more acceptable ways and they began to receive compliments and attention from adults. As they began to learn to take care of themselves, express themselves, and use the resources of the home and family, it became apparent that they were truly developing skills in relating to people in the community as well as in the family.

From the beginning Andrew and Tom were interested in the other people who came to our home and particularly interested in our daughter and son. As time passed they had more opportunity to know Frosty than Jori because she is much more involved with her own family in Maine and is not with us as often. Frosty had come home in the winter of '73 to help us renovate the big house. He was quite sure that as parents we had gone completely mad to work with children who had so little promise. He had been with the children only two days when he made it clear that he did not feel that he could spend many hours at a time with them. For many weeks Frosty's only exposure to the children was during the evening meal and during the playtime hours that they spent at the new house where they occasionally got in his way as he was trying to do his work. Since Frosty could not consider sharing Christmas with us and the two boys, we arranged to have two Christmases in 1973. As part of our celebration with Frosty we made arrangements to go to a Japanese restaurant for a special meal.

The meal may have been memorable, but I do know that the conversation was a high point in the whole experience for us. During the conversation Frosty let it be known that he had assumed that I had coerced his father into the idea of raising the children and that I had selected the children to live in our home. I well remember his face when his father said to him, "Frosty, there's something you need to get straight. Your mother did not push anything onto me, and for your information I was the one who went to the institution and I was the one who selected the children. As a matter of record I came home and told your mother that she wouldn't like the kids that I had selected. But I had selected them because I wanted to try to do something for them." Frosty put his drink down on the table and looked at his father with astonishment. He said to Wade, "Are you telling me, Dad, that you selected Tom?" and his father said, "Yes, I did."

It made a difference to Frosty to learn that his father had a personal commitment to work with the children that was separate from my professional commitment to work in the field of retardation. He had not understood it prior to that conversation. I think that from that moment he began to perceive the experience differently. Frosty is honest and overt about his feelings. When he thinks something he says it, and when he says it, it is as clear as he can possibly make it. It had not been pleasant to realize that he was so negative about our experiences. On the other hand, it was a very special thing to watch his honest growth along with the children during the three years.

From the beginning Andrew identified strongly with Frosty.

Frosty is 6'5" and blond with a moustache and sideburns, and Andrew had about the same coloring. Andy thought it would be "cool" to grow up to be like Frosty. It was Frosty who introduced Andrew to the dogs and taught him how to play with the animals in an appropriate way. Andrew dared to do this because his idol encouraged him.

Frosty frequently spoke of his annoyance with Tom and his unceasing conversation. I had little hope that we would see a very positive relationship between Frosty and Tom. I was pleasantly surprised one day when I went down to the big house to find that Frosty had set up a work area for Tom so that Tom could work beside him in the basement. Frosty was busy stripping the woodwork. He had arranged for Tom to have a certain amount of work to do also, so that they could work side by side. I noticed that Frosty identified certain pieces of wood for the children to play with. I made a big issue of it and said to Frosty how neat I thought it was that he was doing it. His response was, "Well, I had to give them something so they'd leave my stuff alone." That may have been true, but he was beginning to recognize some of their unique needs and how to relate to them. Increasingly I noticed Frosty taking time to show Tom or Andrew how to do something. As time went on Frosty became more tolerant of their behavior at the dining table. Of course, at the same time, their behavior at the dinner table had substantially improved. He left Michigan in March of 1974 and was gone for several months. When he returned he was impressed with the change in the children and commented on this to his father and me. One evening he introduced the boys to one of his friends, calling the friend "Uncle," intending to create a situation that might be difficult for his friend to manage. The trick boomeranged. His friend rather liked it and became comfortable with his role as "Uncle" to the children. He began to show increasing interest in the children. One day I realized that "Uncle" and Frosty were regularly playing pool with the kids. One night "Uncle" realized that there was a particular movie that my husband and I wanted to see with Frosty. To our surprise, he said, "I'll come and stay with the boys so you all can go to the movie together," and that happened. Soon Frosty began to say, "If you and Dad want to go to a show tonight, I'll stay with the kids." Gradually, over a period of many months and with the boys' improved behavior, Frosty's tolerance and understanding developed to the place where he could provide a kind of grown-up brother model for the children. Much later Frosty and Dwight took the boys to the park and out to eat. Based on Frosty's remarks in 1973 I would have thought that he would be embarrassed to be with children who were retarded. Two and a half years later that was not the case. He accepted the children, he *dignified* the children. In 1976 he came home and stayed home for Christmas. Not only did he stay home for Christmas, he celebrated Christmas by preparing gifts for the children and doing all the fun things that grown-up brothers do with younger brothers.

The boys enjoyed Jori and her husband during their visits to Michigan. When they came to visit they brought the boys gifts.

In April 1975, Jori had a baby. It made Thanksgiving of '75 a special time. The boys had been with us two years and our children all came home for the holidays. Frosty and Jori's family were home. Jori shared her daughter comfortably with our foster children. Tom, Andrew, and Phillip had known all through her pregnancy that Jori was to have a baby, and they knew I had been to Maine to be with her. They realized Martha was a special little girl for us, and Tom understood that she had been named after me. Tom talked about Jori's family frequently.

My stepmother lived in Vermont and seldom traveled because she did not care for planes or trains. However, she was so interested in what we were doing that she came to Michigan in the summer of 1974 to meet the boys and to see how we were managing with our new family. She accepted the additional responsibilities as a grandmother and has been a grandmother to the boys ever since. She did thoughtful things like sending them valentines, birthday cards, and Christmas presents. It pleased me very much that she perpetuated a family custom with our new boys. As long as I can remember it has been a tradition in our family to have some gifts of maple sugar for each of the children under the Christmas tree. I was delighted when we opened the Christmas packages in '73 to find that there were boxes of sugar shapes for the boys. This sugar, sent to the boys, was an affirmation for Wade and me. It was as though my stepmother was saying, "If you're going to raise those children, then I too perceive them as part of the family." I think that she was awed by their behaviors for she was not accustomed to children with retardation, but in no way was she patronizing to them. She accepted them in a warm manner. She spent a lot of time selecting the right kinds of gifts for the boys—gifts that were chronologically age appropriate and yet, at the same time, gifts that would be useful for them given their level of functioning. At Christmas 1976 her gifts to them were billfolds.

My stepmother seemed to understand our need for establishing different priorities. She seemed to know that we needed to spend a great deal of time and energy building security for these children and that we did not have time to travel and to visit her or other people as much as we might like. She put no demands on us but let us know that it was acceptable for us to put all of our energies into the children. Since our daughter lived in Maine and my stepmother in Vermont, they were not as far apart as we were from them. They have a fine relationship and they developed an even tighter bond during these two or three years. They became very close and provided support for each other which was enhanced because Wade and I were not as near to them. It was as though Jori and Eleanor could mutually attend to each other and release Wade and me to do what we needed to do with our boys. As the years went on the people who were closest to us, Jori and Frosty, realized that Wade and I needed the children. We happened to be the kind of people who thoroughly enjoy parenting and the boys let us do that.

Pets have always been important in our home. At the time that Tom and Andrew came to live with us we had two dogs—Kai, who was nine years old, and her son Ziggie, who was five. The most venerable position held by an animal in our house was claimed by our ancient cat, Bootsie. Bootsie was seventeen when the boys came to live with us. She had been the queen of the household for years. As a family we deferred to her many idiosyncrasies. Bootsie eased the children's transition into our home. The first time they came to visit, it was Bootsie who permitted Tom to hold her and stroke her during those first uneasy minutes in our living room. When the boys came to stay, Bootsie was initially tolerant of their roughness, but as the days went on she became impatient with their demands and became a recluse. Eventually she fell ill, not as a result of the boys' being there, but because she was very old. During the holidays of '73 she needed to be hospitalized for several days and the boys were concerned about her, especially Tom. Every time Frosty came home for dinner, Tom said to him, "Call the doctor and find out how Bootsie is and find out when she can come home." Eventually Bootsie did come home, having lost much weight and looking very frail. She had difficulty walking. We quickly recognized that the place she most wanted to be was in front of a radiator in the living room. We carefully assembled her bed, cat box, and food on a big mat there. We restricted that area for everyone and began to talk about it as Bootsie's place to get well. During that time Tom, who had only revealed his selfish side, came to me and said he wanted to make a get-well card for Bootsie. I did not think he knew what a get-well card was. He took an old Christmas card and scribbled some kind of a message on it, gave it to me, and asked me to put it where Bootsie could see it. We tiptoed into the room and hung it on the baseboard near her dish. I know it sounds crazy, but it seemed to me that as Bootsie convalesced she began to be more tolerant of Tom, and I like to think that it was because he gave her that card. Unfortunately, Bootsie's convalescence did not last long and suddenly she quietly died. We found her one morning under the sofa, dead. Tom and Andrew watched me wrap her carefully in a pillowcase and put her in a box in preparation for disposing of her body. That was our first exposure to death with the boys. We talked to them about the fact that Bootsie had had a long, good life in our family. We had loved her very much, and she had made us very happy. The boys wondered if we would get a new Bootsie. We explained to them, "No," that since we were going to be moving soon it was not the time to get a new cat. Maybe some time in the future, but we were making no promises. Bootsie had been around for so long she truly was a part of the family and we were not ready to replace her.

To make friends with the dogs was a greater challenge. The dogs were big, Siberian huskies and they appeared more fierce than they really were. Andrew was the first one who made friends with the dogs. I gave Frosty the credit for helping Andrew build the friendship with the animals. He went out in the yard with him while Andy learned to pet them, rub their ears, and eventually become good friends. Frosty gave Andy a lot of recognition for his increasing comfort with the dogs. Over and over again he said, "Cool it, Andy, cool it. The dogs won't hurt you." No attempt was made to work with Tom regarding the dogs. Frankly, he put up such a scene every time the dogs came near the back door where he could see them that we thought he would be a long time in overcoming that fear. There seemed to be so many other things to work on. Nevertheless, Tom was observing from the kitchen window all of the activity between Andrew and Frosty and the dogs. He was dying to go out and try it but he just could not bring himself to do it.

Several weeks passed. One night when I came home, Tom said "I have a surprise for you, Magoo." Sure enough, later in the evening he came down the stairs and said, "Wade said that I can let the dogs in." He went to the stairway and opened the cellar door to let the dogs in. This was a major accomplishment. He and Wade had been working on it for several days. He could get close enough to the dogs to open the door and let them pass by him as they went down the cellar to eat their supper. A year later he was a good friend of the dogs; he walked in and out of their dog yard, patted them on the head, and was kind to them. When Kai, the old dog, lost her hearing, we had to tell the children they must not go near her, or startle her. They must always move their hands to break the air current so she would feel their presence and open her eyes before they touched her. They were able to accept this, and they knew that she was getting old and was going to die someday soon. Tom spoke about this on two or three different occasions with me. He said, "Magoo, Kai is going to die pretty soon like Bootsie died?" and I answered, "Yes, that is so." Wade had the habit of feeding the dogs separately which meant that he brought the older dog in to eat in the basement every evening. She was stiff and had difficulty going down the cellar stairs. To my chagrin Tom made a comparison and said to me one day, "Magoo, you're getting old. You have trouble going up and down the stairs, just like Kai does." I was glad to realize that he was becoming so perceptive, but I did not appreciate the fact that this perception was focused on me.

When the boys came to live with us they needed to be introduced to new doctors and dentists within the community who would be monitoring their health for the years ahead. One pediatrician at a local clinic was especially helpful to us in raising the boys. I had had some professional contact with him and knew of his interest in our plans. This did not prepare me for his offer to provide medical attention to the boys in our home. We were relieved to know that we would have this kind of service. The clinic provided twenty-four hours a day, seven days a week coverage. Because we were nervous about bringing children out of an institution with all of their histories of behavioral problems, hyperactivity, and seizures, I felt the need to have a secure medical resource. To have that resource within a mile of our home was more than I had hoped.

Within a week of Tom's and Andrew's move into our home, Wade took them to meet the pediatrician. He was a jolly, gregarious, kind middle-aged man who immediately put the boys at ease. He gave them physicals and reviewed their medical information.

It was our understanding that before the boys were placed in our home, they had been given complete physicals. Any remedial or corrective treatment needed by a particular child was to have been accomplished before the child came into our home. Thus, we believed that the children came to us free from any contagion or infection, having had a recent medical review and with appropriate prescriptions. As the boys lived with us we came to realize that this procedure had not been adequate in any instance.

Tom came to us at eleven with medication which he continued to use for seizures and hyperactivity. Andrew, who came to our home at thirteen, was on a prescription to stimulate his appetite because he had a history of being a poor eater. He stayed on that medication until the supply was exhausted. By that time he had developed an interest in food and was on a routine where he had adequate exercise, sleep, and a balanced diet. He seemed to be eating well and gaining weight, so he never took any medication after that. Phillip came to us when he was fifteen. He was on daily medication prescribed from the institution. When we introduced him to our doctor, he asked why Phillip was on that particular regime. Records were obtained from the institution and it was found that he was on the same medical program that he had been on since he was five. There was no clear indication as to why he had been put on the medicine in the first place. The doctor suggested we immediately stop the medication and watch for changes in his health or behavior patterns. We could see no difference when the medication was stopped. Therefore, he took no medication after that time. Mark came to join our family when he was fifteen. He was taking phenobarbital, Dilantin, and Mellaril as a way of controlling his seizures.

Three of the boys had received dental examinations and hearing tests. There was no need for eyeglasses and they were free of any infection.

Mark had no record of dental attention, but did wear glasses, which we subsequently learned were no longer needed.

The doctor's office was in an extremely attractive building decorated to help children minimize their anxieties about going to the doctor. This atmosphere was soothing to Tom and Andrew and subsequently Phillip, too. Quickly the boys became comfortable with their semi-annual visits to the doctor. During the entire three years we had no serious emergency visits to the doctor. The boys had their appropriate injections and went to the doctor's office for the necessary completion of forms for school and camping affairs. Over three years' time, the boys had several contacts with the doctor, and all of them were pleasant.

After a couple of years there came a day when Wade was taking Tom for a routine check-up. When they arrived and were seated in the waiting room, having already identified themselves to the receptionist, Wade found to his dismay that he had left the identification card for Tom at home. What to do? Wade spoke to Tom, "I forgot something, Tom that we have to have and I must go back and get it. Do you want to come with me?" To his surprise Tom said, "No, I'd rather wait here." Wade spoke to him briefly about what he would expect of him in terms of behavior while he was gone and then he left him alone in that big medical complex. He was gone approximately fifteen minutes. When he returned Tom had been called by the nurse and was already in the doctor's office. To Wade's pleasure, Tom was handling the experience calmly. Wade and the doctor viewed this as real growth on Tom's part. Without question he was beginning to trust a situation and trust people that Wade introduced. When we considered the tremendous anxiety that had surrounded Tom so much of the time, we were pleased to see this happen.

Early in 1976 Wade initiated the process to have Tom reevaluated at the Epilepsy Center. The doctor agreed that this was necessary in that there were changes in Tom's behavior. He was moving into puberty, growing tall and slim, and it was time for a review of his medications. Eventually a report came from the Epilepsy Center. The news was surprising. Tom did *not* have epilepsy, nor had he ever had epilepsy! It turned out that the Epilepsy Center had records about Tom from having tested him at age five. They reported to the doctor and my husband that at age five there had been no evidence of epilepsy and at age thirteen and a half there was no epilepsy!! Further, they stated that the Epilepsy Center had *never* recommended medication for Tom. Yet for eight and a half years the institution had recorded Tom's use of Dilantin and Mellaril. It was upsetting to think that Tom had been on drugs he did not need. Probably we will never know how it happened that Tom was inappropriately medicated for so long. The experience did little to encourage our respect for the medical attention given to residents of institutions.

Tom was immediately started on a withdrawal process to remove him from the drug Dilantin. After a six-week withdrawal there was no change in Tom's behavior. So by mid-1976 Tom was taking 100 mg of Mellaril a day and the process was started to remove him from this drug.

After three or four months the boys went to the dentist. It was difficult to find a dentist who was willing to work with children who had retardation and hyperactivity. Andrew and Phillip were stoical as they approached a visit to the dentist, but Tom was very frightened. His fears had some reality for his teeth were in bad shape and he needed a major amount of repair work. The dentist who worked with him managed Tom well. He helped Tom accept the fact that it would be to his advantage to have his teeth taken care of. In order to do that he would be expected to act like a grown-up and sit in the dentist's chair without Wade anywhere around. Wade had gone to the dentist expecting that perhaps he would need to be in the dentist's office with Tom but that was not expected. Tom was met in the corridor by the dentist who, in a very positive manner said to him, "You and I are going to do this by ourselves and Mr. Dickerson does not have to come with you." He treated Tom like a man who was capable of handling his own behavior. The first day he had Tom in the dentist's chair, he cleaned his teeth and checked them and explained to him exactly what needed to happen next. Through all of his many visits to the dentist there was only one occasion where Tom yelled and the dentist said that that was a noble record for any child.

It is to be expected that parents and families of children returned to the community to someone else's home may have unresolved feelings about this. Wade and I took the position that we had all we could do to work with the children placed in our home. We did not have the energy, time, or objectivity necessary to provide consultation and support to the family. The agency was agreeable to this and accepted their responsibility to work closely with the parents and to serve as a liaison between natural parents and foster parents. Occasionally I have had second thoughts about our position.

Sometimes I thought perhaps if Andrew's father and mother could see how well he did in our home they would be better able to have him in their home. More frequent visits with his family would have been good for Andrew. Sometimes I thought we should spend some time with Phillip's mother helping her recognize that Phillip could do many things for himself and did not need to be waited upon. But these moments of reconsideration passed quickly. In the process of working with the boys we acquired some information and understanding about the family dynamics within the home from which they had come. It is my opinion that it would have taken a tremendous amount of skill to walk that very thin line between parenting the foster child and, at the same time, teaching parenting to his parents. It was a line that I did not feel capable of walking. Some foster parents might be capable of this, but usually it would take a third person to work with parents, someone very different from the person working in the home with the child.

We wished that each of the boys could go home overnight every other month and out with their family for an outing on the alternate months. It would have been great if the boys could have had extended vacations over Christmas and during the summer time. I believe that such a visitation plan is in the best interest of the child and in the best interest of the family also. When a child is with his family only on holidays when gifts are being exchanged, everyone's behavior is at its very best. Because of the obvious rewards involved, the child and parents have a skewed experience, an unreal experience. In the last analysis a holiday experience does not provide the best opportunity for parents and child to get to know one another's real selves. I believe it would be better for every member of the family to have more frequent contact over a variety of experiences so they would be more accurately in tune with each other.

In Andrew's case, I thought he could learn a great deal if he were able to spend more time with his father, mother, brothers, and sisters. He did understand that they were his family and that they were uniquely different from his foster family. We noticed that Phillip had a much better understanding of gift giving than the other children, and we wondered if that was not related to his frequent contacts with his family. He was beginning to learn that there is a lot of fun in making something for someone you care about. He talked often about his mother and about the particular project he was preparing for her. Because Phillip went home under all kinds of circumstances he was able to understand that parents were not just sources of gifts. He genuinely enjoyed being with them and doing things with them.

Phillip's mother and stepfather were extremely interested in him and they had visited him regularly all through the years that he lived in the institution. After Phillip was in our home, their contacts with Phillip were frequent and friendly. His mother was very cooperative and honored our request not to visit Phillip for the first three months he lived with us so that he could get used to the new situation. After the three-month period had passed, he went home for Thanksgiving weekend and the Christmas holiday and the pattern was started. He went home for every major holiday, spending as much as ten days at Christmas, five days at Easter, five days at Thanksgiving. During the summer he went home a couple of times for a week or more. During the course of a year Phillip probably spent as much as six weeks at home. After his parents knew that he could ride a bicycle, they took his bike home with him and permitted him to ride in their neighborhood.

From the beginning all arrangements for home visits were made through the agency social worker. Usually this involved the parents' contacting the social worker and indicating that they would like to have their son visit at home on a certain occasion. During the last three years there was only one instance where we have asked that a boy not go home. We were planning a special affair that involved Phillip and the parents agreed with us that it would be to Phillip's detriment and disappointment not to go along with the plans that he had made with his foster brothers.

From the beginning we indicated to the agency that we did not wish to entertain family members of our children in our home. The reason was that we thought at the beginning that Tom would never have any company. We did not need to aggravate an unhappy situation for him by forcing him to be around the house when other boys were entertaining family. Phillip's and Andrew's parents have both accepted this graciously.

During the third year Wade and I felt that it was expedient to modify this position somewhat. During the summer of '75 we had difficulty getting in touch with Andrew's parents in order for them to sign a release so that he could be sent to camp. The social worker tried the two telephone numbers that were available innumerable times with no luck. Wade was asked to see if he could reach the family at odd hours, late in the evening and so on. Eventually the contact was made and Andrew's father was gracious and anxious to sign the necessary permission so that Andrew could go to camp. He explained that because the family was out of town and he was working erratic hours it was difficult to make connections. He offered to come by the house to sign the necessary form at our convenience. It had happened that for several days prior to his phone call Andrew had been talking a great deal about his father and wishing that his father could come and watch him swim. He was anxious for his dad to know how well he could swim, how he could dive off the board and so on. It seemed like too good an opportunity to miss, so spontaneously an invitation was issued to Andrew's father: "Please arrange to come sometime when you can go swimming with your son." He arrived one afternoon about 5:30. It was a beautiful afternoon, the weather was superb, and he told Andrew that he had come to go swimming with him. Andrew was so excited that he just could not move to get himself into the pool. His father was patient with him and gave him the kind of encouragement that Andrew needed and eventually he went off the board. Andy and his father had an hour's time together in the swimming pool, playing and splashing. Andrew was so proud of himself and his father was pleased to realize that his son had become so competent in the water. It was a very special time. While this was happening Wade and I took the other two boys and did some special activity with them so that they would not be put in the position of having to be resentful observers of Andrew and his happy time.

There was one other occasion where we were flexible about Andrew's family, Christmas of 1976. It was not convenient for his family to take him home for the Christmas Day itself so they had arranged to take him home for a visit three or four days later. However, again spontaneously, an invitation was extended to them to come by the house on Christmas Eve to spend a bit of time with their son. We were pleased on Christmas Eve that the father and mother arranged to bring all of the children. It was a happy time and Andrew handled it well. Other than those two instances, we have planfully avoided any one boy having a lot of family contact time within our household.

And then there was Tom—Tom who needed so much, who had so many loving experiences due him. He was the child with the least contact from family. As I have indicated, when Tom came to live with us we were under the impression there would be no contact with family so we were pleased that his paternal grandmother could come to see him on his first Christmas in our home. His grandmother told us that she had seen Tom frequently in the state home, and she was upset that he had been placed in the community and nobody had bothered to inform her.

He was very excited to see her. She took him out to lunch and shopping. They returned home with a bagful of toys and clothing. He was almost out of his skin when he returned. He was the most hyperactive I had ever seen him—screaming, bouncing, and jumping. We had to put our arms around him to hold him. During the twenty-four hours following his grandmother's visit, Tom systematically destroyed every single toy that she had purchased for him. This included smashing a transistor radio. However, he did no harm to any of the clothing that she had given him. It was a long time before we realized that that first episode was the way he would act each time grandmother visited.

During the following months there were three more contacts with grandmother. In each instance he destroyed the gifts she gave him during the visit. In each instance a transistor radio was included. On the last of the three visits his grandmother wanted a picture of him. He refused. He screamed and yelled all kinds of filthy words at her. It was sad to watch Tom during this whole interaction. He was very excited and it was obvious that he wanted to go out with her, be with her, and do everything he could with her. She reported to us that when she took him into a big store he said, "I want, I want, I want," and she bought and bought and bought until she had spent all the money that she could afford. After all the indulgence he destroyed everything that was for play and kept only the clothing. For the following twenty months grandmother did not come to see Tom. There was illness in her family and it was not possible for her to visit. She wrote to him many times during that period and in several instances sent him money.

In the early months of living with us he talked about his grandmother a great deal. Every time that he was upset, angry, or frustrated he was sure to say, "I'm going to call my grandmother," or "I'm going to tell my grandmother." Sometimes he just wailed "Grandma, Grandma." As the months wore on he talked about her less and less, perhaps for two reasons. She was not around, and he accepted the fact that she might not be around for a long time. Second, as his security grew in our home and with us as parenting people, he did not feel the need to hang onto that fragile connection.

After many months of no face to face contact, the arrangements were made for grandmother to see Tom during the Christmas season of 1976. Wade told Tom at breakfast that grandmother would be coming at noon. They spent time during the morning discussing the way that Tom should act in order to have a good time himself and to please grandmother. They talked about how Tom could be in control of his own behavior and that he would please grandmother if he would learn to act in a pleasant manner. The discussion between Wade and Tom also included firm statements.

Wade explained to Tom that he was going to ask grandmother not to buy him a lot of sweet food because of his intolerance for it. Also, he was going to talk with grandmother about the fact that it would be better to shop for clothing since that was what Tom seemed to enjoy most from her. Since Wade and Tom had spent the entire morning preparing, Tom was able to contain himself during the conversation between Wade and grandmother. According to grandmother's reports Tom's company on the outing was pleasant with minimal misbehavior from Tom, who had had no need to destroy any of the gifts that his grandmother had brought to him.

The following spring Tom asked if he could send his school picture to his grandmother. He dictated an interesting, newsy letter that was mailed with the picture. It appeared that he had learned to accept and maintain his relationship with his grandmother in a way that was comfortable for both of them.

Mark had little involvement with family members for reasons unknown to us. Mark was not supposed to have any contact with his biological mother. His older sister had called our home a few times and visited with him on the phone. He enjoyed this very much. Although his contact with his family was very limited, nevertheless, they were family and he felt a great void where family was supposed to be.

Of all the children, Tom was the only one who gave any indication of reaching out to make friends. Since Tom was able to carry on a conversation, he initiated a friendship with a gentleman who lived two houses up the street from us. Tom frequently rode his bicycle up to the neighbor's house to help him with chores and he and Tom often talked. The other boys went along too, but they clearly relied on Tom's verbal skills in terms of their relationship with our neighbor. We saw this as a real step in growth for Tom to be able to initiate and sustain this relationship over a couple of years.

As a family we have always enjoyed entertaining and never more than over Thanksgiving and Christmas. We were used to having friends in our home frequently for meals, overnight, and longer periods of time. We were anxious that this activity continue for us and we believed the children could learn to enjoy this experience, too.

A few days after the boys' arrival in our home in the fall of '73 it was Thanksgiving. The day was a fiasco. The boys apparently had no reason to experience the day as different from any other. At the end of the evening when Tom and Andrew finally went to bed and to sleep, I recall sitting on the top step and holding myself tight to keep from crying. I wondered for the first of many times, "What in hell have we gotten ourselves into? What are we trying to prove?"

Thanksgiving had always been my favorite holiday. It had been a time for friends and family to be together in our home. Thanksgiving of '73 we had arranged to be alone. We had decided to give the day to the boys to help them learn about a special day. Wade was tired, disgruntled, grumpy, and irritable when the children finally went to bed and was not available for conversation at all. I was distraught, bitter, and angry. I felt that the Thanksgiving had been ruined for some ridiculous enterprise. One good thing came out of the day. I was prompted to talk with Wade about planning for Christmas. We decided to make it as meaningful as possible for the children, and at the same time to save some of the joy of Christmas for us. We decided that we would celebrate Christmas over a long period of time. Each phase of Christmas preparation would be extended as long as possible, and it worked. One day we went and purchased an artificial tree, the next day we assembled it. On the third day we put on the lights. The tree was decorated on four successive days. Each day we used one box of decorations. At the same time we prepared simple decorations for the house and gifts for Andrew to take to his parents. The boys made aluminum foil stars, popcorn strings, cranberry ropes, and terrariums. These articles were assembled and displayed around the house as the excitement of Christmas heightened. Seven days before Christmas we started presenting the boys with a gift a day. It helped them become used to the idea of receiving gifts in our home.

On Christmas day they could cope with the gifts that had appeared under the tree. There were gifts from friends and neighbors. Several persons who did not normally send gifts to our home sent gifts that year of cookies, toys, and candies for the boys. Wade and I experienced this sharing as an affirmation from our friends and neighbors that they approved of what we were doing. The children received some gifts to share: a toboggan and sled. Each boy received the usual quota of mittens, hats, sweatshirts, pajamas, personalized placemats, and personalized dishes. Each of their gifts seemed to add to the joy of ownership. After that Christmas they became increasingly comfortable about leaving their treasures scattered around the whole house. That day marked the beginning of acceptance of our house as their home—a marked contrast to the former time when treasures went to bed with them.

During the holidays the boys were introduced to candles.

Candles have been special for me and I have enjoyed having them all around the house. In the fall, winter, and early spring I light them frequently, so this was a personal indulgence I hoped to continue. We decided that the boys could learn to enjoy candles also. We talked about how candles were enjoyed by looking and not by touching. I told the boys that they could help put the candles out by using a snuffer if they would not play with them during the time they were burning. Progressively we lit candles. One night one candle, the next night two or three. When Christmas Eve arrived in 1973 the children were comfortable with candles. Candles, flame, matches, fire were never concerns in our home.

Wade and I decided for several reasons that Christmas 1973 would be focused entirely upon the two new foster sons. However, we felt a great need to sustain ourselves with some of the traditional things which we had always enjoyed. In order to do this, we arranged to have John and Noni spend twenty-four hours with Tom and Andrew on December 22 and 23. We spent those twenty-four hours at the big house with our son Frosty. On Christmas 1973 the house was a shambles. Because of the renovation it was difficult to find a place to stand or sit without being in dust or plaster. However, there were a couple of beds on which to place sleeping bags and we did sleep there one night.

That twenty-four hours away from the boys was the first of many such arrangements. It was twenty-four hours of refreshment; it gave us time to call on friends, deliver gifts, go out to dinner with Frosty, and enjoy Christmas breakfast in our home. What a crazy breakfast that was in that shambly dusty shell of a house. There was coffee made in an electric coffeepot, and coffee cake from the bakery. The house was not very warm. We shared coffee and gifts among the three of us and felt warm because we were together. The boys had a fine twenty-four hours with Noni and John in our absence.

Andrew had been more open about his concern and had asked repeatedly where we were. They had assured him that we were away overnight and would be back the next day. By the time Wade and I returned from our short holiday apart, the kids were up and behaving beautifully. They had been cooperative through breakfast and had been on a long walk with John and Noni. I was grateful that John and Noni had seen their pleasant sides because we hoped that John and Noni would come frequently to allow us a day or a day and a half away.

Christmas Day arrived. Three young adults, all of them non-

Christian, joined our family for the day. Many things were new for all of us that day. Our Jewish friends were introduced to Christian customs. Tom and Andrew were introduced to a family Christmas. Tom's and Andrew's behavior that day was no different from Jori's and Frosty's behavior years before. They were excited, curious, and had so many things to do simultaneously that they hardly knew where to start. Somehow, through all the excitement, under all the pressure, Tom managed to stay cool. He had no tantrums the entire day. There were times during the day when he needed to be reminded to "cool it" and each time he was able to do that. Their manners at the table were exemplary and they were delightful company.

Andrew did have a toileting accident.

A couple of days after Christmas, Andrew went home with his parents for twenty-four hours. It was exciting to help Andrew prepare for this visit. He had a hard time not packing everything he owned. We had helped him select gifts for his brother, sisters, and parents. Fortunately, the gifts filled up his suitcase so that he could not pack all of his socks, underclothes, and pajamas. Tom handled the preparation time well; however, once Andrew had left the house he threw a full-scale tantrum. It did not last as long as others. We were patient with him for we recognized how frightened he was to be left alone with us, for the very first time. There had always been two of them and they had been together for eight years. Tom's anxiety around Andrew's absence was eased by the special time he had with Frank. Frank came and took him to the airport, out to lunch, and shopping. Tom enjoyed the time alone without Andrew.

Before Christmas, the children were accustomed to having food only at mealtime. With the advent of the holiday there were plates of goodies around the dining room and living room much of the time. Nuts, Christmas candies, and Christmas cookies were plentiful that year for several friends had shared generously with us. Andrew seemed to understand that a little bit of "treats" went a long way, but Tom would stuff food into his mouth until his sides would split. We had to put down some rules. During the holidays we gave each boy a paper plate immediately after breakfast. The boys were told that they could select treats to last them until the next meal. This technique worked for Andrew. He paced himself and gradually during the morning he consumed all of the treats. Tom, on the other hand, gobbled them up instantly and was reminded all morning, "No, Tom, you may not have anymore." Since that worked for Andrew we continued the plan through the rest of the holiday. A few weeks after Christmas my son had a houseguest for the weekend. As I was setting the table for dinner, Andrew was upset with me because I was not getting out all the fancy dishes. I was using the everyday pottery and the stainless steel silverware. As I mentioned before, Andrew was not satisfied with this plan and insisted that we use best dishes and silver for company as we had done on Christmas Day. I began to realize how important it was to the boys to use best as opposed to everyday articles. During the several weeks following Christmas '73, I made many opportunities for the children to get out the best linen, best dishes, and best silver. I did this deliberately for I knew we were planning to have a reception for our daughter, Jori, in the spring of '74 when she returned from Alaska.

Six months after the boys had arrived they moved with us to the big house. Two days after moving into our new home we had a reception for our daughter and her husband. There was a large group, and we arranged to have refreshments catered. When the food arrived, the children were very excited as they peeked into the boxes of fancy sandwiches and cakes. I took the opportunity to talk to them about how much food they would be allowed to eat at the party. A young couple was serving and tending bar. The children were told that they could have drinks prepared by the bartender. They would be limited to two drinks and could choose between Coke and non-alcoholic punch. Late in the afternoon of the party they practiced walking up to a buffet table and helping themselves and walking up to the bar and asking for a drink.

The excitement heightened in the late afternoon when flowers were delivered. After they had oohed and aahed over the beautiful flowers, the boys went upstairs with Frank to prepare for the evening of excitement. They showered, brushed, polished, and put on their new slacks and sportsjackets. It had been arranged for Frank to take the boys out for dinner. Wade and I and a houseguest went out to dinner also. This plan was an accommodation to me. I did not think I could cope with preparing dinner, as well as an open house reception. Frank had come to work for twenty-four hours to take over the responsibility of shepherding Tom and Andrew through this experience. He had arrived late in the afternoon, supervised their showering, dressing, and trip out for dinner, and would be there through the entire evening, including bedtime. He stayed over that night and was there for wake-up in the morning to help them move through the confusion of the day after. The plan worked well except when Frank, Tom, and Andrew returned home from the dinner. The young couple who were to do the serving had arrived and were waiting on the porch. Tom was upset because we had not been there to let them in. Frank handled this with him, but Tom kept saying, "Where's Magoo, where's Magoo? The party's going to start, where's Magoo?" We arrived soon after, however, and things did get organized to Tom's satisfaction.

When the guests started to arrive, Tom and Andrew were fabulous. They were so proud of their new home that they took everyone on a tour through the entire house. Although many of the guests were new to Tom and Andrew, they handled the strangeness with poise. They liked the fact that most of the women had on long dresses and that the men were all dressed up. They had never been to a party with people in their best clothes, on their best behavior. They kept talking to us about it. They walked from room to room enjoying the candles, conversation, and flowers. Several people had brought gifts. The children realized the gifts were not for them and they were not upset that they were not the center of attention.

Two friends brought a video camera and playback equipment. They televised and videotaped the entire party. By setting up the equipment in one room, they could video the actions in four different areas. They took a lot of footage of the children who were delighted. They thought it was great fun to be in one room looking at a television screen and see the other person. Later in the evening when part of the videotape was played back they were excited all over again to see themselves on the television screen. Of course Tom ate too much, but he is not the first boy that overstuffed at a party. Frank kept close watch on the children and when they seemed to be getting tired, took them upstairs to bed and stayed with them. The day had been so full that they were content to do that. They retired hours before the guests left our home, but they did not resent this. We were very proud of our two foster sons that evening; they had done very well.

That was the largest group of people we ever entertained. After that, there were many occasions when twelve, fourteen, or sixteen family friends would be together with us at one time, but these were informal gatherings. During the summers we enjoyed having pool parties, friends to join us for swimming and supper. Usually supper was cooked out on a grill. Eating and dress were casual. The boys enjoyed that kind of entertaining, too, and they liked having different designs on the paper plates and napkins for each event of entertaining. Informal entertaining outdoors around the pool, around the

grill, was easier for the children to handle. There was more freedom
to leave the togetherness of the party and escape for a quick ride on
their bicycles. Wintertime entertaining was more difficult because
everything happened in the house, so we tried to do more entertaining during the warm months when there was more freedom of
movement.

During the first couple of winters that the boys lived with us,
we were not comfortable entertaining without involving them. They
needed so much attention from us that they could not go to bed or
entertain themselves while we had guests. For many months bedtime was an extended time demand for me as a mother so it was impossible for me to entertain. As time passed, the children became
comfortable in our home and learned to spend more hours by themselves. Eventually the time came when we had friends in for dinner
and did not include the children. I explained to the boys that some
friends were coming to have dinner with us as grown-ups. I prepared
their meal for them ahead of time. It was important to Tom that he
and Andrew have the same food to eat that the guest would have
later in the evening. This was done and he was able to give us some
free time for our guests. When the guests arrived they visited with
the boys for a brief time while I served. When dinner was served the
boys went upstairs to play pool and prepare for bedtime. It was
necessary for them to come down two or three times to check, but
their behavior was not offensive.

Tom very much appreciated fancy food and he was disappointed
not to taste everything that was special. As time passed, we became
comfortable about having guests and not including the boys. No
longer did we need to have someone work with the children so that
we could entertain. All of the boys were able to recognize the difference between a grown-up party and a family-type party. When en-
tertainment was focused on adults the boys greeted our guests and
visited with them for a few minutes. Usually Tom persuaded someone to shoot a game of pool with him. After a half hour of making
sure the grown-up friends knew about "my new shoes, my trip to
the zoo," the boys permitted the adults to be together without
interruption.

Their behavior was similar to the way Jori, Frosty, and their
friends used to act when there was company in the house. The boys
enjoyed the day after a party for they knew that lunchtime meant
party leftovers.

Down through the years the children learned that there were

certain things that we did to get our home ready for a party: we tidied the house, put things away, and made room for other coats and other boots. The children learned from me to associate candles with parties. They came to love candles even as I do and reminded me to light them when it was almost time for guests to arrive. The boys realized that we served wine and drinks to grown-up friends. They talked a lot about growing up and trying these kinds of things. Phillip was very aware that he would be grown-up first. We promised him that on his eighteenth birthday he could celebrate with a glass of wine.

The children also enjoyed the hospitality of our friends' homes. One of the most delightful experiences happened as we delivered Christmas gifts to one home in 1974. It was a special occasion because Wade had made a dollhouse for our goddaughter. The boys were excited, and it was great fun smuggling the dollhouse into the house so that she would not see it. There were many relatives and guests at her home that evening, and I was apprehensive as to how well the boys would behave. The boys were interested in the Christmas tree and all the presents which were visible. They understood that the packages were for the people who lived there. They did not ask to have anything for themselves, even though they were very curious. The boys enjoyed the Christmas treats that were served to them. As the grown-ups were visiting, the boys played with our goddaughter, who was three years old at the time.

Suddenly, one of the grown-ups stood up and asked everyone to join hands. The children were not sure what was happening, but they joined hands with all the others to form a circle to sing Christmas carols. She quickly determined that the boys knew "Silent Night" and "Jingle Bells." We walked around in a circle, singing those Christmas carols over and over again. It was a nice warm time. The children felt very much a part of that home and welcome there. As we were leaving, our hosts gave each of us a package to take home. The boys received the gifts with poise. They thanked our friends for their gifts and carried them out to the car. To our surprise they carried them home and put them under the tree to wait for the next morning to open them with the rest of the gifts.

Another happy time occurred when we went to a friend's home. Our friends were people who were used to being around children with retardation. They were not concerned by the continuous questioning. Our host gave the children specific boundaries within which they were to play outside the house. He explained to them what was expected of them when they came onto the porch where the cooking was being done. As our host, he put down enough limits to give the children some sense of security and yet, at the same time, was permissive enough so that the boys had the feeling that this was an occasion and they were being entertained.

Our neighbor kept a large garden. He permitted the boys to help him with certain tasks. As a reward for their help, he frequently gave them fresh vegetables to bring home to the family. All of the boys were welcome at his house, although he felt a special relationship with Tom, partially because Tom was more capable of sustaining a conversation than the other two children. On three different occasions the neighbor invited Tom to do different things with him. Once, he invited all three boys to attend a baseball game with him. Wade refused the invitation for the boys, judging that they could not handle that long a period of time without incident. He explained that he would be very glad to have any of the boys go with him when not so much time was involved.

A few weeks later, the neighbor took Tom to a choral presentation at his church and subsequently he took all three boys to a Christmas pageant. When he brought the boys home he talked with Wade at great length. He had been pleasantly surprised by the attentive, quiet way Phillip and Andrew had behaved in the church setting, but he had been embarrassed by Tom's lack of attention and unruliness. The situation had been difficult for him to handle since the children were in the congregation while he had been in the choir loft with the rest of the musicians and the singers. He had expected that all three boys would be able to be quiet and participate in the service. Phillip and Andrew were able to do this. Tom, without the constant attention and monitoring of an adult sitting close to him, had behaved poorly. Tom has not been invited out since.

Later, the same neighbor gave Tom a toy that he had salvaged from a garage sale. It was a bouncing horse on springs, generally considered to be an appropriate toy for children up to age five. Tom enjoyed this toy because it permitted him to bounce up and down. We were dismayed to see fourteen-year-old, 5'6" Tom sitting on this infantile toy bouncing up and down. He was doing this in the middle of the basketball court so that his activity was in the way of the other boys shooting baskets. Using the excuse that the other boys needed room to play, we asked Tom to take his bouncing horse into the garage and keep it there. Tom spent a great deal of time riding where few people observed him. He looked ridiculous and we did not want him to become the target of teasing by the adolescents who walked up and down the back street. When the springs on the horse wore out, they were not replaced since we did not appreciate Tom's slipping into such an infantile game. On the other hand, we were pleased that the neighbor cared enough to give him the gift. In a way the horse is symbolic of our dilemma. Because of Tom's abilities, interests, and level of functioning, he enjoyed and preferred this type of play equipment. On the other hand, Tom wanted very much to be able to do what boys his age were doing. As parents, we knew if we continuously urged, supported, and taught Tom to move toward age-appropriate activities, it would be at the expense of his enjoyment of more juvenile toys and equipment.

During the first several months of the boys living with us, Wade and I had little leisure time other than when the children were asleep. It was difficult for us to get away to do anything by ourselves even within our own home. It was difficult to walk out and leave the boys behind even though they were not alone. For the first several times that we went out it worked best to use a ruse. Frank took the boys out to do something special and while they were out, Wade and I left. The boys did not seem to mind returning to the house to find us away, but they had problems if they were in the house when we left. Over the months this changed.

We could pursue our own interests and the boys were comfortable with that. They understood that Wade and I, individually and as a couple, enjoyed certain things without them. They were able to accept our wanting to visit friends, go out to dinner, go to movies, and go away for weekends. They came to understand that when we were gone someone else would be with them. They came to expect a good time, that when we were gone, it was a time for special treats or outings. It was understood that the boys would go out to dinner with Mike when Wade and I went out to dinner with friends.

The morning after such outings, Tom and Mark liked to compare menus. They liked to tell us what they had to eat and they expected me to give them a complete run-down of all the foods I had had. I experienced that as typical teenage behavior. I remembered Jori and Frosty doing that and I recalled asking my father the same question years ago. "What did you have to eat last night, Daddy? When can we have that too?" No longer did the boys need and expect tangible reinforcements from Wade and me when we returned from an outing. They accepted our right to do some things sepa-

rately from them, as well as their right to do things separately from
us.

The boys learned to use leisure time in a manner similar to other
teenagers with one major difference. The boys, alone or in a group,
were never without adult supervision. There was always a grown-up
man or a grown-up couple with the boys in every situation. In the
house, outdoors, and on the back street, the children had increased
freedom, but always with a monitoring adult within earshot. We
hoped that eventually each of the boys would learn enough about
community behavior to permit him to use the facilities in our suburban area by himself, but there were many things to learn before
that could happen. They needed to learn how to respond to traffic
lights, cross a street, use money, and tell time. They needed to learn
the route between one place and another, to school, the drugstore,
and the grocery store.

They learned to be in large groups of people and act in a quiet
non-intrusive way. They modeled their behavior after the friends
with whom they spent so much time. No longer did they need to
handle merchandise in stores. No longer did they want everything
they saw. They needed to be reminded to stay together. They
needed to be warned about cars in parking lots. Often they forgot
the need to pay an admission fee. There were many simple as well as
complicated tasks to be learned before the boys would be able to use
freely a community larger than the boundaries of one block.

One of the ways we hoped the children would grow and develop
was in their ability to take responsibility for themselves. The boys
demonstrated to us something we had theorized about before. That
is, to the extent a person feels good about himself and develops
respect for himself, to that same extent is he able to give feelings of
affection and respect to another person. As each boy began to know
the security of having his own things, space, and time, he began to
permit other persons to have the same. It was as though each boy
came to *understand* that his earned respect for himself was somehow related to that which he gave to others.

11

Ownership

WHEN THE BOYS CAME to live with us, they wanted to have everything they owned with them all the time. We realized that in an institution a boy needed to hold in his hand any article that he wanted to keep, for to put down was to risk loss. This meant that at bedtime all kinds of things were stowed underneath the bed, under the pillow, under the blankets. It was difficult for the boys to learn that there were rooms in the house where certain things could be kept safely. Wade and I realized that we had a long-range goal for the boys—that they could trustingly put things away; they could put coats in one place, toys in another place, pajamas in a third place, and lunchboxes in a fourth place. When they first lived with us, they took everything from one place to the next whenever they moved. For example, the first thing Wade gave each boy was a lunchbox. The boys wanted to take their lunchboxes to bed with them to know that they had them all the time. For many months every new object had to go to bed for a few nights to make sure it would not be "lost." Gradually the boys learned that there were areas or places in the house where it was safe to leave their things. Later they were able to leave bikes in the garage, toys in the playroom, boots in the clothes closet, and medicine on the kitchen shelf.

That took weeks and months of insisting upon two particular details. First, things had to be in a certain place, and second each boy had certain places for his own individual use. In our house each boy had his own cubby where he kept his playclothes, mittens, hats, boots, and lunchbox. As described earlier, the closet was divided into sections by partitions so that each boy had his own area.

Somehow this separate but close arrangement was secure. I think the boys would not have been able to learn to put their playclothes in a closet area as quickly if they had needed to use an open closet without partitions. By having the partitions lined up, side by side, each boy could see his own place or territory, as well as the territories of others. This helped each boy begin to learn the relationship of his clothes to someone else's clothes, the idea of mine and yours. We have tried to emphasize and dignify ownership and territory for each boy with as many different things as possible. We provided different-colored toothbrushes, and it worked. However, the boys still had difficulty recognizing the place to hang the toothbrush. It was not uncommon for toothbrushes to be stowed away in bureau drawers. Each boy had his own bureau, and we insisted that clean clothes were put there. Tom knew that his clothes would be safe in his bureau when he knew that Andrew also had a bureau for his clothes. Each boy learned his ownership and his territory at the same time he recognized that the other person had comparable territory and comparable things to put away.

Even so, anything new that came along was tremendously important. There was a period of time when each boy needed to discover the right place to keep it. For example, one Christmas Tom received Skidoo boots as a gift. He wanted them, I guess, much more than we had realized. For two or three days he wanted to wear them while he watched TV and take them to bed with him. We did not allow that. We insisted that the boots were to be worn outside. "When you go out to play in the snow, that's when you put them on. Where do you keep boots that go out to play?" We kept asking him that question and insisting, after he had given us the correct response, that he put the boots in that place. After several times of saying, "Tom, take your boots off. You cannot wear them while you watch TV," he learned when, where, and how to use them.

For many reasons we wanted the boys to feel a sense of ownership, territory, and privacy about their beds. We thought each boy would more readily accept bedtime routines, bedmaking responsibilities, and the security of his bed for exploration of his own body if his bed was attractive and uniquely his. At the beginning of the boys' living with us, each boy was given distinctive sheets to use on his own bed—different colors, different designs. From the first week the boys could help fold the laundry and identify their own sheets, as well as the sheets of the other boys.

We needed to buy new beds so we took the children with us to pick out the headboards. That was a big occasion. The boys were very excited about the fact that they had selected their own headboards, mattresses, and springs. They understood that the new beds would be delivered to the big house down the street. The boys knew they were going to move down to the other house after Christmas, and they knew the bedrooms in which they would be sleeping once the family had moved. It was with much excitement they awaited the day for their new beds to be delivered to their new bedrooms. We pored over a catalog to select sheets and bedspreads for the new bedrooms. The boys had a voice in the selections that were ultimately made. Several times prior to the delivery of the new linens, the boys would look through the catalog again to point out the sheets and bedspreads that had been picked out for "my new bed in the new house." Subsequently, the boys settled in their new rooms and made up their new beds with new sheets, blankets, and bedspreads. They experienced a great deal of pride. Easily recognizable, individual sheets, blankets, and bedspreads made the task of making beds more enjoyable. The boys enjoy the different patterns and colors of the individual sheets, bedspreads, towels and wash cloths, and it certainly makes the housekeeping easier.

Thus, the boys had many private places and personal spaces: closet, cubby, bed, bureau, bulletin board, toy box, and suitcase. Each boy had belongings that he never had to share with anyone: clothes, toilet articles, bike, sports equipment, craft supplies, and other toys.

As described earlier, when the boys came to live with us, they had adequate wardrobes. Unfortunately, most of the trousers were either olive drab or black. Most of their T-shirts were short sleeved brown, yellow, red, or blue. That was not the "in thing" for clothes in our community that year, when most of the children were wearing levis and long sleeved sweatshirts. Even though Tom and Andrew were well dressed, clean and warm, they stood out in any group because of their institutionalized look. Fortunately, active boys wear out clothes rather quickly. Over a period of a few months the boys' wardrobes became less drab and more individualized. We shopped as needs arose and encouraged the boys to pick out their own clothes. In every instance shirts were picked to go with pants so the boys would remember the particular combination when selecting clothes at home and would wear the combination that looked well for school. The clothing became more individualized, and it was no longer necessary to put identification on shirts and slacks, as had been the case in the institution. The children had come with their shirts and pants labeled with their names. Name tags, and in some instances magic markers, had been used to write their last names in big block letters on the inside of the fabric. In some instances this printing had leaked through and showed on the surface of the cloth. It may have been necessary to do that in order to have the children's clothes kept separate in the institution, but fortunately as the children began to select their own clothing there was no longer any need to label outside clothing. The boys began to take pride in their clothes. They enjoyed folding their shirts, sorting their socks, and hanging up their trousers. They enjoyed selecting their clothes to wear to school in the morning, and soon we began to notice that they had favorite outfits. Some outfits they would want to wear over and over and other outfits they liked to keep for best and when they were going to special places.

One day Wade introduced the children to coat hangers. I never thought that coat hangers could provoke so much excitement for children. It did in our household and I began to realize why. Not many state institutions provide for closet space where clothing is hung on hangers. More usually, clothing is stored in boxes according to size. In our home the boys were enchanted to have clothes hangers like "Big Stuff." They enjoyed looking in their cubbies to see how each had hung up his clothes, so they could hang theirs the same way. For many months there was a pride in clothing. Later the children were very alert to what they owned and what matched what, but they moved on to more typical teenager behavior, and they were very casual about clothes. As with our other children, the boys had special outfits they wanted to wear, and they really did not care if they were tattered or torn. They had favorites that they had selected and they wore them because they were comfortable. Ownership had been experienced. The boys appreciated clothing that other people wore and often made observations about someone else's appearance.

As the children became more interested in clothing they began to recognize that there was some difference between the kinds of clothes that they as boys wore and I, as a woman, wore. After the children had lived with us for about six months, Wade went into the hall where the clothes hamper was kept. Andrew had all of the clothes out of the clothes hamper and had made a separate pile of all my bras and underpants. My husband made no comment except to ask Andrew to put the clothes back in the hamper. The following

Saturday when I was doing laundry, I invited the boys to help me fold clothes. For several weeks the boys helped me fold clothes. They folded bras, underpants, and slips and put them aside for me. We talked about the fact that girls' underclothes were different from boys' underclothes. As I look back now, I realized that that was the beginning of overt sexuality training in our household. Up until that incident the boys had been concentrating on learning to trust the home, to learn the routines of the home, to learn some sense of ownership and pride in themselves. But that curiosity about girls' underwear was the beginning of a whole series of experiences.

In the process of monitoring other boys' behavior, we frequently observed Andrew apparently masturbating. Andrew would be stretched out on his bed face down, mounted upon a pillow (frequently Tom's) making hip thrusts. We kept giving Andrew the same message: "Andrew, that's really OK. Close the drapes, close the door, don't use Tom's pillow." Over a period of time with those kinds of reminders we no longer observed Andrew's masturbation. We believed the masturbating continued, but it was no longer observed. There were a couple of reasons. We no longer needed to go upstairs as frequently to monitor behavior, for all the children were more appropriate. We could call reminders upstairs. For example, "It's almost time for dinner," or "It's time to get ready to go out to play." Sometimes an adult was upstairs in the playroom or in another part of the upstairs talking to the children and noticed that the door to Andrew's room was closed. The assumption was that Andrew wanted to be alone. We hoped that he had the drapes closed, but we never walked in to see. We had a rule in our house that you never walked into anyone's room without knocking. There was one occasion, I remember, when we called and called for Andrew and he did not come. Subsequently, I went upstairs and knocked on the door and said, "Andrew, we're having dinner in a few minutes and you'd better come down." I went on downstairs and he followed soon afterwards. No one asked him to account for his tardiness. We assumed that he had been masturbating and had not wanted to come the moment he was called. We tried to give the children the consistent message that self-enjoyment was all right, but that it needed to be in a place where other people did not observe it.

There was one incidence of mutual masturbation which we observed. One summer afternoon as the boys were playing around the swimming pool in their trunks, they were playing a game they called "grab ass." Specifically, they were grabbing for each other's genitals. At the point I intervened, both boys had erections. I asked Tom and Andrew to come into the house with me because I wished to talk with them. I told both of the boys that I knew that what they were doing felt good and that doing it was not the issue. I wanted to talk about where they were doing it. I went on to say that it made other people uncomfortable to see them involved with each other, playing with each other's penises. I talked particularly about the man who lived next door.

The man next door was a thirty-year-old husband and father who was very cordial to the children and often talked with them. He frequently provided them with little treats and on occasion came to swim with them in their pool. Tom and Andrew thought the neighbor was very cool and they earnestly sought his approval. I took advantage of this and said to them, "He will not like you doing that kind of thing. He will not enjoy watching you boys play like that with each other. It may make him stop coming over here to swim with you guys anymore. If you want to play like that, there are places to play like that, but out in the backyard is not one of them." Andrew showed no emotion during this discussion. He just listened and took it in. It must have made an impression because I observed no "grab ass" games on his part after that day.

Tom's way of handling that situation was different. As I indicated, the boys were mutually involved in this game and I had called them both in. Andrew left and went out to play but Tom stayed with me. He seemed to want to have more discussion. He appeared genuinely perturbed and on the verge of tears. So I said to him, "Tom, I really do know that it feels good to play with yourself. Everybody does it and everybody knows it feels good." And I went on to say to him, "Does everybody go to the toilet, Tom?" And he answered yes. I asked him, "Does everybody eat, Tom?" And he said yes. "Well Tom, everybody masturbates and it's really OK." With that, Tom began to weep. He cried and cried and cried. I sat there and held him in my arms and experienced the time as though Tom had found his way back to the human race. I believe that up until that conversation he had thought that what he was doing was something terrible. He appeared to be weeping with complete relief. I believe I was the first person who had ever told him that what he was doing was all right, that everybody else did it. I went on to say to him, "Does Big Stuff go to the toilet? Does he go to the toilet alone?" "Yes." I asked the big question. "Does Big Stuff masturbate?" His face reflected his acknowledgment of the possibility. His eyes became as big as saucers. It became clear to me that it had never crossed his mind that anyone like "Big Stuff" might masturbate. I hugged him, I told him that it was really OK and he needed to know that it was really all right to enjoy himself. The important thing was that people did not like to watch other people enjoy themselves. We do not like to watch other people have bowel movements or urinate. We do not like to watch people masturbate. I said to him, "Do you know what masturbate means?" And he responded, "Yes, play with myself." So I knew that he really understood the word and the concept. It was one of the most meaningful exchanges I ever had with Tom and I felt that it was a turning point in his relationship with our family. I think many feelings of guilt slid off his back during that conversation.

There were two other incidents with Tom that relate to his developing sexuality. A year and a half after this incident we became aware that Tom had decided it was fun to urinate behind another neighbor's barn. Wade and I did not see that it was all that unusual for Tom to explore the idea of urinating outdoors. We knew that many, many boys have that experience while growing up. We did not make a big issue of it with Tom except to tell him that it was not sensible to urinate outdoors when you could easily come home. We told him that some people would be turned off by the fact that he did not know enough to go home to go to the toilet. It worked and there was no recurrence. Tom seemed to be learning to explore his own body in privacy.

Last summer, on an extremely hot day, the swimming pool was over-chlorinated and the children faced a day of no swimming. My husband and I were painting some furniture and the boys were playing around trying to keep cool and amused. I missed Tom and looked for him in all of his usual haunts outdoors. I could not find him so I went in the house. I called up the stairs and heard a mumbled voice answer me. In a very annoyed manner, I said, "Tom, what are you doing upstairs? Come on down and join the rest of us. We're all outdoors and we're going to make lemonade. Come on down and be with us." He took his time and five minutes later he came tumbling down the stairs. I said to him in a most sarcastic manner, "What in the world were you doing." He just looked at me and with a long suffering sigh answered, "I was playing with myself." I put my arm around his shoulder and said, "Oh, Tom, I'm so sorry I intruded upon you. Do you want to go back?" And he looked at me again in the most forlorn way and said, "No. I'll go outdoors." I was very angry with myself because he had met all the expectancies of other people. He had gone off by himself to do what he wanted to do and I had intruded upon him. I am grateful I did not walk in on him, but I wish I could have been more aware that he had a right to be alone in his room with his door closed. He had met all of the family's rules and I had not been fair.

Andrew has an interesting use for my bathing suits; we became aware of it in a humorous way. I had two bathing suits so I would always have a dry one for swimming, yet, my bathing suits always seemed to be wet. Day after day I would go to get a bathing suit and they would both be wet. One day we noticed that Andrew was on the pool deck with one of my bathing suits, dipping it in and out of the water. When I spoke to him, he wrung it out and hung it on the clothesline. I just filed that incident away but began to realize that Andrew did this very frequently. He often played with my bathing suit and, on occasion, he took my bathing suits off the line, took them to the basement, and played with them in the washtubs. Neither Wade nor I did anything about it that summer except to tell Andrew to leave my bathing suits alone. We really did not think much about it. During the third summer we surmised that Andrew was masturbating to orgasm using my bathing suit.

One morning Wade got up early to play golf. The house was totally quiet. He went out to the kitchen and Andrew was coming in from the backyard. He was in his pajamas and had obviously been prowling around outdoors.

We had two concerns: Andrew was not ready to wander out by the pool unsupervised. Second, he was again playing with my bathing suit, for there was water splashed all along the pool deck and the suits were dripping on the clothesline. That morning we talked to him about being out of the house without permission; we told him that boys were to stay upstairs until other people were up for the day. Wade talked to him about the fact that the daily routine started when everyone greeted each other good morning and that he was to adhere to that rule. A few days later my husband went down to the basement for some errand and found Andrew playing with the trunks of two of my bathing suits. He asked him to wring the water out of the suits and hang them out on the clothesline.

The next thing we noticed was that Andrew always asked to hang up my bathing suit after I had been swimming with the children. We had viewed it as a courtesy and let him do this. Now we observed that there was a whole sexual thing around this errand: Andrew would have erections while he was playing with my bathing suit. Although we actually never observed this, we assumed that he had been masturbating to orgasm with my bathing suit trunks and washing them out in the washtub or pool. Finally, I found Andrew one day with my bathing suits. I told him I wanted to talk to him about what he was doing with them. Immediately he was defensive and said, "Oh, I wouldn't put them on, I wouldn't put them on." He repeated it two or three times which made me think that part of his game had been to put the bathing suits on. I told him I really did not care whether he put them on or not but the fact was that he could not play with both of my bathing suits. I told him that he could have one of them but he was to keep his hands off the other one. I held out both pairs of trunks to him and said to him, "Which one do you want. You may have it and you can do anything with it you care to." He selected the orange trunks. I told him that he could keep the trunks down in the basement. He could hang them on a particular hook and he was welcome to go down there anytime if he was alone and play with the bathing suit in any way he wished to. He was to wash it out and hang it up again when he was through. From that day on he was expected to leave my other bathing suits alone. He was to leave all of my other clothing alone. That was to be a "guide post" for him from then on.

During the third year, the boys were beginning to get some sense of body parts, body differences, and body changes. All of the boys were beginning to develop hair on their bodies, and Mark was beginning to get some facial hair. Phillip, Andrew, and Mark were having complexion problems. I tried to help them learn good skin care—lathering and rinsing their faces thoroughly, using facial ointments and so forth. One day in early summer it seemed to me that it would be good to have the children have a good facial cleansing. I prepared claypack facials for two of the children. My thought was that if their skins were thoroughly cleansed, the summer of exposure to the chlorinated pool and sunshine would clear their skins of acne. The boys were pleased to have this kind of personal attention from me. As I smeared the claypack across their foreheads, noses, chins, and cheeks, I explained to them that this process would help get rid of some of the muddy places around their noses and chins and get rid of some of the blackheads that were beginning to form there. I saw no need for putting the claypack on Tom's face for his skin was as clear as a baby's and it did not seem to need any particular attention. He felt differently, and clamored for a facial. I told him that he really did not need one and he asked me why. I suddenly realized that I was in a situation to help the children learn some facts about body changing. We talked about the fact that as boys matured and became men, for a period of time their skins were apt to be grubby and oily. We talked about the things that happen to their bodies. How they grew taller. How their arms grew longer. How hair came on their faces and around their penises and their armpits. How they were beginning to be stronger and were able to lift things and do things that they had never been able to do before. All three of the boys were comfortable, contented, and without embarrassment, talking about the changes in their own bodies and how they could see that their bodies were beginning to become more like the full-grown men that they knew in their lives. At my suggestion, we began to talk about some of the changes that happen to girls when they become women. Andrew and Phillip did not seem to have any awareness of the bodily changes experienced by girls. Tom and Mark clearly understood that when a girl became a woman it meant that she was old enough to have a baby and that a baby lived inside of the girl for a while. Tom's sharing of these facts was heard by Andrew and Phillip with great disbelief. When I attempted to expand on Tom's facts and give more detail, all of the boys lost interest. There was no evidence of embarrassment, just disinterest.

A few days later, they asked me if I would give them facials again. I was in the middle of some work that seemed more important to me and I answered, "Not right now, I have other things to do, but at a later time I will do it for you" and went on with my work. After a while I found myself wondering if the boys were really asking me to open another discussion with them about the changes that boys and girls experience as they become men and women.

Later, I sat on the porch, polishing my fingernails. The boys began to talk to me about the fact that only ladies wore fingernail polish. We then talked about some of the other things that ladies did that men did not. They talked about lipstick, earrings, dresses, and other superficial items. I asked, "What are some of the ways that women are different from men." Andrew and Phillip wanted to continue talking about the fact that women had shoes different from men. "Women have lots of shoes and theirs are pretty." They did not want to talk about anything else. I did not feel that I was getting anywhere in the discussion. I asked them, "Let's think about the things that are different between a woman and a man from the top of the head down." They could immediately recognize the fact that women did not have beards and moustaches. They talked about the different men they knew, starting with Wade, who wore beards. They commented that it was funny that women's hair could be the same as men's hair in terms of being short or long.

I prompted them by saying, "What are other parts of women's bodies that are different from men's?" They seemed unable to identify anything else beyond the presence or absence of facial hair. Then I said, "What about breasts?" One boy was not sure what I meant by breasts. As I pointed to my own, I tried a street word, *boobs.* "Oh" was the response. I asked the boys, "Do you have breasts or boobs as I do?" "No." We talked about that and Tom appeared anxious. It seemed that Tom was ambivalent about the way the conversation was going; he was glad to have it discussed but he was very nervous about it. The other boys quickly became disinterested. They were satisfied to talk about the fact that because women had breasts it meant that they wore brassieres which meant that their underwear was different from the kinds of underwear that boys and men wore. They knew what brassieres looked like for they had seen them in the wash. I was ready to continue the conversation with them, but the boys decided that they wanted to play. That experience was rather typical of the types of conversations we had that fell under the broad heading of sexuality.

Even though the children were in their teens, their interest was more comparable to children of much younger age. They seemed to want a clear answer to the immediate question and perhaps some introductory idea to the information that might logically follow. Their timing seemed to be that they would take one piece of knowledge, digest it, think about it, make it fit into other information that they had and then, later, come back and ask for another piece of information. Sometimes I needed to remind myself that they were incorporating new ideas and new information into their heads and their experience at a slower pace. Perhaps it was not surprising that Tom was the most ambivalent because he was the one who was the most knowledgeable. Tom learned more quickly than the other boys the appropriate phrases such as penis as opposed to prick, and we heard him reminding the other children. We permitted the use of street language to a certain extent in order to open up communication enough to validate curiosity and to permit the introduction of a preferred word. I believe that Tom understood some things more quickly than the other children and that we were able to support his pride by helping him become a teaching, sharing person with some of these things. Mark was the only boy who understood the how and why of intercourse, but both he and Tom comprehended the fact that a baby lives within its mother before birth. They understood pregnancy of cats, dogs, and humans. They understood that babies are within mothers for growth reasons, but they did not seem to understand how conception occurs. I was not sure that any of the boys would really understand this until we used graphic material. Except for Mark, they did not comprehend the act of intercourse because they had no awareness of female body parts.

Parents often do not know the various sexual experiences their children have during their youth. We were equally in the dark about our boys. We had no idea as to what type of sexual acts they may have observed or participated in within the institution. We tried to help the boys understand and accept the concept of privacy. The fact that two boys shared a room left the opportunity for experimentation to take place between them. There might have been almost any kind of sexual activity between the boys in their own rooms, but I am confident that there was no exploitation of one boy by another, and that is the important issue. I think that if there was any mutual masturbation or other sex play between any two boys, both boys were willing in the exploration. There was no evidence that any boy was coerced or forced into an experience he did not want.

There was one observed incident in the house where one boy was lying on top of another boy fully clothed. There was no evidence of roughhousing. One evening Dwight went up the front stairs to do something with the children. As he walked down the hall he passed one of the bedrooms where the door was open. Two fully clothed boys were observed lying with each other. He said nothing. He continued down the hall to the poolroom. Immediately the two boys joined him there. There was no indication of clothes being disarrayed and no indication of arousal on either boy's part. However, it would have been naive not to recognize that there could have been sexual experimentation.

Looking ahead after three years, this is not an area of heavy worry for us. I think that because of our personal preference we would rather the boys move toward heterosexual experiences. However, we will not be concerned if the boys have homosexual experiences. Wade and I accept the idea that same sex exploration is a part of growing up, one way of learning about one's own body in relation to someone else's. The important issue for us is to teach the respect of oneself and respect for another person and respect for others outside of the twosome. We believe that the boys are learning that. They are learning that they do not have to be part of something if they do not want to be, but that it is acceptable to be a part of something with another person if both desire the experience. The adherence to privacy, self-respect, respect for another person is preparing the boys to be tender, caring, touching in consummating types of relationships with other people in ways that are respectful. If that means that the boys will go through stages of same-sex experimentation or arrive at maturity where same sex is their preference so be it.

The opportunities for heterosexual relationships for retarded citizens is very limited at the present time in Michigan. Pragmatically, in Michigan in 1977, given the level of functioning of our boys, given the rigidity of the state system, given the choices that are out there in terms of alternate living for them as adult males, it is quite likely that their sexual expression will be limited to the same sex or own self. As foster parents, we would like the boy first to learn self-respect, and then respect and caring for another person. It is not of primary importance to us if the person is of the same or the opposite sex. If a boy, girl, man, or woman can learn to care respectfully for self, flagrant or inappropriate public behavior will not occur. We hope the boys in our home will learn that touching is necessary and wonderful. To experience caring, attending, touching, and loving with another person is a wonderful thing that should happen for everyone. If our boys are, in fact, destined to be limited to consummating experiences with their own peers reflecting similar levels of development, it may be of even greater importance to emphasize the opportunity to learn to touch and care. Wade and I have had many experiences with men and women who grew up in state institutions who were not taught either self-respect or respect for other people. Unfortunately, after leaving the institution these young persons were apt to have bizarre experiences that were injurious to themselves and extremely offensive to the community. We want something different for the boys who live with us.

It is our intention that before the children leave our home as young adults, they will understand the range of options open to them as adults including masturbation, homosexuality, and heterosexuality. We hope that the boys will learn that there are responsibilities that go along with the privileges of being sexually involved. We hope the boys will learn to protect themselves from unwanted pregnancies and to care for themselves in terms of hygiene and protection from venereal disease. We hope they learn that sexual expression is a part of a total relationship. We hope that they can avoid promiscuity. We will not teach these boys that marriage and family are necessarily for them. We would try to help them recognize all the responsibilities that go along with being a husband and father and help them recognize for themselves whether or not they are capable of meeting those responsibilities. We expect to be able to do that.

We are very aware that the boys have learned that they cannot meet the responsibilities of driving a car. They are learning in our home that driving big machinery is not possible for them because they cannot accept the big responsibilities. We hope that before they leave our home they will begin to understand the responsibilities of marriage and family and that they are not able to accept those responsibilities. However, that does not say that we think they should be refused the right to learn in our home how to be private, sexually knowledgeable young men.

In order to help the boys learn about their bodies and the responsible enjoyment of them, we have attempted to respond to all questions as they are asked. Unfortunately the boys do not ask questions very often. We have intentionally opened discussions about sexuality and have introduced facts and ideas. We try to take advantage of every opportunity to discuss the responsibilities and privileges in human relationships.

Once Mark learned to use the phone, he enjoyed calling a girl he had met at school. Like other teenagers they enjoyed lengthy conversations. Since both of them were very dependent upon parents and teachers, the telephone time was very important for it was a rare time to be spontaneous and unsupervised in their interaction. Mark became troubled when his girl friend began to pressure him to marry her. "I'm not old enough to get married, but she wants me to marry her in the church," Mark shared with us at the dinner table. "She says you get babies by eating popcorn." We were relieved when Mark assured us, with a laugh, that he knew babies did not come from popcorn.

Over a period of several weeks and innumerable phone calls, Mark reported that the girl friend wanted to talk too much about marriage. "I just want to be friends," he said so he decided to "cool down" the relationship. He handled her threats to tell Wade that they had been kissing in the school bus, by saying, "I've already told him." He had also discussed with us what parts of her face and body were all right to explore while kissing her on the bus.

We have in our home some simple drawings that were prepared for distribution by the Planned Parenthood Association in Seattle, Washington. This set of ten illustrations depicts facts about sexuality that we believe the boys should learn. Through studying the drawings the boys should be able to learn the difference between men and women, boys and girls, and the differences between the adult and young person of the same sex. They will get some understanding of masturbation, information about the erect as opposed to flaccid penis, and facts about intercourse. During the next several years these pictures will be used over and over again. They will be studied and looked at, questions asked and answered repeatedly.

Presently Phillip is the only one interested in picture books. He is the only one who enjoys going through a magazine, catalog, or a book of any sort but his fascination is related to numbers. I have no way of knowing how long it will take or how many different ways we will answer the questions or how many different ways we will introduce the material. We are confident that this sort of material will be the resource that we will rely on most heavily to buttress our own candor and commitment to the boys as we try to help them learn the important aspects of privacy, ownership, and territory as they apply to human fulfillment.

12

Difficult Behavior

SOMETIMES IT WAS DIFFICULT, but Wade and I tried to remember why the boys lived with us. They lived with us so that they could begin to assume responsibility for themselves and their actions in an ever-broadening range of situations. Because of the great disparity between their chronological ages and their level of functioning, it was important for Wade and me to establish goals for growth and development *for* the boys, not *with* them. This was a challenge for us. Both of us tended to view Tom, Andrew, and subsequently Phillip and Mark as persons who functioned at a level comparable to their ages. Yet when we stopped to think we remembered that Phillip was a boy with retardation and speech delay. When we stopped to remember we realized that Tom presented several behavioral concerns, as well as retardation. Frequently, however, in the immediacy of a situation we were tricked into assuming that we were negotiating with a thirteen-year-old, a fifteen-year-old, or an eleven-year-old. We had to remind ourselves constantly that these children were not able to negotiate on their own behalf. We had to learn to back up, slow down, and accept the awesome responsibility of planning *for* teenagers, as opposed to planning *with* them as we had with Jori and Frosty. This was not all bad, for because Wade and I had a tendency to see them as functioning at age level, we had a tendency to open up their world with high expectancies.

We began to realize that each of the boys needed to learn what it meant to be responsible for himself, for owning his behavior, for knowing what he was doing. It would have been a great achievement if each boy could also have learned *why* he did what he did in a

particular situation. Given the age of each boy and the level of functioning that he presented at the point that he came to live with us, it
seemed to Wade and me that we should try to help each boy learn to
match the appropriate action to a situation at the right time in the
right place. If it was possible to help the boy learn the reasons *why*
an action was taken, we were grateful. However, we did not believe
that the nuances and complexities of understanding the why of behavior was within the reasonable reach of any of the boys. We
settled on a couple of trite phrases that we used as a way of interpreting to the children why a particular behavior was appropriate,
expected, and respected in certain situations. We relied on saying to
the children, "Other people will like you better if ____ " or "Other
people will accept you better if you know how to ____ ." The constant repetition of those two statements was the extent that we
tried to help the children understand the reasons behind what was
expected of them.

As we approached the management of behavior we thought of it
in positive terms. Wade and I believed that we did not need a long
list of restrictions, a long list of don'ts.

Andrew and Phillip responded very well to the limits set upon
them. It was a different story with Tom.

Tom needed to test. He had quickly learned to respect property,
so over the years any willful property damage was always directed
at his own things. Gradually in our home he discontinued most of
his self-abusive behaviors. He retained the habit of pretending to
bite his arm as he threw an obscene gesture at whomever was
bothering him. Frequently, he approached another person with his
left arm up to his mouth as he pretended to bite it while with the
right hand he reached to grab and pinch the other person. This
behavior began to diminish, but it did not seem to be enough to
remove him from the situation or to deny him privilege. On one occasion when he pinched one of the boys rather severely, Wade asked
Tom if he had any idea of what it felt like and Wade pinched him.
That served to be a good deterrent. Wade told the other boys they
did not need to take any kind of pinching or slapping from Tom.
After that the other children were capable of saying to Tom, "Get
your hands off. Don't you touch me. Don't you pinch me," and Tom
was able to restrain himself when so reminded.

On one occasion Tom missed the school bus and as a result the
following day the bus was not scheduled to stop. Wade believed that
Tom was capable of going to the foot of the sidewalk and flagging

down the school bus so that it would stop for him. I was apprehensive about this idea because we lived on a very busy street. Wade assured me that it would be perfectly safe. There was no question but that the bus driver would see Tom and stop the bus, slow down traffic, and Tom would safely get on the bus. I kept protesting, "What about all the other cars whizzing by before the school bus comes." But Wade stubbornly stated, "Tom will know to stay on the bottom step of the porch steps until he sees the bus coming." I was incredulous and continued to protest. Finally, out of exasperation, Wade said, "Do you remember our deal? I've listened to all of your ideas, I insist that it be this way." I was furious. But I backed down and went into my bedroom from where I could look out upon the busy street to see what would happen. It happened just as Wade predicted. Tom stayed on the bottom step until he saw the bus coming down the street at which point he went to the foot of the sidewalk and waved. Since that day Tom has been responsible for catching the school bus and coming in from the school bus without having a parenting person stand at the door. A big lesson was learned.

That was typical of many situations that developed during the three years. Wade was more able than I to let the boys take risks. I knew that about myself so I frequently backed down when Wade was insistent upon a point. In every instance, it turned out that his position was correct. But then there was the one time Tom was in need of a new bicycle. He had grown so tall that he had outgrown the bicycle that Wade had given him a couple of years before. I wanted Tom to be able to have the bicycle for Christmas of '76. Wade just as emphatically did not believe that was appropriate since Tom was persistent in dismantling his bicycle and resistant to the task of reassembling it. We both had our reasons that we adhered to so stubbornly that we arrived at an impasse. However, Wade was agreeable to having a discussion with a third person whom we both respected and felt would be objective in such a discussion. Subsequently we discussed the issue of Tom's receiving a larger bicycle for Christmas of 1976 with our friend. He helped us move to an acceptable compromise.

We decided that Tom would be given a new bike for Christmas with the understanding that he absolutely could *not* take it apart. He would be helped to understand that the upkeep and maintenance of the new bike would be under *Wade's* exclusive supervision. He would be permitted to dismantle and reassemble his old, smaller bike as frequently as he wished. That has been the only incident where we have felt the need to have someone help us with our concerns about our own feelings and attitudes about what should happen with the children.

When the boys came to live with us there was nothing they liked better than eating. Anything they could put in their mouths was about the best reward of all. The traditional things such as candy, ice cream, cookies were highly prized. Soon they began to realize that to go out to eat combined two pleasurable things—an outing and food. That became the most powerful reward that we had. Each of the boys was anxious to be socially acceptable and so they loved to go places. As with all of us they enjoyed being praised and they enjoyed being praised publicly. We have found that for one boy to receive praise in front of the other children served as a great motivator for the other children to attempt to catch up to also get that praise. Each boy enjoyed special times when he was the one child with a particular adult. As they grew older the sharing of time became the most prized reward for the boys with the possible exception of Tom who still liked to taste his pleasure immediately.

As the boys learned more specific behaviors, more sequences of behaviors, and more patterns of behaviors, it was no longer possible to give immediate praise for each accomplishment. Periodic reminding of the fact that something had been learned and learned well was acceptable.

During most of the last year Tom did not need to say to me, "I don't mess my clothes anymore, I don't dirty my underpants anymore," because he had internalized his pride. He was proud that he could take care of himself so well. That did not stop me from occasionally saying to him, "Gee, Tom, it's hard for me to remember that there was a time when you did not do that. And look it's been months since you've had an accident. Isn't that wonderful!" So the children got recognition for their growth steps immediately, occasionally, and sometimes in the historical perspective. We learned that if a child was having a great difficulty with one particular unit of behavior at the dinner table it helped to take the pressure off by recognizing publicly something that he did with excellence. Tom was being monitored constantly about the rapidity with which he ate and it must have been an irritation for him. I'm sure that he took heart when he heard one of the adults at the table saying, "Gee, Tom, you know how to serve salad very nicely."

There were times when the boys felt inadequate in dealing with situations. Mark tended to wheedle. Andrew was more capable of asking for assistance and support in a non-whining or compromising manner than the other boys. Phillip tended to wait and see what was going to happen and then cautiously followed the lead of the adult. Tom responded to a situation that he expected to be a problem by having a tantrum. Gradually his self-confidence developed and he began to approach new situations with less need for acting out. I believe that Tom was able to try more and more things because he saw the other boys doing it with safety. He experienced the encouragement from the parents involved and he was daily more secure in his home setting.

The boys required a tremendous amount of affection. They needed a lot of hugging and horseplay. Wade and I had some difficulty with this. We were, by nature, somewhat reserved people, and it was not our habit to be demonstrative in public places. I knew there were times when each of the children wanted more public display of affection and attention from us than we were able to provide them. I felt a little guilty about that. Wade was practical and took the position, "That's the way I am and the boys need to know that I love them the way I do. They cannot have everything on demand. That's not the way the world is." But I got caught up in my own guilt at times and thought about what it must have been like to be those children when they were little boys, growing up in a barren institution where there was never any cuddling, hugging, or attending by parenting people. I sometimes felt as though I ought to replenish all that was missing, but I was extremely uncomfortable with myself doing that. So once again I had to deal with my own ambivalence. There was no question in my mind but the boys knew how much we cared for them and how much we were committed to living, learning, and loving with them. There were times when I wished that I could be more cuddly. But it did not come easily for me—which brings me to the whole business of handling a crisis.

When a boy had a crisis a parenting person had to help him get in touch with his pain, his anger, his hurt, his frustration, his anxiety, his physical need. As an outsider I had to communicate somehow to the boy who was having the crisis that I must be in touch with it, be a part of it, and share it. I never believed that it helped anybody to say to them, "I wish I could take that from you" if I could not touch the person when I said it to them. Even though it was difficult for me to be joyous and physically free with affection in easy times, for some reason I had no problem in reaching out and using myself overtly and physically in situations when the boys were in pain. Certainly Wade and I were called upon to do this many times through the years with Tom as he needed to have a tantrum. It seems to me that when a person is in a tantrum they are experiencing themselves as scattering through the winds totally out of control of their feelings and actions. Somehow, someone has to hold onto them until they can regain control of themselves. It makes sense to me to hold physically a person who is in tantrum. It makes sense to me to put my arms around the person and allow them to feel the control of my body, the warmth of my body, the strength of my body enveloping them. I do not believe it makes any sense to try to talk a person down from a tantrum when the person's ears are not ready to hear. Tom needed to feel, he needed to feel my body caring enough to commit itself in time and space to help him get his body under control. The only thing he heard was comforting, soothing sounds, like, "Now, Tom, it'll be OK. Get it together, boy. Get it together, calm down. I'm here, hold on."

There were three or four things I tried to remember when a boy was in a tantrum. First, help him protect himself from hurting me or somebody else, and protect him from hurting himself. Second, help him avoid damaging any property. It is bad enough to have to come out of a tantrum and deal with the shame and embarrassment of having lost control of *yourself* without having to add to *your* total shame because you hurt somebody or ruined some article of furniture or damaged the wall or something else. Because of these thoughts that we shared there was no question in our minds as to how to work with Tom during the early months when his one recourse when frustrated was to go into a tantrum. We held him and helped him get it under control. We did this for many months.

We learned to hold him in certain parts of the house and before long the place itself became a security for him. We could say to him, "Hey, come on Tom, you're getting high. Stand in that corner. Face the corner. Sit in the chair, just hold onto the chair." We would seat him in a dining room chair, feet flat on the floor, holding onto the bottom of the chair, facing into the wall. We stood behind him and helped him do that. The concentration that was involved in keeping his feet down and holding onto the bottom of the chair was a discipline that served to help him begin to get himself under control. As the weeks and months went past we were able to recognize when Tom was escalating toward loss of control and moving toward a tantrum. We would say to him, "Hey, Tom, looks like you're getting high. Why don't you go and sit in the chair and face the corner for a few minutes and get it together?" Over a period of time we were able to arrange for a quieting down place practically anywhere we were—the bottom porch step, the bottom step going out of the kitchen, a particular chair in the dining room, the rocking chair in his bedroom, a certain beanbag in the playroom. Over the years Tom began to know ownership of his own behavior and he no longer needed to have the extreme tantrum outbursts that formerly were frequent. He still had times when he cried. He still had times when he screamed. He still had times when he swore and gestured. But he went for months without losing total control of Tom. It was possible to say to him, "Tom, are you getting high? Do you need to sit on the bottom step?" Generally, his answer was no. At that point we could say, "Count to three, Tom." We counted with him, one, two, three, as a reminder to him to collect himself. Every time he tried and won his battle for control of himself, we quickly tried to give some kind of pleasantry to him so he realized that we respected the fact that he was trying to polish this part of his social behavior.

Phillip always tried to maintain control of himself and generally he handled his frustration and anxiety in appropriate manners. Mark tended to sulk. Andrew attempted to emulate Phillip's behavior with his own variations. One day, quite by accident, we learned that Andrew's habit of putting a mask on his face to conceal his feelings could be modified. Frank had observed Andrew throw a play watch of Tom's into a swampy area of the park. It appeared to be deliberate on Andy's part. It was impossible to retrieve the watch. Andrew denied any knowledge of the affair. Frank, Wade, and I joined Tom in being very angry with Andrew. The play watch meant a great deal to Tom; the teacher had given it to him as a reward for some good behaviors. Andrew refused to respond to any questions or comments made to him. He was sitting at the dining room table staring straight ahead. In my anger I slammed my hand onto the table so hard that my hand smarted. It jolted Andrew, his mask of composure slipped, and he answered the question that had been just asked of him.

Subsequently we learned, when he tried to play the "masking game" as we called it, to clap our hands very sharply in front of his face. We did not touch him, but our hands clapped within an inch of his nose. At the same time we said his name sharply, "Andrew!" He would blink and drop his mask and respond. That sharp sound seemed to force him into a reality and he moved to take on responsibility.

As the months went by we no longer needed to clap our hands that way. We could say to him in a sharp voice, "Listen, Andrew," and he would own up to the situation and respond. His answers were tentative and soft-voiced, more softly spoken than usual, but he did answer and he did engage himself in the real situation. Later I noticed that he tried to play the game with new people, but in each instance, as soon as we clued the new person into the way to circumvent his game, the game ceased. He was beginning to be responsible for his own behavior and made progress in accepting responsibility for his mistakes and minor accidents.

Tom would have tried the patience of a saint. If there were ninety-nine options I swear he would find a hundredth. He was very, very challenging. Tom could stand in front of you, stare into your face, pull a caper, and deny it. It was as though, even as he was doing it, he was saying, "Not me, Wade; not me, Magoo"—after having just done it! Later, however, there were two incidents which allowed Tom to move ahead by leaps and bounds in terms of accepting responsibility for himself. He was involved in an incident where a decanter was broken and some liquor spilled on the Chinese rug in the dining room. There were two issues: roughhousing indoors and property damage. The incident happened one evening when Mike was working with the children so we heard about it when we returned. Michael told us that the boys were aware that they had broken a limit and they were very worried. Frankly, I was so angry by what had happened that I made the decision not to do anything about it that night. That was hard for me to do because it was my father's decanter that was broken. When we went upstairs to tell the boys good-night, they were wide awake expecting to stand accountable. We said nothing except good-night.

Next morning I had to handle the situation alone because Wade had gone off to play golf and it was my morning to follow wake-up routine. The boys were on their best behavior. It was clear that they had been worried for some time about what I was going to do about it. I told them to go into the bedroom and wait for me. I sat on the edge of the bed and said, "Now before either of you guys says anything I want to tell you something. Nobody gets punished in this house for telling the truth. I'm going to ask you some questions and you tell me the truth and there will be absolutely no punishment at all. It is very important to me now that you tell me the truth. But I will tell you that if you lie to me I will know it and I will punish you." At that point I said to Tom, "I want to start with you. Will you please tell me what happened last night." And he said, "We were roughhousing." "Where?" "In the dining room." "What happened?" "I pushed Andy into the cupboard." "Then what happened?" "The bottle fell over." "Then what?" "It broke and spilled all over the rug." At that point I said to him, "Tom, I am very pleased with you. That was very, very good to be so truthful and tell the truth." I talked for quite a few minutes about why it was so great that he had acknowledged his responsibility. Then I turned to Andy and said, "OK, it's your turn now. What happened last night?" Obviously, he had seen that Tom had safely survived telling the truth so he presented the same story. I told them I was pleased with them for having told me the truth and that was the important thing.

They needed to know that I was hurt that the decanter was broken for it had been my father's and there was no way of replacing it. I went on to assure them that we could get the stain out of the rug and that was not a concern. I asked them how they would feel if all of a sudden their bikes were broken. They both acknowledged that they would feel very badly. I said, "Yes, the difference would be if I ran over your bikes with my car, I could buy you a new one. But with my father's beautiful bottle I can't go buy a new one. So you need to understand that I am hurt by that, way down deep in my stomach. But that's my problem now, not yours. It was an accident, you did not do it on purpose, you didn't break it to hurt me, I know that. I know that you did not intend to be mean to me. It was because you were careless and you were roughhousing where you should not have been." Then we talked about where people should roughhouse. It was an outdoor game and it was wrong to play in the house where accidents could occur. I told the boys that I was going downstairs to start breakfast and as far as I was concerned there was no need for any more discussion. I was ready to be friends again. I told them that I had not talked with them about the accident the night before because I was so hurt and angry that I did not know what I would do.

That was the end of the incident as far as I was concerned. About a half hour later I was asked, "Can I help you put the rug back and the things away when the rug dries out?" I felt that was a real attempt to make it right. There has been no conversation with the boys about this since then. However, I did tell everybody that came into the house for the next two or three days how responsible the boys had behaved and always so they could hear. As I think about it now I am sure my father would have believed that that was a good use of the decanter. If all it takes to have a boy learn to be honest and acknowledge a careless accident he has experienced is to break a decanter, it is a small price.

Three days later Tom had another big test. He was roughhousing on the porch with Michael. He raised his head in such a way that he hit Michael on the chin, causing him to bite his tongue. Hurt and angry, Michael said to Tom, "Get out of my way. I will sit here and cool off before I do anything." Tom went into the kitchen and started playing around with the electric stove. He turned the stove on and ignited a piece of paper toweling that he had in his hand. He was scared when he realized that the paper was burning and attempted to put it out by opening the kitchen door and throwing it outdoors. In the process he dropped it on the porch carpeting. At this point Michael saw what was happening and stamped the fire out, but not before a hole was burned in the carpeting.

When I arrived home the other boys were quick to tell me what Tom had done. He was out playing somewhere so I called him to me. Again, I said to him, "Tom, I want to remind you that you do not get punished for telling the truth. Sometimes there may have to be some kind of consequence that will have to happen. But you are not punished for telling the truth. Now let's start and you tell me exactly what happened this afternoon." He again went through every step of what happened and acknowledged every action. "I was roughhousing. I hurt Mike. I played with the paper towel in the kitchen. It caught on fire on the stove. I threw it out on the porch and burned the rug." Again, I gave him full praise for being truthful. It seemed to me that Tom needed to feel some unpleasant consequence because the naughtiness concerned fire. We talked about how dangerous it was for anyone to play with fire because someone could be hurt or the house could burn down. We would all be in serious trouble, with no place to live. I told him that there had to be a punishment. There had to be some unpleasant happening so he would always remember and never play with fire again. Knowing how much he loved to go out to eat, I said that he would have to forego that pleasure. The next time anyone went out to eat he would go along but he would have to sit there and have nothing. That was the punishment.

The following weekend the boys went out to dinner. Tom went along too, to a newly opened pancake house. Everyone was excited and had complete dinners. Tom sat through the entire meal without so much as a glass of water. He understood why he was denied the special treat even though several days had passed since the unfortunate affair. He told me, "I can't have anything to eat tonight because I started the fire." In our judgment it turned out to be a fair way to handle it. He was given a lot of recognition and praise for being truthful and acknowledging his action. He had to pay the consequence and he was reminded that he had done something to make it right. He had paid the price, or the fine. He had a clean slate. That made everything all right again. Later, when he looked at that burnt place on the carpeting he did not have to feel badly about it because he had paid for it. We thought we had learned how to help Tom continue to be truthful. We said to the children in a situation such as that, "Tom, before you say one word, remember, there's no punishment for telling the truth. We will respect you for being truthful and acknowledging what you did. We may have to do something to make the mistake right." It seemed to work with the boys.

It bothered me to know that lying had worked in the state institution. If Tom learned honesty in our home, it might not work for him in the future depending upon where he might live later on. It was a value in our home to be honest, to stand up and be responsible for your own behavior. As long as he lived in this type of situation it would be good for him to be trustingly truthful. How could I guarantee that when Tom left us to live in a group home somewhere or to work in a sheltered workshop that his ability to stand up and be responsible would be equally valued? I hated to think that he would be in a situation sometime where he would be punished for having followed through on a value that he had learned in our home. I hoped that what we were teaching him would not turn out in some way, somehow, to be dysfunctional for him.

Tom was so overt in all of his behavior that it seemed as though we were forever concerned with him. Andrew, who gave the impression of being well-behaved and well-mannered a good share of the time, was capable of pulling sneaky tricks on people. I expect that when two or three boys live together there's bound to be a certain amount of jealousy and acting out upon that jealousy. We certainly had some of this in our home, especially on Andy's part. He was apt to destroy some precious article that belonged to whomever he was angry at at the time. This destruction was always directed at one of the boys; it was never directed at one of the grown-ups. Andrew was apt to let his resentment build up against Phillip over a long period of time and then he would be hateful in some particular way. For

Christmas of '74 Phillip received a record player. Andrew was resentful of this, but limited himself to making angry remarks. Finally he walked into Phillip's room, removed the needle from the record player, and threw it away—a pretty explicit message to Phillip as to what he thought about that. In this instance Andrew acknowledged that he had thrown the needle away and accepted the punishment that was given to him. A few months later on his birthday we gave him a record player for his very own. We told him that he was getting the record player because he had done so well in the recent weeks in respecting Phillip's property. Now he could have one of his own.

I am not sure that he understood all that. It seemed important at the time to tell him because there were times along the way when we noticed that Andrew identified someone's very precious belonging and needed to destroy it. He may have done that because he was covetous about the other person's having it, but he knew that he could not have it, either. That may have been his motivation when he destroyed Tom's watch. I think that Andrew's covetousness had become more pronounced because Tom had been willing to share. It was an extremely hateful action for Andrew to throw it away. Subsequently, as described earlier, he acknowledged he had thrown it away but he was not able to tell us why he needed to do it. The punishment that we designed on that occasion we hoped fit the situation. We told Andrew that we were going to take Tom upstairs with him and that Tom could select anything of Andrew's that he wanted and he could have it. Tom went to the toybox and selected a toy of Andrew's and took it. Wade, Frank, and I said, "OK, from now on that belongs to Tom, you may not play with it again." Andrew was terribly upset. He sat down and cried and cried because he knew he could not have it any longer. I believe that he did experience some kind of pain, some kind of punishment, maybe even some kind of remorse for that act, but I am not convinced that he necessarily learned a lesson.

The last incident we had with Andrew just before this narrative closes had to do with his taking Michael's wedding ring. In order to do some task that was messy, Michael had taken his wedding ring off and put it on a table. When the task was over he went looking for the ring and it was gone. We searched and searched to no avail. Eventually the wedding ring turned up because Andrew remembered that he put it in the lilac bush. Once again, when he was confronted, he acknowledged that he had taken the ring. We think that he may have picked up the ring to carry it around because he liked Mike so much. We talked to Andrew a great deal about how it was a mean thing to do to pick up Michael's wedding ring. We explained that the wedding ring meant very much to Michael and that if it ever had been lost he would feel badly. I think he understood and in the future will leave Michael's ring alone. I really do believe that in that particular case Andy had such a deep affection for Mike that he wanted to have something of his, to own, to have with him. We also noticed that Andrew hung onto his most precious objects. There are certain articles of clothing that he wore over and over again. When he got a piece of mail he carried it for days and weeks until it was frayed.

Managing behavior when children are in crisis is a challenge to foster parents even as it is to biological parents. Children with whom we have lived as long as we lived with these boys become a part of your family, part of your world. We began to have family expectancies, parental expectancies. We wanted the boys to look well, to behave well because they were extensions of our ego, our home. We began to feel irritations and frustration because they did not reflect as well upon us and upon our child-rearing techniques as we wanted them to. I knew that there were many times when I was very angry with one of the children and after the experience tried to come to some understanding as to why I had been so provoked. When I really thought it through, it was my disappointment in the way they were not meeting my expectations for them as a result of my *magnificent* parenting! Thank God we had access to so many resources, so many skillful and talented friends, so many good books. We tapped our friends for spontaneous and informal consultations. We read a lot and learned new techniques daily about working with the children. As I reflect about our learnings and the things we came to do with the children, it is amazing but true that most of the things we learned had to do with how we managed ourselves and our own behavior.

The boys began to feel good about themselves and proud about their accomplishments. At the end of three years the boys were able to completely take care of themselves and assume total responsibility for such tasks as toileting, bathing, dressing, eating, and playing. Tom still needed monitoring at mealtime. Each of the boys needed monitoring and assistance with hair brushing, tooth brushing, and the use of deodorants. It was still ahead of us to teach the boys how to shave and to attend to their adolescent complexion problems.

The boys enjoyed clothes and had complete wardrobes. They had each learned to put away their clothes using the closet and the bureau. They knew to put soiled clothes in the laundry. With an occasional exception they all knew how to dress appropriately for the situation and the weather. Each of the boys knew where to put winter, outdoor clothing, and rain gear so that it could dry appropriately. Each of the boys kept messy dresser drawers but inasmuch as their clothes were primarily of the wash and wear variety it did not create too great a problem. Each of the boys was able to take care of his own bed completely, including changing the linens from top to bottom.

The boys also knew how to take care of their sports equipment and toys. They understood that large outdoor equipment was stored in the garage and that smaller outdoor equipment such as a baseball mitt was stored in their cubbyhole. Their ice skates hung on nails in the basement. Each boy knew that his record player, radio, model car, or toys belonged in his own room when he finished play for the evening. The children took care of their own rooms, the playroom, and the bathroom. They learned to close the drapes when they were dressing or undressing and together they were able to pick up, vacuum, dust, and clean the bathroom. However, no one boy knew all of the tasks; it was a team effort. We needed to rearrange the assignments so that every boy would learn every part of maintaining his room.

In terms of doing chores that benefitted the entire family, the children knew how to set and clear the table, carry out the trash, run the vacuum cleaner, and put things away. Out of doors they were helpful in putting things away and raking leaves or shoveling snow. Gradually, step-by-step, the boys learned how to do the clusters of tasks that I have listed. They accepted the idea that everyone had tasks to do and that the sooner the tasks were done the more quickly everyone was ready to go on to activities of choice. Generally the boys did all chores easily and without resentment. Tom, occasionally, needed to resist and to check out whether the demands were the same as they were the day before. But his needs to test the routine were less frequent and the testing time itself was shorter in duration.

Much of this learning took place because the boys had a series of important rewards that were desirable to them—a treat, a trip out, or praise given verbally. Initially the rewards were always treats. Gradually we reduced the idea of a treat and emphasized the trip out. The next step was to eliminate the treat and just have a trip out. Finally we emphasized the praise and began to eliminate the trip out. Many, many times the verbal praise alone was adequate. It was not uncommon to hear one of the boys saying to another or to one of the parenting persons, "I've done a good job today, haven't I?" I am sure they were more able to accept the responsibilities described because they realized that Wade and I assumed similar responsibilities for ourselves. They were never asked to make our bed. They were never asked to clean our bathroom or to vacuum our living quarters. They were not asked to hang up our coats or put our things away.

We were often asked whether we experienced much damage or breakage with the children. There was little of this. I, too, was expecting that there would be a great deal of breakage, so for the three years I kept a record of the accidents that occurred in which things got broken or got spilled. With two exceptions all of the breakage, all of the spilling, was due to the carelessness of Wade, Frosty, or me. On one occasion Tom, in a tantrum, willfully kicked a pane of glass out of the playroom window, and there was the time the two of them broke the decanter.

Tom was hard on furniture, but this was not a willful thing. In the first three years Tom lived with us he wore out two beds; at the end of three years we bought his third set of box springs and mattress. It is true that there was some use of the bed for a trampoline in the early stages of Tom's living with us, but more important he was an extremely restless child in his sleep. He thrashed around and the bed did not stand up under his harsh treatment. In the playroom the children each had large beanbags that they lounged in when they watched TV. It was Tom's beanbag that split in the seam. Again, this was not willful damage but because of the harsh treatment it got when Tom was in his quiet time, watching television. We considered the replacement of the bed and the beanbag a small investment in terms of the overall operation of our home.

Mark presented some unique problems because he faked seizures. When Mark had been with us a month he decided one morning that he was not going to get up and go to school. Wade talked with him, asked him if he was ill, and he said, "No." Wade explained to him, "Well, Mark, if you are well, you go to school. If you are not feeling well enough to go to school, then you will spend the day in bed." Mark laughed at him and said to him in the most seductive voice, "Oh, you wouldn't do that Wade." So Wade walked out of the bedroom, went downstairs, and said no more. After the school bus had come and gone, Mark came downstairs and asked if he could have breakfast with me on the porch. I permitted him to do that. When he was sitting on the porch with me he told me that he had stayed home so that he could help Wade mow the lawn. I explained to him that he was not going to be able to do that. As soon as he finished his breakfast he was going directly to bed to spend the day without television or toys. Since he had made the decision "No school," I was making the decision that he was going to have to stay in bed. He told me that I would not do that, and I said, "Oh yes I will." In about 30 seconds Mark managed to have a seizure and pitch forward so that his face was in his bowl of oatmeal. I reached over and took his head and lifted it up and said to him, "I will give you exactly 30 seconds to go in and get a washcloth and wash your face and then you come out here and clean up this mess." That was all I said, but I said it in my most angry, assertive voice. He instantly moved and cleaned up the mess. I prepared him another bowl of cereal which he ate. When he finished his breakfast, I said, "Now you *will go* to bed," and he did. He was permitted to get up for lunch and again for dinner. During the day he was aware of the things the other boys were doing. That evening, Wade and I were going out for dinner and Michael was working. The children and Mike started dinner on the porch as Wade and I were leaving. Wade said to Mark, "When you finish your dinner you will go immediately upstairs to bed and you will not play with the boys or Michael after dinner. When I come back I'm going to ask Mike for a report and if you have not followed the directions you will settle with me tomorrow morning." When we returned later that night Michael said that Mark had griped because he had to go to bed after dinner, but that he had done so and had not attempted to watch television. The next morning when Wade went up to see how the kids were doing with wake-up routines, Mark said to him, "I learned something yesterday. I didn't think you really meant it." And Wade said, "I did," and Mark said, "I know you did." So the two of them had a good discussion recalling the previous day. Wade explained to him that "You'd better understand that whenever I tell you that I'm going to do something, I will do exactly that. And there will be no negotiating." Mark was quite impressed by this.

The days passed and we continued to record how many seizures happened every day. We realized that on some days there were as many as five or even eight. A couple of weeks later Wade was making breakfast and packing lunches with the boys when Mark faked a seizure in front of the kitchen stove. The other three boys were standing in the kitchen not knowing what to do. Wade firmly said, "Boys, go in the dining room now and have breakfast." He continued to serve the children and take their food to them. Perhaps as much as five minutes passed. Wade was aware of the fact that during this whole process Mark was watching him with one eye open to check out what was happening. In a sharp voice, Wade said, "Mark, I will give you exactly two minutes to decide whether or not you are going to school or staying home. If you're going to school, get up, get washed, and get into breakfast. If you're going to stay home, get ready for bed." Instantly Mark was on his feet and on his way to join the family for breakfast. We decided that it was time to have a family conversation about Mark and his seizures.

That night after dinner we told the boys we had a serious topic that we wanted to discuss with them. We told them that we had a problem to solve in the family. We talked about the fact that some people had some things that were not quite right about them and that they had to take care of them. For example, Wade had glasses and he had to be responsible for those glasses. He was the one who had to wash them, and know where they were. We talked about the fact that I had arthritis and often it was difficult for me to walk, but, nevertheless, I had to do my own walking. Nobody else could do it for me. Then we talked about seizures. We pointed out to Mark that he had seizures. He knew it, and so did we. It was unfortunate, but he had to learn to live with them. We were going to help him learn to live with them like a man. We were not going to help him or wait upon him, but rather we were going to help him learn to take care of himself. We assured him that whenever he needed to have a seizure that we would get out of his way so that he could have it all by himself. We talked about the fact that as he grew older he could predict more accurately when he was going to have a seizure, and the better it would be for him. He would learn to recognize a feeling, an aura, that would tell him that he was about to have a seizure and that he should respond to that feeling and sit down or lie down, whichever was possible. We promised him every time we saw him moving to sit down or lie down we would get out of his way so that he could do it easily. We also told him that we were not going to talk about it. We were not going to offer to help him or to extend any kind of sympathy messages like "Oh, we're so sorry it happened." We talked about the fact that there were times he pretended and that was something we were going to try to help him learn not to do. We told him that there were ways he could get attention without pretending to lose control of his body because that way of getting attention was not acceptable. Once again, Wade and I stated firmly that we were not afraid of seizures, we were not impressed by seizures, and that it did not matter to us if he had a seizure. We expected him to live by the rules of the house. He would have as many privileges as anyone else, no more and no less, and the fact that he had seizures had nothing to do with it. The final statement that Wade made was, "Oh, by the way, Mark, any day you have a seizure you had better not use your bike or get into the pool."

We began to give him feedback on the days that were exceptionally fine for Mark. At dinnertime a remark would be made such as, "Gee, Mark, you didn't have a seizure all day today. That's really cool." or "Mark, it was really great that you didn't have to pull a fake today. That is really nice." On the occasions that he had slipped, we developed the same style. First, we ignored him until he decided to rejoin the action and the group, at which point the adult nearest to him would say, "Mark, you just faked it. You know it and so do I. Why did you feel the need to do that? That wasn't very cool." In several instances Mark was able to tell us, quite accurately, why he had felt the need to fake. In one instance he said, "I wanted you to do something with me." In every instance we explained to him that when he faked, he only delayed the experience that he wanted so much. Simultaneously, as we saw Mark experiencing a real seizure we gave him positive feedback for managing it. Remarks such as "Gee, Mark, it was neat that you got yourself to sit down that time. That was good." For several weeks Mark reported nightly as to whether or not he had had seizures. This whole process was certainly accelerated by two factors: Mark loved to swim and ride his bicycle. They were very important experiences for him. To lose those privileges because he faked was a strong deterrent to faking.

After living with us for a few weeks, Mark stopped faking seizures in front of Wade and me. He never tried that game with Wade or me, but he might put on a show for a newcomer. He needed to test Michael and he needed to test Bill. I am quite certain that if we had a guest in the home for a week, Mark would find it necessary to fake a seizure in the guest's presence. Recently, our friend the contractor needed to see us about a renovation. Mark felt the need to fake a seizure for some attention. Fortunately for us and for Mark, our friend had been around our home enough and trusted the way Wade managed the other children so he did not react visibly to Mark's behavior. He took his cue from Wade and the two men stepped over Mark's body and went on into another room and continued their business transaction, quite ignoring him. Later we began working with Mark to help him learn not to be as physical with the other boys, and he made tremendous progress in this area. Eventually we will begin to focus on helping Mark stop his whining, wheedling, and cajoling attempts to get his own way. So many people are turned off by his ingratiating attempts that I shall be pleased when he develops a more acceptable way of approaching people with a request. As Mark receives more positive responses for presenting himself as an assertive person with legitimate requests, he will no longer need to be so self-deprecating. He will have developed one more skill in getting along with others.

13

Living with Foster Children

EVEN AS THE BOYS LEARNED how to get along with more individuals outside their peer group, Wade and I needed to learn some things about living so intimately with boys who had handicaps.

Wade maintained an objective attitude with the boys, and his involvement was more detached than my involvement. In addition to his detachment, he was always consistent in his expectations and rigid in his enforcement of limits. I, on the other hand, did not maintain detachment or consistent modeling as well as Wade.

One of the most difficult things for me was sharing Wade with the boys on demand, their demand. I certainly did not anticipate that this would happen. As I look back I realize that I had become accustomed to the many benefits of living alone with my husband. There had been several years when our natural children had been away from home before Tom and Andrew arrived. I had enjoyed the spontaneity that can happen when two people live together, to be able to pick up at any time and go to a movie, go out to dinner, be casual about dress, or to disrupt the routine for whatever reason. I had not anticipated how I would feel about accepting schedules and routines that needed to be maintained for the good of the children. I had been prepared for a few transition weeks, or even months, for the boys to become comfortable in our home and learn to live with us. I recognized that there would be an investment in time that we would have to make, but I had expected that after a few months Wade and I would again move toward the free style of relating to each other that we had been used to for several years.

For the first several months of the boys' living with us, we were caught up in the excitement and the novelty. We were getting used to the boys and they to us. We were renovating a home and doing all the exciting things about refurnishing and decorating an old house. During those exciting days I do not recall being aware of any resentment or feeling that I was being intruded upon by the boys. I had been flattered by all the attention I experienced from Wade as he planned and developed the privacy suite for us on the main floor of the new house. It was fun furnishing those rooms and putting in the mementos of our earlier life together. Then things seemed to change, and I felt suddenly insecure about my place in our family.

From the first day the children lived with us they received the message that they were the highest priority to Wade during all their waking hours. He was with them as their model, teacher, monitor, their authority, referee, and limit setter. He was the person who cared for them every single moment they were awake in his home. When he was not with them, another man was, who followed the directions developed by Wade. Andy quickly accepted Wade and related to him as the authority person in his world. During the first months of living with us, he referred to Wade as Mr. Wade. Gradually, over a period of time he became less formal and called him Wade.

Early in the relationship Tom called Wade "Big Stuff." There was no question but that this was supposed to be a put-down. We surmised that somewhere in an earlier experience Tom had heard people refer to other people as "big stuff" in a derogatory way and he started that in our home. Wade and I turned that around on him; we began to refer to Wade as "Big Stuff" as a family nickname, and finally Tom accepted it on this basis also. Andy had comfortably moved into a pattern of accepting Wade and all the different ways that he related to the boys, but Tom had difficulty with this. Tom needed to test and challenge, thwart and sabotage, every step of the way. There were numerous altercations and confrontations between Big Stuff and Tom, far too many to record. They happened many times each day in those early months. Authority was a big issue for Tom. On one occasion after the boys had been with us for two or three weeks, Wade gave a direction to Tom and Tom turned to him and said, "You can't make me. You haven't got the keys." That struck us as both funny and logical because Wade and I had been around institutions enough to know that attendants carry bunches of keys in a conspicuous manner. People who live in such places quickly come to realize that the person with the keys is the person who has the final say, and since Tom never saw Wade with keys he challenged his authority. One day Tom found some rings that are used to hang shower curtains. He strung them on a thread, tied them on his belt, and went around for several days saying, "I'm the boss. I have the keys."

Down through the months, as the boys learned more and more behaviors that allowed them to function independently, Tom accepted Wade as his foster father. For most of the third year he called him Dad. It was a term that Tom used with affection. There was much evidence that he saw Wade as the most important person in his world, certainly the most important person to love and be loved by.

In the early weeks of living with the boys, I had been caught up in the routine. As soon as I was up in the morning or when I returned from work in the evening, there were several things that I needed to do to help the family function. As the weeks went on, however, and the boys became more competent, they needed less and less of my time as a teaching person. They achieved such a level of independence in self-care, use of leisure time, and houshold chores that they did not need me to provide anything but monitoring, limit setting, and supporting remarks. I was no longer needed at home to be involved in a number of tasks, and home was no longer a constant training experience for me. It became a living experience which meant there were several levels of sharing that took place between the boys and Wade and me. There was a deeper level of sharing. Now the boys wanted to talk with me about all the things that had happened to them during the day, the things that concerned them.

From the beginning Andy always called me Martha, and when Phil and Mark came to live with us they learned to call me that too. In the beginning Tom used to call me Mama and Mommy. I always felt that he was trying to wheedle and manipulate me when he addressed me in those terms. I felt a real insincerity about him, so I did not encourage it. As the weeks and months went on he began to call me a nickname that he devised, Magoo, and Magoo I remain to Tom most of the time. Occasionally I am Martha, but Magoo is his term of affection for me.

Gradually I began to recognize some change in my needs. When I returned from work I knew that I did not have to be involved with heavy responsibilities and so I came home wanting to have some time alone with Wade. The boys were not too anxious to let me have that, and Wade was understanding of that. He thought that if I spent some time with the boys immediately, later on in the evening we would have time to be by ourselves and talk. However, sometimes I had difficulty and really had to surmount my own resentment. I came home, parked my car, dashed into the house, bursting with things I wanted to share with an adult, and I could not do so. I had to siphon off that enthusiasm into another direction for a while. Many of the things that I wanted to share with Wade were not appropriate for family sharing because they would be far beyond the boys' comprehension. It would have been closing them out for us to carry on a conversation that excluded them. I did not think that was fair, but I had a personal struggle in that sometimes I wanted time alone with Wade immediately when I came home. There were times when I wished I could just sit down, put my feet up, and have a drink before dinner with my husband. I realized that it was different twenty years ago with our own children when the roles were reversed and Wade came home at the end of the day because we could share all discussions with our children as their understanding and ability to share in a discussion developed.

Fortunately for us, the boys did very well about respecting our territories. The rule in our house is that we do not invade their privacy areas and they do not invade ours. They learned that lesson well. They never walked into our rooms. They were alert to knocking, and after the first year there was no problem in terms of invasion of territory. The boys never snooped in our papers or things that were lying around on the desk. I knew that I could leave items on my desk or bureau and they would be safe. Often I left different projects on which I was working on the porch or on the table. The boys never got into them. I never went back to look for a needle to find it missing.

Wade thought that the kids had occasionally been in his workshop and had messed around with his tools, but it was not a big issue for him. He seemed to blow his cork when it happened and then he forgot it. He did not seem to need to do anything about it except ventilate. I was bothered by my own feelings about intrusive behaviors, however. I noticed that I began to get a little more comfortable with being able to say to the kids, "I need to talk to Wade alone now." There were many weeks and months, though, when I felt that I owed it to the boys to be available on their demand. Because I felt that I owed them attention, I kept my resentment bottled up in myself, which now seems unfair to me. Finally after two and a half years I tried to be more open about that and to be more comfortable in saying, "Hey, guys, I need to talk to Wade by myself right now. Let us have some conversation by ourselves."

During the third year I also felt the intrusion at swimming time. The first summer every time I went swimming I was teaching children how to swim. The only time I was ever really able to be in the pool for my own enjoyment was late in the evening after all the children had gone to bed. Once all the children learned to swim I was able to step back and assume the role of a lifeguard. I even got to the place where I could sit on the deck or on the porch and monitor them in the pool. I began to find that I preferred to monitor them during their swimming time and then go swimming after they came out. I found that this meant Wade and I could have some time alone in the pool. It reminded me of the old story of the mother who bought the playpen so that she could get in it so that there would be a place that the children could not reach her. I began to realize that in a way the swiming pool was like that for me. I spent two or three hours on a weekend afternoon watching the boys as they swam. When they came out to dry and dress, I jumped into the pool. It was as though I was in the pool and inaccessible, and I could not be intruded upon. Without any discussion on anybody's part we had a whole new routine.

The boys were often swimming when I got home from work in the summer. When I drove into the garage they left the pool to shower and get ready for dinner. While they went through that part of their routine, my husband and I swam. It proved to be a nice time for us. It gave us an opportunity to get caught up with each other after the day and to get tuned in to where the other person was as we approached the evening with the boys. However, I also realized that the boys were beginning to send me messages like, "When are you going to go swimming with us?" These remarks were directed to me because Wade swam with them during the day. He was in and out of the pool several times during the day. He played ball with them, romped with them, in and out of the pool, but as it worked out the children had little in-pool time with me. During the summer of '76 there were many comments like, "Come home early and go swimming with us and teach us how to swim." They already knew how to swim. Obviously they seemed to think I would only swim with them if I were teaching them. I was ambivalent about this, feeling that sometimes I should be able to take that time and spend it with them, but on the other hand, there was another piece of me that did not want to feel that I had to give up a piece of the day that so nicely met my own needs. I rationalized that I had the right to this time because the boys were so insensitive about conversations and interruptions into conversations.

I can remember Jori and Frosty being like that when they were so involved that they would come flying into the house and interrupt whatever was going on so that they could have immediate attention. The boys were typical teenagers and behaved the very same way. I had trouble with that simply because I had had so many years of being the center of attention late in the afternoon. It did seem to me that they always picked a time when Wade and I were right in the middle of something or other that was very important to us, that was exclusive to us. They seemed to know that that was the time to ask the questions. Wade did much better with this than I, because obviously I had not yet resolved it. I was still far too subjective and found myself saying too frequently, "This is my time with Wade, please do not interrupt me." As I said, I justified that to myself by saying they needed to learn that they could not always be the center of attention. They could not intrude upon people in other situations. Although I had all kinds of justifications to make it all right for me to feel this way, I also had some ambivalence about my role and responsibility to them. I was concerned about how deprived they had been and thought that I had to "fill the buckets that were so empty for so long." But another piece of me said, "That's not real. I have a right to attend to me and maintain the most important relationship for me." It was further complicated for me because Wade, most of the time, was able to handle the intrusions with more patience than I. I both respected and resented him for his ability to do so. How tired I was, how weary I was, affected my level of patience or tolerance. Sometimes I think this was the most difficult challenge in parenting for the second time. We had known two different times during more than thirty years of marriage where we had been able to do a lot of things spontaneously together: the first years of our marriage and those years between our two families.

So I lived with my joint feelings. Sometimes I felt selfish: "What's the matter with me that I need to insist that these children let me have this time alone with my husband?" On the other hand sometimes I thought, "Why should I not have that privilege?" At the end of three years I had not resolved it and I am still working on it. I hope that I can work it through so that I do not become bitchy with the boys, so that I can help them realize that I, as well as each of them, have a right to my own feelings. I have a hunch I may struggle with this as long as the boys are with us but that someday the struggle will be easier.

After the first two years I no longer did household tasks for the boys. By that I mean I no longer cleaned their bedrooms or changed their beds. I did not gather up their soiled clothes. I still did all the laundry every weekend. It was something to see such a stack of slacks, shirts, and underclothes piled up. I happened to enjoy that task. The weekends were the only times I went upstairs to check on the bedmaking routine. I made two trips upstairs each week. I went up and down frequently three years before. Now the boys take full responsibility for cleaning the bedroom, changing the beds, cleaning the playroom, and cleaning the upstairs hall. I did not have to do any of the typical housebound tasks for the boys.

People often ask me how the boys viewed me as the absent worker, which was the reverse of most families. In our suburban community the usual pattern was that the father went to work and the mother stayed home, or both parents went to work. The boys never questioned our arrangement. That was the condition of our living when they came to our house. From the first day they knew that Wade was home most of the time and I was at home part of the time. They grew accustomed to my comings and goings. It was interesting to hear how they patterned some of their comments to me after what they heard Wade say. The boys were very apt to say, "Have a good day," and when I returned at the end of the day, "How was your day? How did it go today?"

The boys understood that I worked at the University of Michigan and they told their friends that. They were pleased that I brought them things like T-shirts and sweatshirts that had U-M insignias. They told people, "That's where Martha works." They knew that when I went out the door with my briefcase it meant that I was going to work. When I took a suitcase, as I occasionally did, they realized that I was going to be working away from home for a day or two. That was difficult for them to get used to because they associated suitcases with vacations. Later, they realized that a suitcase and a briefcase meant that I was working. Wade with a suitcase meant a vacation. At first the children thought that I was a secretary and they were very interested in knowing about my skills as a typist. Gradually they came to learn that I was a social worker and a teacher. They understood what each of these professional persons did because they had a social worker assigned to them from the agency, and, of course, in the school system they were familiar with teachers.

The boys were usually comfortable with my comings and goings. After three years with us, Tom was fourteen. He was the one who was apt to have an attack of anxiety on occasion. I learned that it worked very well to take Tom aside and say, "Tom, I'm going to tell you something now. I want you to know that I'm going to be away overnight. I'm going to Grand Rapids. I'm taking a suitcase. I'm going to drive and I won't be back until tomorrow night in time for dinner. I want you to be responsible for making sure the other boys understand. Every time they ask, you tell them that I went to Grand Rapids and I drove my own car and that I'll be back for dinner tomorrow night." Tom happily accepted his assignment as the newsbearer and the repeater of the message. As he, with great authority, spread the news to the other boys as to what Magoo was doing, he handled his own anxiety in a way that was responsible. I began to realize that this was a technique we should use more often in introducing new material to the boys. Generally my relationship with the boys was a warm experience.

Unfortunately I had more difficult times with Tom than with the other boys, and some of those times have been quite unpleasant. Tom had to test us in every single way possible. He threw tantrums when he came to live with us and it was not uncommon to have to hold Tom physically until he was under control. Sometimes the holding would last for several minutes during which time I risked getting bruises on my arms and legs. I never minded that. I always felt that when Tom was in a full-scale tantrum he was not in control of his behavior and, therefore, he was not maliciously trying to hurt me. Such was not the case the day Tom deliberately "farted" in my face.

I was sitting in the hallway outside the bathroom waiting for the children to complete their showers so that they could start the bedtime routine. Wade was in the bathroom monitoring the showering, and Tom came streaking out of the bath, running into the bedroom to get his pajamas naked as a jaybird, and as he went by me he deliberately sashayed as close to me as he possibly could and passed gas in my face. I never even thought. My hand whipped out, cracking him a sharp slap on his fanny. I was furious with him. He was so surprised that I had slapped his bottom that he turned around, eyes filled with tears, and began to cry, and I just glowered at him and in my sternest voice said to him, "Don't you ever do that to me again." He has not. Tom needed to learn that he had been extremely insulting. He had offended me, and I am not sure that he had ever had such a straight-out confrontation with what his own behavior did to other people.

There were some beautiful times with Tom, too. In our third year together, there was a most unusual occasion in our home. On this particular evening, when we had finished dinner, Tom asked to be excused and he came back to the table carrying a large piece of birthday cake which he gave to me along with a hand-printed birthday card. He wished me a happy birthday. It was not my birthday. There had been a party at school that day and there had been a piece of cake left over. Tom had gone to the teacher and told her incorrectly that it was Magoo's birthday. So the teacher had helped him make a birthday card and wrap up the birthday cake to bring home to me. Tom brought it home and put it in the refrigerator and left it unwrapped until dinnertime. At the appropriate time he presented it to me as a surprise. He was most insistent that I not share it with anybody including him. I had to eat it all by myself because it was my birthday cake. To me that experience was a demonstration of Tom's growth. This child three years before had crammed every morsel of food he saw into his mouth unless he was carefully monitored. This child had had difficulty with secrets and delayed pleasures. It was a meaningful sharing and, of course, Wade and I gave him *much* positive feedback because of it. As time went by the children came to realize that they were accepted and respected in our home and that this idea was acted upon and not discussed. They came to trust us and rely on us. I believe that it was because of this trust that they were able to move toward establishing meaningful relationships with other people.

All the boys changed, developed, and matured a great deal during our three years together. Now I am glad we kept all those records for we can document their progress and brag about how they have achieved their goals.

Of all the boys Tom demonstrated the greatest progress and he gave evidence of being able to achieve still more. We had mixed feelings living with Tom. On the one hand, when we reflected about the changes in him in the last three years we were pleased with him. On the other hand, when we identified those irritating actions that Tom persisted in doing we became quite aggravated with him. After attending two years in a special classroom for trainable boys, Tom began to attend a special program provided by our school system for teenagers and young adults. He made reasonable adjustment to his new situation—reasonable in terms of Tom, difficult in terms of the school teacher, psychologist, principal, and others.

Tom looked like a different boy than he did three years before. He was very tall and quite slim. No longer did he pull out his hair, pinch, or bruise himself. We no longer observed him biting his arms, although the scars of earlier episodes were still evident. He would still rather run than walk, and he approached every flight of stairs as though they should be accomplished in units of threes or fours. Generally his way of getting into a chair or sofa or onto a bed was to attack it, a running jump toward it. However, we were beginning to notice some changes in this. He was able to sit still longer and attend to a situation for more minutes than before. We still saw him standing by the gate, jumping up and down in one place when there was nothing else to do. However, increasingly he had more to do in that he had a wider choice of activities when he went out to play. Cautiously I make the statement that he was doing better at the table. He had quickly learned to be a considerate boy in terms of "Please," "Thank you," and "May I be excused." He always had been gracious and helpful in passing plates and serving dishes. Of all the children he was best able to serve himself neatly from a salad bowl. However, it was difficult for him to learn to eat his meal slowly and try to chew his food with his mouth closed.

Tom took complete care of himself. He no longer had any kind of toileting accidents, although Wade still got him up at 11:30 to go to the bathroom. Wade told me that it was not uncommon for Tom to be almost awake when he spoke to him. We expected that it would not be long before Tom would find himself waking up to go to the toilet in the middle of the night. Tom liked his clothes and enjoyed putting on his very best outfit for special occasions. Tom no longer had to miss outings with the other children. That indicates how much he had his behavior under his own control.

Tom really was doing *very* well. It was true that he was the most aggravating, irritating, demanding boy in the house. At the same time he was the most affectionate, lovable, generous, and forgiving. There were times when Tom was so happy with himself and the way he was getting in harmony with Wade or me that he would fall apart; he disintegrated. He made me think of a little puppy that had just had a bath and had to shake all over to shake the water off. That's just the way he appeared—he was so happy, so pleased with himself, so pleased to feel the acceptance coming from this man whom he adored that he seemed to be momentarily shattered with that joy. Sometimes it was more difficult to help Tom after one of his joyous highs than it was when he had had some minor disaster. Tom was doing so well that that in itself caused a dilemma.

Obviously Wade was right years ago when he identified Tom as being a child who had the instinct to survive and a lot of strengths that would help him survive. Because he had done so well and learned so much, we had a tendency to become impatient because he did not learn *more* things faster. It was as though he taunted us; he acquired a long list of things he could do and then to control the situation he refused to learn the next thing. For example, Tom had never learned to count beyond two. He absolutely could not comprehend beyond that unit. Three, ten, twenty, could all be the same. He seemed to have no sense of which one of those words indicated a lot or a few, nor did he recognize written numbers. He had some interesting ways of compensating for this. He would name articles. You could tell him that you wanted enough apples for everyone in the family and he would name apples so that there were enough. But it was not possible for him to count. Wade and Dwight had great difficulty with this. They both believed that there was a way to teach Tom to count and understand numbers. They were convinced that he was refusing to learn as a way of being obstinate, naughty, and in control. Wade, Dwight, and I had some spirited discussions about that.

Of all the boys Tom had shown the most progress in getting in touch with himself and liking himself. Most of the time he assumed responsibility for the way he acted or talked. His language improved considerably, although he sometimes could be heard swearing when he was by himself. Gone were the days of tantrums, screaming, yelling, flailing out with fists and feet, swearing, and name calling. Instead, we had arguing, negotiating, wheeling and dealing, cajoling, pleading, or begging, all carried on in a reasonable voice. Whatever approach Tom used at any given time he used knowing that the result would be determined by the adult working with him. Increasingly the grown-up would say to Tom, "What do you think, Tom? What are you supposed to do now? What is the thing that you're supposed to do now?" It worked like a charm to say to Tom, "What is your name? What are you going to be responsible for right now?" His repertoire was without limits: "Shower," "Wash my hair," "Brush my teeth," "Chew slowly," "Carry out the garbage bag."

Somehow to have Tom acknowledge who he was and acknowledge what his next task or action was going to be helped him realize that he would be responsible for it. It had an extremely positive effect upon his behavior. He showed us that he was learning control of his behavior from within himself.

As a result of all of our talking we began to realize that each of us, in our own way, needed to deal with the fact that it was all right for Tom to (a) not know his numbers; (b) not use his numbers; (c) be retarded; or (d) be brain damaged. We began to realize that this was the issue. The other children in our home had not made fantastic progress and we were not acting as though we expected a miracle to take place for them. In Tom's case, because he had done so well, we had allowed ourselves to slip into the trap of thinking that with a little bit more effort on his part and a little bit more effort on our part, a miracle would take place and Tom would catch up.

We wondered how many parents had done the same down through the years. How many parents had found it difficult to accept the real situation: the limitation or handicap of their child. How many continued to impose the expectation of a miracle on their child and upon the child-parent relationship. It was hard for us to put the dream of a miracle away. It was as if Tom's not learning all of those things was a sign of our failure as parenting people. Of course that is not true, but it felt like a truth for a while. Tom had safely made the transition into the community. He had a long way to go and many things to develop about himself, but he was beginning to realize that he, Tom, had a lot to say about what could happen to him.

At the end of three years Andrew was sixteen. When I remembered what Andrew was like three years before and thought about the way he appeared and acted at sixteen, it seemed to me that there had been little progress compared to the progress the others had achieved. Andrew was in good physical condition. He no longer needed to take an appetite stimulant. He had learned to swim, ride a bicycle, and bowl since living with us. He was very interested in clothes and took good care of himself, including independent toileting. Andrew was a well-mannered boy.

I recall the night I took Andy with me to a large department store. Some clothing had been purchased for him that did not fit, so we went to exchange it. He was a delightful companion. He enjoyed all the new things about going into the store: riding the escalator, moving through the crowds, looking at all the things on display. I had reminded him just as we walked through the revolving doors

"Look with your eyes but don't touch things." If he could get through the experience without touching, I promised to stop and buy a treat on the way home. We exchanged the clothes for Andy, and he was doing so well I asked him if he would be willing to go with me while I did an errand for myself. He said he would like to do that with me. We went up to the ladies' apparel department, and, as luck would have it, I found a couple of articles that I wanted to try on. With much trepidation I asked him if he thought he could sit quietly and wait for me to try on the clothing. "Yes," he thought that would be just fine. So I found an empty seat where I asked him to sit down, and I gave him my coat to take care of because I thought if he had some responsibility it might help him stay in one spot. I was feeling irresponsible when I went into the dressing room because I was aware that Andy was the boy who wandered. I hurriedly tried on the first garment and went whipping out to see how Andy was doing. Andy was sitting in the chair where I had left him and was carrying on a very pleasant conversation with one of the saleswomen. I continued with my personal shopping, finished my purchases, and Andy very graciously stood up and helped me on with my coat. He had been a marvelous boy in that store. On the way out we stopped at a confectionary so that I could make good on my promise. I told him that he could have anything he saw in a certain section of the counter. He looked at me and his first statement was, "Can I get one for Tom too?" I could not resist hugging him right there in the store. I said, "You certainly can. You pick out what you want and we'll buy two." So he picked out a small article of candy and we did buy two. I was pleased with Andy and down through the months and years came to learn that that was a typical way for him to act. He wanted very much to do as well as he possibly could.

Andrew was anxious to be accepted and liked by other people and attempted to mirror the behavior of any person he was with. But he was instantly responsive to any kind of approach made toward him. This was a great concern to us for we perceived Andrew as being extremely vulnerable to such things as sexual exploitation given his good looks, his desire to please, and his inability to make decisions for his own safety. Andrew could be easily influenced into situations that he was not prepared to handle. Andrew was stoical about pain. He seemed to have the notion that it was better to take any kind of hurt without whimpering. A most recent example had to do with skating. Two of the boys wanted to go skating on a bitter cold day. Wade tried to help them accept his recommendation that it was just too cold, but they were just as sure that it was warm enough because the sun was out. Wade and the two children dressed warmly and went down the nearby park to skate. It was so cold that Andrew had a lot of difficulty lacing his skates, soon gave up on the task, and just sat on the snow until Wade asked him, "Are you cold? Don't you think we'd better go home now?" Even with the direct question, Andrew had difficulty acknowledging that he was cold. When they returned from the ice rink Andrew was chilled through. His hands were so cold that it was very difficult for him to put his skates away and take off his heavy boots and jacket, and no one helped him so the process was even longer. Eventually he was out of his winter clothing and was ready to come to the table for lunch. As we walked to the table it was clear every step hurt him, we assumed because his feet were so cold. We said to Andrew and the other boys that when it was cold outdoors, we felt cold and it was OK to say so. The other three boys were perfectly capable of saying they were too hot or too cold, but Andrew just endured. We wondered if he understood the concept. There was one thing we were certain of: he undoubtedly would have stayed at the skating rink all day until some responsible adult had given him the direction to go home. The next day Andrew's knee was swollen and Wade insisted upon a medical check-up. Subsequently it was determined that Andrew had a hair line fracture of his knee cap. He was placed in a knee cast. During the days that followed, as before, there was not a whimper from Andrew, no acknowledgment of pain or discomfort.

During our last three years together we learned some techniques for helping Andrew get in touch with himself and become more responsible for his own actions. He was much more open in his behavior, and he was not as apt to be sneaky in action. After a while he was more likely to answer a confrontation by acknowledging, "Yes, I did it." After two years with us he no longer tattled on other people's behavior. However, he gave little evidence of taking something that he had learned from one experience and applying that knowledge to a similar situation. Andrew did become more comfortable in indicating preferences about many different things: television shows, food, colors, and girls.

Andy liked girls and talked about them quite a bit. He was shy as he discussed the girls in his class, even though he was comfortable with saying such things as, "I kissed her today."

Andrew still continued to have some difficulty remembering the names of individuals. He remembered that he had a father, mother, brother, and two sisters, but he might not remember the names of his sisters and his brother. Andrew continued to attend the special education program provided in our school and did well. The school was content with his progress. They, as well as we, recognized that Andrew was on the verge of learning many things about appropriate sexual expression.

Andrew had also made considerable progress in learning to keep his hands off people. When guests arrived at our home, he might still turn to Wade or me and ask, "Shake hands?" However, his need for reminders was weakening. He had not done as well in learning to keep his hands off *things,* but I reminded myself that "hands off people" was more important.

It was relatively easy for Phillip and Mark to join the family because they came with a certain amount of maturity and behavioral sophistication that put them on a par with Tom and Andrew. They quickly trusted the experiences they observed Tom and Andrew having, and in no time at all they also had a warm relationship with us. There was a certain amount of rivalry among the children, but nothing that was unusual or different from boys in any other family.

Andrew and Mark became friends, and Andy was positively influenced by this relationship.

Phillip also did well in our home. He quickly learned the routines and easily accepted and honored privacy rights. Until Mark joined the family, Phillip had a room to himself. After that, he shared a bedroom with Andrew. This was an amiable relationship for they respected each other, although they were not very close friends. But then Phillip was not close to anyone.

Phillip's mother was surprised that he had learned to ride a bicycle. One day when she came to pick him up she said to Wade, "Do I understand Phillip correctly? He said he had a bicycle?" Wade assured her that that was the case. His mother wondered why Wade had bought him a bicycle when Phillip could not ride it. Wade assured her that Phillip could ride his bicycle. Immediately Phillip was called upon to make a demonstration. He went and got his blue bicycle, climbed on, and rode a hundred yards down the street and back. His mother was amazed and very pleased. She told Wade of their attempts to get Phillip on a bicycle that had training wheels. They had despaired of his ever learning to ride. But ride he did. Phillip was more in touch with his body. He took good care of himself. He was anxious to understand more about it. He was curious about body parts and was beginning to be interested in women. Recently he joined a teen club at a local church. We saw this as an additional opportunity for Phillip to have contact with boys, girls, men, and women with whom he could communicate.

Language was still a problem for Phillip. In the fall of '76 we took him to ISMRRD for a speech evaluation. We learned at that time that there was no physical impediment to Phillip's speech. The evaluators determined that Phillip had an extensive vocabulary that he understood and was able to respond to when other people used it, but he was not using the words himself. The speech evaluator said she believed that he would show an increasing interest in the use of words as he became more interested in relating to other people. We noticed that this was true in our home. Phillip was anxious to make friends and to get along with other people. He learned the names of many people and appropriately used them. He began to understand that to make the effort to talk would make it easier for him to make friends. We learned not to respond to some of his gestures, signals, and gibberish that we understood. Rather, we insisted that he attempt to say the word as slowly and as clearly as possible. We were grateful that he no longer spoke so loudly. Phillip took correction more easily that he did when he first came to live with us. He seemed to understand that we were trying to help him. No longer did he cry or whine when he was confronted with a mistake or was asked to correct some behavior. He was proud of being the oldest boy and knew that he was eighteen.

His eighteenth birthday was an important day. In our home it was not uncommon to have wine with meals. However, wine was never served to the foster children. We told the boys that wine was for grown-ups and that when they were eighteen they could have wine along with other grown-ups at the table because they would be grown-ups too. Phillip knew this and knew that when his birthday came he would be able to have a glass of wine. Of course, we made a big occasion of his eighteenth birthday. There were gifts and a birthday cake, but they were of little importance compared to the bottle of wine. Frosty sat beside Phillip and opened the bottle of wine and served all of the adults including Phillip. As he poured the wine he talked about how Phillip was now a grown-up. He gave Phillip some specific instructions on how to drink the wine: slowly sip it, make it last through your whole meal. It was a nice time between the two. Frosty treated Phillip as a mature eighteen-year-old, and Phillip responded to it. Frosty's bond to Phillip was probably the strongest of all the boys. Phillip had an infectious giggle and his sense of humor was beginning to be apparent and understandable to the rest of us. Frosty and Phillip enjoyed a certain amount of teasing, pushing, and shoving. Phillip was beginning to understand that some of this activity between him and Frosty was the kind of thing that was acceptable to do between men. He was also learning that he should treat me, and other women, in a different way.

Phillip's mother and stepfather were pleased with the progress Phillip had made in our home. They asked if he could be permitted to stay beyond his eighteenth birthday. Wade and I considered this and decided that he could stay at least one more year. Wade thought that as long as the boys got along well together and continued to help each other grow, it would be good to have Phillip stay with us. He agreed that on Phillip's nineteenth birthday he would again assess the situation and discuss with the agency social worker and the parents whether or not Phillip would be better off in some other situation than here with the younger boys.

Mark proved to be a good addition to the family. The other boys accepted him and recognized him as a leader. He served as a model for them and that made him feel competent. It was good for the children to be able to compare their behavior with a person of their own age and to try to acquire some of his skills. Most of the things that the boys learned from Mark were positive.

Mark brought religion to our family. Wade and I had not been involved with a formal church for many years, and that is our preference at the present time. Mark came to us having lived in a home that was rich with religious structure and he seemed to miss that. To meet this interest and need, we arranged for him to join a teen club sponsored by a church in our community. This particular church followed an ecumenical approach to providing religious experiences for people with developmental disabilities. The emphasis of the teen program was to help children and young adults learn the kinds of behavior that would allow them to participate in church services. They were taught some of the words of religion: "God," "Jesus," "Mary," and "Easter," with the intent that they should learn to use these words with reverence and in the appropriate manner, and they had an opportunity to do so. They had an opportunity to learn some of the traditional music, prayers, and rituals of the different churches. Mark enjoyed his participation in this group. However, it did not seem to meet his needs completely. One day he asked me, "When can we go to church as a family?" We will probably have to handle the larger issue with him soon.

Mark accepted the normal routines, schedules, and expectations of our home. He quickly and easily became comfortable with the ideas of privacy, territory, and ownership. Over several months Wade helped Mark assemble a wardrobe and the type of sports equipment that the other children had who lived in our home. It appeared that Mark had never had this kind of attention before. Mark saw this as a statement of affection and acceptance of him by us as his foster parents.

Mark was much more capable of talking about his feelings than the other three boys. He was able to acknowledge that he was very angry, that he hated, liked, or loved. We began to hear the other boys saying the same phrases, but we questioned whether or not they understood the meaning of those phrases as Mark appeared to. He was doing well and Mark would stay with us as long as it seemed to be a growth-producing experience for him. We hoped that that would be a long time because we understood that he had never lived in one place long enough to feel rooted. We hoped that we could provide this for him.

I am sure that his feeling of belonging was a large factor in his virtual ceasing of all fakery about seizures. He no longer needed to do that for attention. It was evidence of his maturity that he learned to recognize the aura or onset of a seizure and hastened to sit down in order to protect himself. No longer did he handle situations by fighting, but rather he learned to talk about his feelings and concerns.

At the point that Wade decided that he would be willing to keep Phillip beyond age eighteen, we had to apply for an adult foster care license. In the state of Michigan, a different licensure was required than the one we had to operate a foster care home for children. Once again, the process started. We had to fill out an application form, find references that would attest to our ability to parent, have our home inspected for health, safety, and security factors. Eventually this was done and we were duly licensed by the state of Michigan. One person, Phillip, was in adult foster care. It made no difference in the way the family functioned. The major difference was that Phillip was now an adult and there were certain privileges that went with that stage that we are trying to help him experience.

Perhaps it was too soon to say, but Wade and I thought that as the other boys approached eighteen we might petition the agency to switch each of them to family care so that they could continue to live with us as a family unit until Tom becomes eighteen. It had been our thought that the boys should move on to other living arrangements by the time they were eighteen. We hoped that within our home they would learn the kind of skills that would prepare them for the kind of life provided in a group home or some other type of sheltered living situation. We began to see that there might be some value in keeping the young men together until such time as they could leave as a group.

I do not believe it will be easy to find the next homes for any of the boys. We have "adultized" them for so long that they will not be content in settings that do not provide the challenge of risking and growing. Unfortunately, many of the homes available to adults with mental retardation provide comfortable custodial care at best. Homes that provide the ever-expanding opportunities to "grow and go" are few and far between. Phillip and Mark are ready for that kind of experience. Andrew and Tom will require situations that have definite structure, limits, and rules that protect even as they allow for growth.

Wade and I have seen some amazing growth on the part of four boys as they have become young men. But that growth and energy on their part only makes more definitive the challenge we must now address. We must help each of them secure the best place possible for growth to continue for them as adults. We must now prepare them to leave us, leave our home, even as Jori and Frosty did so many years ago. The separation is some years away, but it is important to start the weaning process now. Perhaps when they do leave us, we will finally be ready to cease active parenting.

Many things happened to the boys and to the Dickersons. We knew a tremendous satisfaction in the progress that the boys made in our home. We appreciated the rhythm of our life now that we were again a family of adults and children. There is a rhythm in the routine of children. There are expectations when there are children in the home that keep the parents vibrant, engaged, and involved. I think Wade and I needed that, and I know we enjoyed it. We became tired, terribly tired. We got bored. We got resentful about being tied down, but those were passing feelings. Most of the time we felt pride in the fact that we were doing a good job and we were helping some children lead a better life than they would have otherwise. We began to be confident with our techniques that we had learned with and from the children and we are happy to share them with other people. The sharing of our ideas is also validation of ourselves.

I think we needed the children as much as they needed us, and it has been mutually beneficial. It was a joy raising Jori and Frosty. They were, and are, delightful people to live with, but unfortunately, just when they finally got us trained to be reasonable parents they went off to do their own things. They were ready and well prepared to do so, but Wade and I wanted more of that parenting experience. I often think that one of the wonderful things the four boys did for Wade and me was that they kept us so involved with them so that we were protected from being too intrusive into the lives of Jori and Frosty. I am sure Jori and Frosty are grateful for that. We love our children profoundly and we are interested in what they are doing, but I think that if we became meddlesome it would be disappointing to all of us. Some parents have had enough of parenting by the time their children are eighteen and twenty and go away. I am glad that we were different. I like to think that four boys are also glad we are different.

As parents we were pleased to see the change of attitude that Frosty experienced. Initially, in his honest, forthright manner, Frosty had shared with us his feelings about the boys and his misgivings about our involvement with them. It was wonderful to watch Frosty's original lack of tolerance be replaced by understanding and acceptance. It was heartening to watch Frosty gear himself to learn that which he did not care to learn, to deal with that with which he did not want to deal. I am sure that initially Frosty's intent to grow and change attitudinally was based on his wish to give support to his father and to me. He would eventually realize that it was his own humanness that needed to be tested and developed, and in the process of reaching out to understand and accept four boys, he learned a great deal about understanding and accepting himself. In 1973 I never thought that three years later Frosty would prepare dinner and supervise evening and bedtime so Wade and I could go out. But he did and he volunteered!

During the last three years I have observed Wade's commitment to the boys deepen. He has revealed unusual parenting skills. He seemed to know intuitively the most appropriate thing to do to help the boys grow well. I do not think Wade ever felt sorry for the boys. To Wade it is demeaning to feel sorry for any other person. Rather, he accepted their condition of retardation as one aspect of their humanness. He acted as though, "They have retardation—so what? Now let's move on to help them do what they can." Wade always acted on the belief that to permit a child the right to develop and grow did not deny the child's limitation, but, rather, it put the limitation in the right place. Because Wade always held a positive view of the boys, he permitted himself to be an initiator, a model, a supporter, and a teacher, but never a caretaker. He could provide the boys with the safe home setting within which each of them could take risks. He permitted each boy to "grow and go." The boys and the parents were not permitted to run away from stressful situations, for Wade insisted that we work to eliminate the cause of the stress. Through it all Wade was the primary person to maintain a home of stability, a home with the security of routines, limits, and individualized rules, a home where each person was respected and honored and held accountable for all of his own behavior.

It was not always easy for me to accept the fact that Wade was the primary parent at home. With Jori and Frosty I had been the primary parent and he had given me tremendous support. Even though we discussed, planned, and negotiated, there were times when I chafed under the agreement that we had made. I found it very difficult that I could not have the last word about raising the children. After all, was that not the mother's role and was I not the one who had spent years studying and reading and learning in the field, as well? Gradually, my resentment of Wade's authority dissipated as I began to recognize the actual points of irritation, which always had to do with risk taking. As a young mother I had found it difficult to allow the children to take growth-producing risks, and often I was tripped into a smothering role with the children. In each instance Wade insisted upon having his authority honored, he was proven right. I challenge him less now, but then maybe I am learning to take risks too.

As time went on I began to realize that my experience with the boys and Wade in this new family structure was affecting my professional growth positively. I shared our experiences with my colleagues, and they provided a fine sounding board and made many suggestions that were duly reported back to Wade. In many instances the ideas were woven into the family's style. My credibility as a social worker was enhanced. I was asked to do some training for other foster parents who wanted to work with children with retardation. As I developed this training program I found that I repeatedly used examples of Wade's work with the children. Suddenly I realized that Wade had invaded my professional territory without my ever having planned it. I found myself saying publicly in training programs, "My husband has taught me this, my husband has taught me that." I freely quoted him. Subsequently, I developed a training manual for foster parents that was based on my training as a professional social worker and secondary parent to a family of foster children. Since we lived with children who had limitations, Wade and I may have been more sensitive to the needs of other families. In any event, I believe that my counseling skills improved and that I am better able to relate to parents than I was three or four years ago.

Wade and I often wonder where the boys will end, where they will live, what they will do when they are twenty-five, thirty, and thirty-five. We looked around the community and were discouraged by what we saw. Although we believe that we live in a county that has exceptional service designed for the person with retardation, the need is still greater than the service. We began to wonder how far our commitment would take us. When was enough? Where was done? I became involved with a group of other people in a nonprofit effort considering new living alternatives for persons with retardation. I look to this group as a possible way of continued involvement in this field.

I think about our boys. Our boys do not need or want pity, charity, sympathy. They want to be dignified in themselves. They need to be permitted to do mutually satisfying tasks and activities with others of their choosing. They do not wish to be tragic and pitiful; they want to be liked, accepted, and loved. The more our boys learn to be socially integrated persons the more acceptable and likeable they will become. They need practice in order to develop strengths through these skills. They need an opportunity to be proud of themselves and of their accomplishments. The more practice they have the more they will be equipped to deal with a normal society. We do not see society providing all the gradations of experience that the boys need in order to continue their growth and achieving, but, still we want our boys to be accountable. We want them to own and experience their lives. We know that it will be difficult for them to escape the well-meaning rejection and condescension of other adults who excuse them and treat them as children because of their retardation. We would like our boys to know adults who only help them when they ask for help. We want the policemen to scold our boys when they break the rules. We do not wish to see our boys exceptionalized and infantilized by a society who feels sorry but does not care. We hope that they will live in that part of the community where they are held responsible and accountable for who they are and what they do. We hope that they will be respected for what they do well. We hope that they will be provided with the opportunity to continue to grow and learn, experience and love. I imagine that Wade and I will continue to put our energies in that direction. We will try to do what we can in our community and in our county to ensure improved living experiences for adults with retardation.

Loving has not always been easy. I think when the boys came to live with us I had the fantasy that they would become to me comparable to my own son and daughter. I naively thought that over time and proximity I would come to love them in a very subjective way. This did not happen, and it caused many mixed feelings for me. I never felt that Phillip or Andrew wanted mother-loving from me. They were content to experience me as a special adult woman in their lives. My relationship with these two boys has been comfortable. It has a lot of spontaneous affection, impromptu touching, and occasional hugging as part of the messages shared between us. I occasionally call them by pet names and they have their ways of showing their affection for me. Never have I felt the need to be mother to Phillip or Andrew.

Tom and Mark cry out for mama and daddy relationships. When I realized that I could not spontaneously respond to this need, it troubled me very much. There was a piece of me that had felt as though I had a responsibility to give to each of the boys what they had never had. When I realized that I was not able to do that with sincerity I went through a period of wondering what kind of deficiencies there were in me that I could not share myself freely with two children who needed me so much. I am not sure that I have it resolved yet. I know that it would be completely dishonest and artificial for me to pretend that I have the same mother feeling toward Tom and Mark that I have toward Jori and Frosty.

Deep inside it feels like this: I could die for Frosty or Jori without a second thought. In a time of crisis for Tom or Mark I would look at all the options and respond in an objective manner. My practical self tells me that these children need consistent, objective, thoughtful parenting. The other half of me says that every boy and girl is entitled to have a parent that would fight like a tiger for them, but I cannot give that to these children. I do the best I can and the best I can is to provide consistent teaching, training, model-ing, support, and affection. I never have any problem at all using my physical self when a child is in a crisis. I have held Tom through innumerable tantrums and have had no problem with that kind of use of myself. On the other hand, it would not be possible for me to go up and warmly embrace Tom. I distrust what he would do with that. I distrust and fear what he would do with me. I am not com-fortable with my dilemma, but accept it as it is.

I finally realize that I can only be a mother to Jori and Frosty. There is a difference between the profound feeling I experience toward my own children whom I forever wanted. I respect, like, at-tend, and have feelings of affection and feelings of advocacy for the foster children who live in my home. This has never been an issue for Wade. He never deluded himself into thinking that he could be these children's father. His pragmatic set made it easy for him to accept the reality that they were not his boys, they were boys whom he would try to help make it in this world. But they are not his sons. He has not seemed to need to deal with conflicting feelings about fathering, but this certainly has made no difference in the results that have been accomplished with the children. I imagine it goes along with the way he feels about the condition of retardation. "So you have retardation—tough! So you never had a mother—tough! Those are the breaks in life. Now let's get it together and look at all the things that you do have."

Our marriage has been affected by these last three years. We have learned a great deal—each other's strengths and weaknesses. It has been good to know that in most ways we complement each other and supplement each other in mutually comfortable ways. Wade is comfortable with being the doer in the family and accepts my role as the person who talks about what is being done. There have been times along the way when I have resented that the boys were the priority. Frosty was right; there have been times when I have gone home and wanted to say, "Let's go out for dinner," and it was not possible because there was no one to work with the children. There were times when I wished that we could take extended holi-days and it has not been possible because the boys would have felt too insecure to have us away for so long. Gradually, over time, it has come together. For the first two and a half years Wade and I were never away from home together longer than forty-eight hours, but we had lots of fun using those forty-eight hours. We became very knowledgeable about the resources in the various communities within 35 miles of our home. By spending a weekend at a nearby community we would have some respite and the worker on duty would have us close enough to be in touch in case of emergency. Wade, of course, was right when he insisted that we take the time to build our home securely so that the children could realize that home continued even when parents were away for extended periods of time.

After many weekends, probably as many as thirty different weekends away from the boys, Wade felt that the time was right for us to take a vacation. We arranged for Bill to live with the children so that we could have a two-week holiday, thousands of miles away from responsibilities for children. It was a marvelous time! After the first twenty-four hours we worried about the children not at all. Our time away from the children and their time with us away was so satisfactory to all of us that six months later we went away again for another two-week period with the same happy results. This careful use of respite time demonstrated something clearly to us. As we read articles and talked to different people about respite, we got the impression that most people viewed respite as an opportunity for parents to have time away from a difficult, challenging situation in their home. Sometimes parents arranged for respite for themselves by having the child live somewhere else for a period of time. Always the emphasis was on providing a rest for the parent and/or family. Wade and I realize, from our experience, that it is just as important for the children to have respite from us. Most normal children growing up in healthy homes have endless opportunities during their growing up years to try their wings with other grown-ups. For example, they go to camp, they go to grandma's, they go to friends to slumber parties, they go on trips with neighbors. All of these opportunities for the child of normalcy to have time away from family are ways of helping that person prepare for separation from family. All of those experiences help the child get ready to go away to school, to go away to college, to go away to service, to be married; to leave mama and daddy. It suddenly occurred to us that children with retardation do not usually have this kind of opportunity. We began to realize that quite by accident we had incorporated into our home a very growth producing experience. The boys grow when we go away and let somebody else be with them. They grow even more than we get rested.

There is no question that the boys truly understand that our house is their home. We come and go, they come and go, but the house is the central place. It is our responsibility to work with these boys to prepare for living somewhere else, but always with the understanding that our house is home. Whenever the boys do leave us, wherever they do go, it is our intention to provide for them the same kind of transition into maturity that we provided Jori and Frosty. They will have the opportunity to come home, to get reunited and then re-readied to be out in the world again. It is our hope that we will so prepare them that they will happily go and happily return and that this cycle can continue for the rest of our lives. Obviously it is a great pleasure to me that we can come and go more freely now, and it is our intention to be away from the children frequently and for extended periods of time.

Life does move in cycles and this never ceases to amaze me. When I was a little girl I remember the day my father brought a beautiful Tiffany lamp home to hang in our dining room. He hung it with a great deal of ceremony. Down through the years that Tiffany lamp symbolized many things to me because I recall sitting at that table for meals, sitting at that table doing my homework under my father's supervision, playing cards, and discussing all kinds of plans. When we were grown and my father was deciding to whom he would give different articles in his home it was my good fortune to get the Tiffany lamp. I had always dreamed that someday that Tiffany lamp would hang in my home. When Wade and I moved to renovate our new house I, of course, assumed that the Tiffany lamp would never hang in my home until the foster children had passed through our lives. But that was without taking into consideration Wade and his impossible dream. Wade was determined three years ago that children would honor, take care of, and respect beautiful things. In 1976 we brought the Tiffany lamp back from New England and hung it in the kitchen window in our home. There it hangs today and Wade is right. The children love it and I am certain that no harm will ever come to it. Two of the boys understand that that lamp hung over the dining room table in the house where I grew up as a little girl a long time ago in a part of the world a long distance away. Yes, we hung the Tiffany lamp, and somehow that action confirms and enhances our commitment to the four boys in our home. The boys are growing up, and as Wade constantly reminds us, "We are raising men, not boys."

OUR FOUR BOYS

was set in 10-point Compugraphic Century Textbook and leaded two points,
with display type in Century Schoolbook,
by Metricomp Studios, Inc.;
printed on 55-pound Warren antique cream,
Smyth-sewn and bound over boards in Columbia Bayside Vellum,
by Maple-Vail Book Manufacturing Group, Inc.;
and published by

SYRACUSE UNIVERSITY PRESS
SYRACUSE, NEW YORK 13210